Machine Learning

This book includes

Basic Concepts + Artificial Intelligence + Python Programming + Python Machine Learning. A Comprehensive Guide to Build Intelligent Systems Using Python Libraries and Advanced Features.

D1089499

By: Ethem Mining

First book

Machine Learning for Beginners: *A Complete and Phased Beginner's Guide to Learning and Understanding Machine Learning and Artificial Intelligence*

Second book

Artificial Intelligence for Business Applications: *Use Artificial Intelligence for Scaling Up Your Business Using AI Marketing Tools*

Third book

Python Programming: *A Comprehensive Smart Approach for Total Beginners to Learn Python Language Using Best Practices and Advanced Features.*

Fourth book

Python Machine Learning: *Understand Python Libraries (Keras, NumPy, Scikit-lear, TensorFlow) for Implementing Machine Learning Models in Order to Build Intelligent Systems.*

Table of Contents

11

Machine Learning for Beginners

A Complete and Phased Beginner's Guide to Learning and Understanding Machine Learning and Artificial Intelligence

By: Ethem Mining

Introduction

While many people have heard about "artificial intelligence" or AI, not as many people seem to know what machine learning is. With that being said, machine learning is a subfield of AI and is, in many cases, the basis for AI technology. The goal of machine learning technology is to understand the structure of data and fit that data into specific models that are able to then be understood and used by humans for various applications throughout life. Machine learning is recognized as a field of computer sciences, however it does not carry the same approach that traditional computer sciences carry. Whereas traditional computer sciences are driven with algorithms that are human-created and managed, machine learning is driven by algorithms that the device itself can learn from and grow from.

Beyond that, they are often built with a very specific purpose that enables them to specialize in specific areas of "knowledge" or capabilities. These days, anyone who has used technology has benefitted from the power of machine learning in one way or another as it has become built into common, everyday technologies. Devices such as your cell phone, tablet, smart watch, computer, and other smart devices have all been designed using the power of smart technology, or machine learning technology.

Everything from the face recognition capabilities in your phone to the self-driving technology in cars is derived from specialized forms of machine learning technology. It has become, and continues to become, a highly relevant and well-researched part of our modern world.

The more we continue to develop new technologies and put these new technologies to work in our modern society, the more we are putting machine learning to work for us. As a result, computer scientists continue to research machine learning capabilities and expand on this unique form of technology so that they can be used in newer and even more revolutionary devices. In this book, *Machine Learning for Beginners,* I want to elaborate on what machine learning is, exactly, how it works, and why it is something that people need to educate themselves more on.

Whether you are a computer scientist or aspiring computer scientist yourself, or if you are a technology enthusiast, I hope that you will find great value in what you learn here within this book.

Inside we are going to cover everything to help you begin to understand machine learning and it's many uses so that you can develop confidence in what it is that you are talking about, and learning about, when discussing machine learning technology. As you read through this book, please note that the primary goal is to help you learn about and understand machine learning.

This particular topic is an incredibly vast topic with a seemingly endless number of subfields and areas of focus, all of which are devoted to different methods of advancing or utilizing this particular technology. For that reason, there is no way that I could possibly discuss every single aspect of machine learning technology in a single book. However, with this foundational knowledge you will be able to take your basic understanding of machine learning and use it to develop even more knowledge in your chosen area of research, should you desire to pursue machine learning in any way. So, if you are ready to get started, let's begin!

Chapter 1: What is Machine Learning?

In the introduction, we briefly touched into what machine learning is exactly. In its essence, machine learning is a form of computer science technology whereby the machine itself has a complex range of "knowledge" that allows it to take certain data inputs and use complex statistical analysis strategies to create output values that fall within a specific range of knowledge, data, or information.

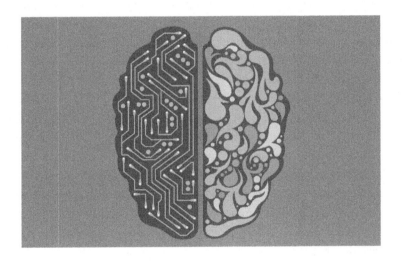

This sounds complex, and that is because it is. However, once you begin digging into what machine learning is exactly it becomes easier to understand how this particular technology works and what can be done with it.

In order to help you really start to dig into machine learning, we are going to start with the very basics. That is: what machine learning is, the history of it, what it can do and how it is applied, what benefits it has, and practical everyday examples of how machine learning is used.

Definition of Machine Learning

The definition of machine learning is one that is relatively difficult to summarize because it is often described or explained differently by different people, or groups. With that being said, the generally agreed upon definition of machine learning is:

"machine learning focuses on the development of computer programs that can access data and use it to learn for themselves."

Machine learning devices essentially take data, and use to look for patterns and other pieces of specified information to create predictions or recommendations. The goal is for computers to learn how to use data and information to be able to learn automatically, rather than requiring humans to intervene or assist with the learning process. In other words, rather than having to push updates or adjust the coding, machine learning devices should be able to recognize its own "needs" and "learn" the upgrades accordingly. This means that the device itself would be able to create and push its own updates and become more functional based on what it was meant to do in the first place. With that being said, this definition is not always entirely accurate, as there are different types of machine learning methods. Some of them, such as the ones described previously, is completely unsupervised and should require absolutely no human intervention to be able to function and learn or evolve entirely on their own. Others, however, require moderate to consistent supervision to ensure that they are operating properly. We will discuss more these different categories of learning methods in Chapter 2, when you can discover what each one means and when that particular learning method would be applied to a machine learning device.

History of Machine Learning

Machine learning may seem like new technology, especially because we are now starting to see more "futuristic" devices in play with our smartphones and our cars fostering more advanced forms of technology.

With that being said, the concept of machine learning is certainly not new, and has actually been around for exactly six decades at the time of *Machine Learning for Beginners* being written and released. That means that the term "machine learning" was first introduced in 1959!

The term machine learning was introduced by Arthur Samuel when he worked at IBM back in the 1950s and 1960s. Samuel was an American pioneer when it came to computer gaming and artificial intelligence, and has largely been recognized as the original inventor of the concept of machine learning. Following his discovery and description of machine learning, Nils J. Nilsson released a book called Learning Machines that discussed the earliest forms of machine learning as we know it today. Back then, these machines were ultimately capable of recognizing patterns and classifying them.

At the time, it was a massive move toward something new, but looking back just 60 years later it seems like such a basic form of the machine learning technology we have grown used to in today's world. Throughout the 1970s and 1980s, machine learning technology was continually upgraded to identify even more patterns and categorize them more effectively. At this point, computers and the internet were not yet a common staple in the average American household, so this technology was still largely private amongst computer scientists and engineers. Later, in the 1990s, computers became more popular in the average household and machine learning was starting to make its way into people's everyday lives. By the time computers were becoming more popular, systems had begun to be put into play so that computers could mine data. This way, anyone who was plugged into the internet could, technically, "feed the machine" so to speak by allowing their devices, and other devices, to collect data about their computer usage habits. This lead to the devices being able to create more favorable experiences over time, such as with search engines being able to offer more relevant search results, or more recently with social media platforms being able to customize advertisements for users. As machine learning capabilities have continued to grow over time, we have seen our lives being massively impacted by them. At this point, machine learning is used to optimize the functionality of computers and their software, has helped build statistics and growth, and has helped customize user's experiences on the internet, and with other software they might use.

The Future of Machine Learning

The scope of machine learning, or the future of machine learning, is still largely unknown. At this point, we can only prophesize what we think is going to happen, however the future is looking rather incredible with machine learning included. There are many ways that machine learning will be included in the future of our world, in ways that can touch nearly every area of our lives. Machine learning could come to affect everything from the way we shop to the way we commute, and even the way we interact with each other or with our technology. At this point, anything is possible.

Some of the futuristic ideas that computer scientists have come up with include things like ending the industrialized era so that we can allow AI to completely run our industries. Many argue that this would be far cleaner than using fossil fuels and human labor like we have been using to date. For many machine learning could indicate freedom from lives that have otherwise been spent engaged in active labor for decades upon decades.

In a time where many struggles to even retire, machine learning could enable the entire working class a new lease on life, so to speak. As people engaged in work-free lives, they could also use technology like completely self-driving cars, digital assistants, and other smart city technology.

In many ways, the machine learning we are coming to know will transform finances, manufacturing, shopping, media, and even the healthcare industry. We could see changes in how we track, manage, and use our money, and how we shop altogether. We could see our products being manufactured completely by AI. As well, we will likely see machine learning technologies continue to customize the media we see and how it is presented to us so that we are consuming media in a more enjoyable manner. In the healthcare industry, you could see anything from better personal healthcare information monitoring systems to better technology that can be used for diagnosing and discovering illnesses or abnormalities in people's health. So much can be moved over to machine learning technology and changed as we know it, as long as we continue to explore it and learn how to practically apply it to our world. Many people think that we are in for an AI revolution. At this rate, we would find ourselves amongst a completely new era were, rather than being fueled by the foundation of the industrial revolution, we would be fueled by the AI revolution.

In this sense, modern fuels, manufacturers, factories, and even engines and transportation forms as we know them would become obsolete as the AI era took over instead. While we cannot claim that this would be the perfect revolution, chances are it would support us in healing much of the problems that fossil fuels and carbon emissions have caused to our planet. In many ways, it may be the revolution we require in order to undo the damage that the industrial revolution has done to our planet.

Application of Machine Learning

To date, there are 44 different ways that machine learning has been applied in our modern world. These different applications have served in two different ways. On one level, they have provided computer scientists with the opportunity to discover, explore, and understand how machine learning technology can work in different applications of our modern world. In many cases, these aspects of research remain private and have yet to be introduced to or used by the public. On another level, these applications are regularly being interacted with and used by the public as a way to help revolutionize and evolve our way of living.

This is both an opportunity for us to implement and enjoy new technology, while also being able to get a feel for how well this machine learning technology holds up in massive ways. The more successfully it is applied and used by the general public, the stronger the technology becomes and the more it can be applied in other areas of life, too. So far, the 44 applications of technology involve being used in industries such as the technology industry, the agricultural industry, the medical industry, the financial industry, the marketing industry, and even the human behavior industry. Below is a breakdown of where machine learning has been applied in each of these industries.

Technology Industry

- Adaptive websites
- Affective computing
- Computer networks
- Computer vision
- Data quality
- General game playing
- Information retrieval
- Internet fraud detection
- Machine learning control
- Machine perception
- Machine translation
- Optimization
- Recommender systems
- Robot locomotion
- Search engines
- Sequence Mining
- Software engineering
- Speech recognition
- Syntatic pattern recognition
- Telecommunication
- Theorem proving
- Time series forecasing

Agricultural Industry

- Agriculture

Medical Industry

- Anatomy
- Bioinformatics
- Brain-machine interfaces
- Cheminformatics
- DNA sequence classification
- Medical diagnosis
- Structural health monitoring

Financial Industry

- Banking
- Credit-card fraud detection
- Economics
- Financial market analysis
- Insurance

Marketing Industry

- Marketing
- Online advertising

Human Behavior Industry

- Handwriting recognition
- Linguistics
- Natural language processing
- Natural language understanding
- Sentiment analysis
- User behavior analytics

Benefits of Machine Learning

You can find a vast number of benefits from machine learning no matter where you look. These benefits can be categorized by industry, or looked at as an entire series of benefits from machine learning itself. Because this book is about machine learning in general, and is not biased to any specific industry, we are going to look at some of the many benefits of machine learning as a whole. If you want to go even deeper into understanding the benefits of machine learning, take a look at machine learning for the industry that you are most interested in to find ample benefits relating to that particular industry.

One of the biggest advantages of machine learning is that it makes identifying trends and patterns incredibly simple. Trends and patterns are important in many types of data, ranging from medical records to behaviors, and even demographics and other basic information. Having a machine capable of both tracking or mining and reading over the data makes identifying trends and patterns much easier.

In the past, trends and patterns had to be looked over by humans through having humans search through massive amounts of information.

This could take days, weeks, and even months or longer depending on how much data was available, and was often inaccurate as people could easily overlook pieces of information and miss trends or patterns.

Computers, however, using machine learning technology can identify patterns and trends in minutes after searching through hundreds of thousands, of not millions of pieces of data. Another benefit of machine learning is that there is no need for human intervention, which means that the devices can continually improve themselves using automated behaviors. Having devices that are capable of completing complex tasks on their own, without the intervention of humans, and with their own continuous improvement means that we can start seeing massive changes in the way technology is developed. To date, technology has been designed by human brains which, while incredibly imaginative and productive, are also highly prone to error. The human brain can also miss things, or struggle to identify new patterns, trends, or needs when something stops working. This means it could take months or even years for developments to be made exclusively through the human mind. With the application of machine learning devices, this time can be minimized and the process of evolving technology can be further simplified as technology ultimately beings improving itself.

In addition to the aforementioned, machine learning can be applied to a wide variety of applications, and can handle multiple different aspects of information or developments. As mentioned earlier, machine learning can revolutionize everything from how we shop to how we diagnose and treat medical illnesses, or even implement government programs. When we have machine learning fully tapped into and in force, we can use it to improve virtually everything in our modern world in such a way that we will find ourselves experiencing life different from how we know it to be today.

Practical Examples of Everyday Use of Machine Learning

Machine learning already exists in so many areas of our modern lives. To help you get a feel for what a life with machine learning looks like, let's look at nine different ways that machine learning is already being practically applied to our modern world so that you can begin to understand how, and why, it works. Through recognizing machine learning capabilities in your own world, you will likely see just how powerful and useful this particular form of technology is.

One big way that machine learning has been introduced in the past few years is through image recognition. These days, many smart phones, tablets, gaming devices, and even computers are capable of recognizing certain faces and doing things based on what they see. For example, your smart phone may have image recognition technology that enables it to unlock anytime you look at your device.

Another way that machine learning technology has been implemented is through speech recognition. For just under a decade now we have been using speech recognition as a way to interact with our devices to request support, launch applications, and even use our smart phones while we are driving. Speech recognition is continuing to be implemented more and more with the development of in-home "smart assistants" such as Google Home, Alexa, and Apple's Home Pod. Machine learning has also been applied to medical diagnosis already, with machines being developed that can screen patients using various tests or collections of data to help identify possible ailments that the individual may have.

So far, this implementation has helped hundreds of thousands of patients receive diagnoses by first discovering what that patient likely has, then using manual methods to validate the diagnoses and treat it accordingly. In the financial industry, many different trading platforms and programs have been developed as a result of machine learning. Through this, trades and investments are being made and managed automatically as a result of the machine learning technology. In fact, most modern trading platforms have machine learning built in where users can input certain parameters and the device will manage their trades accordingly, ensuring that they enter and exit trades at the right times.

This way, they are capable of maximizing their profits and minimizing their losses in their trades. When it comes to user behavior and the internet, machine learning has been used to make associations between things that an internet browser would likely want to view or purchase. By recognizing what their typical browsing behavior looks like, machine learning can propose new pieces of media or new objects for people to purchase through the internet based off of these recognitions.

In the financial industry again, machine learning is being used as a way to classify people. This way, banks can input certain forms of data and identify whether or not people are eligible for things like loans or credit cards, based on information such as how much they earn, what their debt to income ratio is like, or what their financial history looks like.

Machine learning is also being used to predict many different things. By looking at certain pieces of data, machine learning devices can predict things from weather to probable outcomes in businesses or even in various voting-based programs such as presidential elections. Machine learning is powerful at identifying and highlighting probable results or outcomes based on the data inputted into the machine.

Extraction is another method that can be used with machine learning. With extraction, machine learning technology can help extract web pages, articles, blogs, business reports, and emails based on certain parameters that a user uploads. For example, if you are looking for a certain piece of information out of an email you could place that in a search bar and based on smart technologies you would receive the emails that contained that information in them.

In addition to helping people grow or extract things, machine learning can be used for regression. Using regression you can identify possible outcomes and optimize information by removing unnecessary information or data, or "regressing" to a point where you have a more optimized plan forward.

Chapter 2: Machine Learning Methods

When it comes to machine learning, there are four methods of machine learning that are recognized. These four methods include: supervised learning, unsupervised learning, semi-supervised learning, and reinforcement learning. Each of these methods has its own unique benefits, uses, and applications in the industry. Some people believe that the ultimate goal of machine learning is to get to the point where everything is automated, or works in a completely unsupervised manner. While this would be fascinating, the reality is that there are a lot of moral and ethical debates surrounding this idea that result in people believing that it should not be done. For that reason, the likelihood of us seeing an AI revolution where all machine learning technology is completely unsupervised is highly unlikely. Instead, it is more likely that we will see a future where there are various machine learning technologies that exist with varying levels of supervision based on their unique purpose and the sensitivity of the data they are working with.

To help you understand what each method of learning does, and to explore the moral and ethical implications of each, we are going to explore each of these four learning methods. This will help you better understand the degree to which each machine learning technology has "control" over itself, or any of the functions or systems that it operates.

The more you can understand how each of these methods works, the more success you will have in understanding how machine learning can be used, what the future of it really looks like, and where different methods of application would be most beneficial.

Supervised Learning Method

The supervised learning method is comprised of a series of algorithms that build mathematical models of certain data sets that are capable of containing both inputs and the desired outputs for that particular machine.

The data being inputted into the supervised learning method is known as training data, and essentially consists of training examples which contain one or more inputs and typically only one desired output. This output is known as a "supervisory signal." In the training examples for the supervised learning method, the training example is represented by an array, also known as a vector or a feature vector, and the training data is represented by a matrix. The algorithm uses the iterative optimization of an objective function to predict the output that will be associated with new inputs. Ideally, if the supervised learning algorithm is working properly, the machine will be able to correctly determine the output for the inputs that were not a part of the training data.

What this means is: the training data essentially "trains" the machine on certain parameters so that it can apply those parameters to different pieces of information in the future. Supervised learning methods can be complete with both classification and regression algorithms. The classification algorithms can be used to create outputs that are restricted to a limited set of values, meaning that there are a limited number of "actions" that the machine could take. The regression algorithms are outputs that can have any numerical value within a specified range determined by the machine's programmer. There is an additional area of machine learning that falls within the supervised learning method, which is called similarity learning. Similarity learning is an area where the machine learns something that overlaps with classification and regression. With this particular algorithm, the machine measures the similarity between two related objects and then "ranks" the similarity factor between multiple objects.

You can easily recognize this similarity learning as something that you see in advertisements on the internet or when you are scrolling through social media. When similarity learning has been applied, you might notice that you receive advertisements for things that would likely interest you, even if you have never actually researched them or looked them up online.

Supervised learning is a great application that can be used in conjunction with things like business, finances, and the medical system. With it, information can be accessed and retrieved without there being any implications with morals and ethics. This way, the information exists and is accessible, but we do not have to worry about it being tampered with or otherwise manipulated by the presence of a completely automated device. With supervised learning methods, everything can be interrupted by human intervention if need be.

For example, if an algorithm began to show things that were too personal or too private in advertisements, the company running that advertisement company could intervene and create new parameters that ultimately prevented those results from ranking. This way, humans can still have a fairly active level of control over the capabilities and functionality of machines.

Unsupervised Learning Method

Unsupervised learning is a set of algorithms where the only information being uploaded is inputs. The device itself, then, is responsible for grouping together and creating ideal outputs based on the data it discovers. Often, unsupervised learning algorithms have certain goals, but they are not controlled in any manner. Instead, the developers believe that they have created strong enough inputs to ultimately program the machine to create stronger results than they themselves possibly could.

The idea here is that the machine is programmed to run flawlessly to the point where it can be intuitive and inventive in the most effective manner possible. The information in the algorithms being run by unsupervised learning methods is not labeled, classified, or categorized by humans. Instead, the unsupervised algorithm rejects responding to feedback in favor of identifying commonalities in the data.

It then reacts based on the presence, or absence, of such commonalities in each new piece of data that is being inputted into the machine itself. One of the biggest applications of unsupervised learning algorithms to date comes to the field of density estimation in statistics.

Unsupervised learning has the capacity to summarize and explain data features, essentially helping data analysts gain a better understanding of various aspects of data. This way, they can develop a greater understanding of things like economics, demographics, and other statistics to create plans and strategies for whatever area of application they may be focusing on.

Semi-Supervised Learning Method

Semi-supervised is another form of a machine learning method where computers are programmed with some of the training examples missing any training labels. Still, they can be used to improve the quality of a model, allowing the device to ultimately function more effectively. Semi-supervised learning methods can range from more consistently supervised learning methods to weakly supervised learning methods. The degree to which a method is semi-supervised on this sliding scale depends on how the labels for training examples are created.

In weakly supervised learning methods, the training labels are noisy, limited, or imprecise, which often helps create more effective training sets in the long run. In more strictly semi-supervised learning methods the labels are either there, or missing, there are never labels that are incorrect or sloppy. The goal of semi-supervised learning methods is to improve the outcomes of a device without making it completely unsupervised. This way, the device can be even more effective and complex, but is not entirely left to its own "devices," so to speak.

Reinforcement Learning Method

The reinforcement learning method is a method that is concerned with how software agents should take action in certain environments to maximize some notion of cumulative reward. Reinforcement learning is often used in game theory, operations research, control theory, information theory, multi-agent systems, stimulation-based optimization, statistics, swarm intelligence, and genetic algorithms. For machine learning, the environment is typically represented by an "MDP" or Markov Decision Process. These algorithms do not necessarily assume knowledge, but instead are used when exact models are infeasible. In other words, they are not quite as precise or exact, but they will still serve a strong method in various applications throughout different technology systems. The most common use of reinforcement learning is in games where there are "computer players" or a player that is represented by the computer and plays against human opponents.

In these "computer players" reinforcement learning enables them to respond in a way that is not exact and precise every time, but instead in a way that actually challenges the human. This way, games cannot be memorized and overcome, but instead feature some diversity and uncertainty to them. As a result, it makes the game more enjoyable for players.

Other Learning Methods

In addition to the four aforementioned learning methods, there are some additional learning methods that are used by machine learning technology. These additional learning methods are not typically talked about as they are not significant or standard methods, but they are still important to know about. While they may not be used on a widespread basis just yet, they are being researched and may find themselves being used more and more frequently as we continue to explore and implement machine learning over time. The additional learning methods that can be used with machine learning include: self-learning, feature learning, sparse dictionary learning, anomaly detection and association rules. Typically, these are used in very specific areas of technology, and not in pieces of technology that are used every day by average people.

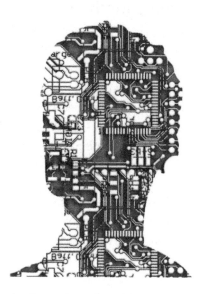

The self-learning method was introduced in 1982 and essentially means that there are no external rewards, or teacher pieces of advice. Instead, the device is designed to be driven between cognition and emotion so that it can educate itself in a way that is meant to resemble the human brain. The device features a memory matrix that it uploads information into so that it can continue to recall previous lessons and build on them.

Feature learning is a system of several algorithms that help machine learning devices experience better representations of the inputs provided during training. These algorithms can also be called representation learning algorithms, and their goal is to preserve the information in their input while also transforming it into a method that is useful. This is completed as a pre-processing step before the device then completes a classification or prediction method. Sparse dictionary learning means that the machine learning device is uploaded with training examples that are a linear combination of basis functions. The method itself is believed to be a spare matrix, and it is difficult to solve approximately. This particular method, although complex, has been applied in many different contexts, including classification and even image de-noising. Anomaly detection is relevant to data mining, where anomaly detection can identify rare items, events, or other anomalies that raise suspicions because of how much they differ from the majority of the data being processed.

A great example of this technology being used in today's world is in banks where the technology is used to detect and prevent fraudulent activity from taking place. Future applications might include medical screening technology where the devices can detect anomalies in DNA, or other genetic cells.

Lastly, association rule learning is a rule-based machine learning method that allows the device to discover relationships between a series of variables in large databases.

In this particular learning method, the machine learning device requires "rules" to identify what relationships it is looking for so that it can bring those relationships to people's attention. Often, the device itself will also learn new "rules" based on what it discovers, allowing new information to come to light for those monitoring the system, too. A great example of how association rule learning has been used in today's world is in the point of sale system in grocery stores. The rule that people who buy onions and potatoes are more likely to buy burgers was identified by an association rule learning method, which allowed grocers to start advertising burgers or ground meat products around the areas where they were advertising potatoes and onions, too. This way, they could improve burger sales by targeting what their audience was likely to want when shopping for onions and potatoes, too.

Of course, this particular learning method can be used in many ways beyond just choosing how to sell groceries, but this is a great example.

These five additional learning methods are not the most commonly focused-on methods because they tend to be more specific, or they may be built in as "add on" methods to technology that has already been developed with a more generic method like unsupervised learning. With that being said, they are powerful and they do represent what technology is capable of, if we give it the opportunity.

Chapter 3: Big Data Analysis

Big data analysis is one of the biggest benefits that machine learning offers people who are looking to create certain outcomes with their data. For example, if you are a corporation looking to pinpoint a specific demographic within your audience that would be most likely to buy a certain product, big data analysis would be incredibly useful for you. In the past, big data analysis had to be done manually by people and it took massive amounts of time to be completed. These days, big data analysis can be done by computers, and often in a way that is far more reliable than when it is done by humans. This is because, rather than having to rely on the memory or possibly faulty organizational systems of humans, machine learning technology can rely on the technology within it to store certain pieces of information and organize it more effectively.

Virtually every machine learning device is capable of analyzing big data, and often uses this as a means for completing its required outputs. Because of how relevant big data analysis is to machine learning technology, it is important that people who are learning about machine learning take the time to learn about big data analysis, too.

In this chapter we are going to discover what big data is, how it is used, and why it is so relevant and necessary in the functionality of machine learning technology.

What is Big Data?

Put simply, big data translates to extremely large sets of data that are analyzed by computers to reveal certain patterns, trends, or correlations between the information being presented in the data. Often, this data represents human behavior or interactions, either with each other or with certain objects being represented by the data. For example, this data might reflect how often certain demographics interact with each other, or it might reflect how often certain demographics interact with something such as a specific object or type of marketing strategy. While big data in and of itself is a fairly simple term, there are countless types of data that can fall under the hat of being considered big data. For example, big data might include hundreds of thousands, or even millions, of demographic-related data, such as where people live, what age they are, and what career or education level they have. Another type of data might include what types of illnesses people have, where those people live the most, and what type of access they have to medical care.

Or, big data might include what areas of websites are being visited the most, what types of emails are opened the most, and what social media platforms are used the most. As you can see, big data can be used in many different forms of data collection, and data organizing or sorting. When it comes to collecting big data, machine learning devices can do just about anything. It can be used to identify trends and patterns, to discover anomalies, to locate certain trends and patterns that are relevant to a specific set of parameters. As you will soon find out, this can serve many purposes, from allowing the machine learning device to complete certain tasks on its own, to allow it to provide relevant information for humans to perform certain tasks. How this information is used and what the output will ultimately depend on what the device was created for, what the purpose of the big data analysis was, and how the humans running the program want to use the information.

Why is Big Data Important?

The importance of big data revolves less around how much data you have, and more around what you actually do with that data. When it comes to business, for example, you can take data from virtually any source and analyze it to discover answers that will help you improve your business in many ways. You might be able to use this data to help you do anything from reducing costs or time in business, to developing new products or making wiser decisions that will have a better impact on your bottom line.

Combining big data with high-powered analytics can help you accomplish tasks ranging from identifying the root cause of failures in business, or defects nearly the instant they happen, to detecting fraudulent behavior before it ever even affects your business. You could even use it to help generate new coupons, or improve your marketing strategies based on consumer buying habits. Outside of business, big data can help in many ways, too. For example, in government big data can help a government identify what matters most to the people they are supporting and how they can make decisions that will improve their civilizations and societies in a meaningful way. In schools, big data can help teachers identify where students are having the most troubles learning and implement new learning strategies to help those students learn better. In sciences big data can be used to identify certain anomalies in scientific findings to discover new patterns, or identify new areas to research or study.

Also in sciences, big data can help predict things such as new strains of illnesses, weather patterns, or certain changes that are projected to take place in various eco systems over time. There are countless ways that big data can be used to help various parts of our modern society, ranging from businesses and corporations to government and educational systems, and even sciences and beyond. Big data is important because, when used properly, it can give us the best understanding of what is going on in a certain set of analytics and what problems we may be facing. When we use this to identify problems that may cause detrimental impacts to our businesses, our societies, our eco systems, and even our bodies, this can be used to offset those impacts. As a result, we can experience a more meaningful and purposeful evolution in our businesses and societies that improves our quality of life altogether.

How is Big Data Used?

Big data is used either entirely by machine learning technology, or by humans as a way to perform a multitude of different functions. We see big data being used exclusively by machine learning technology when the technology is developed to create prediction models, or to project various different outcomes based on a series of inputs that have been made into the system. Big data can also be used exclusively by machine learning technology to produce results, such as with search engines, or to help individuals make decisions, such as with decision trees. There are countless practical applications that this type of technology can introduce, much of which we will talk about in the next section:

Applications of Big Data in Today's World.

When it is used in conjunction with human intervention, big data can be effectively applied to many different things as well. For example, the machine learning technology might provide an organized sequence of data that represents various analytics in such a way that humans can then take that information and turn it into a plan or a strategy to complete something. In business, for example, the machine learning technology might inform a business of the needs and interests of their consumers so that the business can go on to conceptualize a new product or service that would serve their consumers. In this case, technology plays a vital role when it comes to big data but not so much when it comes to conceptualizing the new product or service. Regardless of whether machine learning technology works solely on its own, or with the collaboration of humans, it can play a vital role in many different things in our modern society.

From helping us resolve problems in supporting us with generating new solutions or probable outcomes, there are many ways that big data is used in today's world.

Applications of Big Data in Today's World

To help you further understand how big data can be applied, we are going to discuss practical applications of big data in today's world. In most cases, actually seeing how big data is already working with our modern world to support us in various applications is an easier way to understand what big data can actually do, why it matters, and what benefit it can offer us and our society.

In today's world, we are seeing big data being used most by six different industries. These industries include: banking, education, government, health care, manufacturing, and retail. Each of these industries is benefiting from big data in its own unique way, so we are going to discover what these methods are and why big data is so necessary to these industries. In banking, big data is used as a way to help banks manage their customers and boost their satisfaction. Through this, banks can understand what customers' banking needs are, and how they can create new products or services that will serve their customers' banking needs. They also use big data as a way to analyze what is going on within their systems to ensure that fraudulent activities are not taking place either from internal sources such as those who work at the bank, or external sources such as those who try to commit bank fraud. Using big data, banks can stay one step ahead of their customers, and fraudulent activity, to serve in the most effective and protected manner possible.

Big data does not just come into play in educational systems when we talk about students who are taking courses that educate them on analytics and technical analysis. Big data is also useful for educators who are looking at how they can improve school systems, support their students better, and evolve their curriculums. When an educational system is able to analyze big data, it can identify and locate at-risk students and put them in touch with helpful resources or tools that may improve their educational career. They can also help students progress at an adequate rate, and support them should they be having trouble with their progress. In addition to helping implement new systems for students, big data can also help teachers and principals improve their own methods of teaching, while also ensuring that they are implementing the best possible methods.

In other words, it can help everyone stay accountable and move toward a more effective educational system. In health care, big data has helped things get done more quickly and accurately than ever before. From patient records and treatment plans to prescription information, big data support health care practitioners in many ways. As with the government, it is critical that the big data in the medical system is transparent, protects privacy, and meets stringent industry regulations. For that reason, while it is used, it is also a necessity that any information provided from a machine learning model is also validated by a team of specialists to ensure that they have received accurate information. This way, they are able to improve patient care and increase effectiveness in medical treatments without overlooking the ever-important aspect of ethics.

In the government, big data has been used to manage utilities, run agencies, prevent crime, and deal with traffic congestion.

By using big data, they can identify what is needed, and what may not be needed, so that they can refine their management systems and have greater success in running effective systems for their society.

With that being said, based on the nature of the government it is also important that they are able to address issues relating to transparency and privacy, as many are concerned that the data could be biased or botched to serve the government's preferences. In manufacturing, big data helps boost quality control, increase output, and minimize waste associated with the manufacturing process. In today's market, these are all highly necessary to the competitive market that products are regularly being created for and released into. In using analytics, manufacturers can actually improve the quality of their products, making them more competitive, while also making the creation process more competitive. As a result, they are often also able to reduce manufacturing costs and improve overall service. For the modern world, greener manufacturing solutions and improved quality of products are two of the most important purchasing considerations that people take into account, which means that improving these aspects can massively improve sales in companies.

Beyond manufacturing, big data can also help when it comes to retail. With big data, companies can manage and monitor customer relationships and ensure that they are ultimately building the strongest loyal following possible.

Retailers do this by identifying the best way to market to customers, discovering the most effective methods for handling transactions, and identifying the most strategic way to bring back repeat business. In order for all of this to take place, companies track and monitor data and use this to improve their sales numbers, directly through improving relationships. Ultimately, this is how companies gauge "who" their audience is, and build their brand and mission accordingly.

Big Data Analysis Tools

There are countless different big data analysis tools that are being used to help companies track and monitor analytics in their businesses so that they can improve the quality of their customer relationships and, therefore, sales. These tools are ones that can be used by the average person, although it may be complex to use them if you are not entirely clear as to what you are doing right away. Working with the right tools is a critical opportunity for you to find ways to use analytics to help you make decisions, identify strategies, or improve outcomes based on the information you input into the system. When we talk about big data analysis tools, what we are really talking about are types of software that can be used to compute big analysis. This software can be used on virtually any computer, making it highly accessible to just about everyone. With that being said, there are eight great big data analysis tools that anyone can start using on the market. These include: Zoho Analytics, Cloudera, Microsoft Power BI, Oracle Analytics Cloud, Pentaho Big Data Integration and Analytics, SAS Institute, Sisense, Splunk, and Tableau. To give you an understanding of how these tools use big data to support their users, we are going to explore each one in greater detail below.

Zoho Analytics

Zoho Analytics is a self-service option that's a primary focus is to help users transform large amounts of raw data into actionable reports and dashboards. They are capable of tracking business metrics, determining outliers, identifying long term trends, and discovering a multitude of hidden insights within a business.

This intelligence platform is a powerful one that can transform business-oriented analytics into new strategies to help you maximize your audience and move forward in a strong manner.

Cloudera

Cloudera is a great fit for larger organizations that want to use Hadoop technology, which is an open-source framework used to store data and run applications. For this particular tool, larger organizations can create and process predictive analysis models effortlessly using several different tools that have been integrated into this unique platform. You may require the support of an IT or technical analyst to help you navigate this particular tool.

Microsoft Power BI

This particular technology has been a favorite amongst organizations for a long time, likely because the Microsoft platform is recognizable and reliable. This particular analysis platform is great for organizations that are looking for an easy way to get into analytics and leveraging analytics to help them grow their business. In addition to offering all of the analysis tools within its software, it also offers cloud based analytics and is able to perform multiple different types of data analysis and monitoring at the same time due to the way it was built.

Oracle Analytics Cloud

Oracle moved into big data analytics as a self-service company that enables companies of all sizes to leverage its platform to create different types of analytics findings from big data. The core focus of this particular tool is to ingest data and support users in finding trends, patterns, and predictive models that can support them in releasing bottlenecking and improving the quality of their company.

Pentaho Big Data Integration and Analytics

Pentaho, owned by Hitachi, is another big data analytics company. This particular company specializes in Enterprises, and is built on an open source platform. It is excellent for companies that have many varieties of data and massive data sources, meaning that they are using data in multiple ways, in multiple areas in their business, and on a large scale.

Based on how it is built, it can reasonably and effortlessly handle the bigger tasks and support larger businesses, like Enterprises, in running stronger companies.

SAS Institute

SAS Institute is one of the most well-known big data tools out there because it has been around for so long. This particular company is often used for deep analytics, although it features a drag and drops functionality which means that it is extremely user friendly. With that being said, it is great for building advanced visualizations for what you want to create within your business, and can help you share that information across multiple devices. This tool can either be used locally, or in the cloud service.

Sisense

Sisense is said to be a company that makes tracking big data as easy as possible for anyone to do, no matter how new they might be to tracking big data. With its capabilities, it can support users of any size and knowledge level in getting into tracking analytics so that they can improve the quality of their companies or organizations. This particular company is excellent for larger organizations that want fast implementation time with a company that offers incredible customer service. They have a data visualization service built-in, as well as predictive modeling. This particular platform can be used on mobile or web, and can be used locally or with the cloud based service.

Splunk

Splunk is a tool that is user-friendly and web based, making it easy for many to get started with. This particular company makes it easy to collaborate with other people in your business, so if you have multiple people tracking analytics and monitoring big data you can keep all of your findings and comments local in the service. This way, entire teams can collaborate seamlessly via the internet. This particular company is best known for creating graphs and analytic dashboards which makes tracking and presenting analytics much easier.

Tableau

Tableau is one of the top companies in the industry, and is recognized as being a great option for scientists who are known as "non-data" scientists.

It works excellent no matter what sector you are working in, and is perfect for Enterprises. This particular company uses data visualization technology, and is capable of creating data visualization without the user first needing to organize the data, which is incredibly useful. This particular platform can also help reuse existing skills to support improved big data findings so that companies can have improved analytics discoveries.

Big Data and Machine Learning

Big data and machine learning largely overlap, although they are not the same thing. Big data is a specific term referring to large categories of information that are used by software or other machine learning systems to create certain outputs. For companies and various organizations, big data is an opportunity for them to create a strong thesis around what they can do to improve the quality of their company. For machine learning, big data is frequently used to create training examples that train machine learning technology to behave in certain manners. This big data can be used to train machines to create certain outputs, to self-learn, and to complete other tasks depending on what the intention of that particular machine learning technology was designed for. While big data and machine learning do intercept, it is important to understand that they are not actually the same thing. Big data is a pool of data on certain topics, and big data analysis is process of analyzing those pools of information for certain things.

Machine learning, on the other hand, is a form of technology used to allow machines to behave in intelligent and complex manners, depending on how they were programmed and what they are intended to be used for.

Chapter 4: Machine Learning Algorithms

Machine learning technology relies on algorithms as a means to function, as algorithms are what programs these machines to perform the tasks that they were designed to perform. In some cases, these algorithms are stored on servers that are accessible by other computers through open networks such as the internet. In other cases, these algorithms are stored on servers that are accessible only through closed networks, meaning that only certain computers or devices can access the network. In either case, the algorithm is designed to make the system function in a specific manner so that it can have a certain preferred outcome. Search engines, for example, are designed with a type of machine learning algorithm that enables them to return the best possible information from the internet on any given search parameters that a user inputs into the search bar.

Search engines are not the only example of machine learning algorithms that are used with this particular form of technology, however. There are actually countless algorithms that are used to program machine learning technology so that these devices can complete their intended purposes. In addition, these algorithms are regularly being modified and improved so that they can complete different tasks all the time.

Researchers are regularly looking for new algorithms and programming strategies that enable them to push the boundaries of computer sciences and program machine learning models to do new things on a regular basis.

Despite how many algorithms there are, those who are new to machine learning should focus exclusively on the models that are more relevant to beginners. These algorithms include: the K Means Clustering algorithm, artificial neural networks, decision trees, the naïve Bayes classifier algorithm, random forests, the Apriori algorithm, and linear and logistic regression. These are the most important algorithms to know about as a beginner to machine learning as they are the most commonly used, and explored, algorithms that presently make up most of the machine learning technology that we use today. As well, these are the basis for most of the new technology being developed within the machine learning industry to date.

Before we get into learning about what these algorithms are, it is important that you understand what an algorithm is in the first place and how machine learning algorithms are used. This way, you have a stronger understanding as to how these programming methods train or program machine learning technology to function in a specific manner.

What is An Algorithm?

First things first, let's look into algorithms. Algorithms are specifically defined as: "a process or set of rules to be followed in calculations or other problem-solving operations, specifically by a computer." This definition is proposed by the Oxford American dictionary. Based on this definition, we can conclude that while most algorithms are based on computers, some algorithms are completed manually as a way to help people identify certain pieces of information or access certain pieces of knowledge. Arguably, even the rules you learned in your mathematics classes in elementary school are a form of an algorithm as they define specific rules that are to be followed during calculations. With that being said, the algorithms we are talking about with computers and machine learning models are significantly more complex than the BEDMAS technique you learned in Grade 7.

What Are Machine Learning Algorithms?

The algorithms used in machine learning ultimately program the technology or device to function in a specific manner. Essentially, the developer or programmer defines a specific set of rules and uploads that into the technology in the form of an algorithm. Following that, the device then responds in specific manners that allow the device to ultimately function in a specific manner, too. The types of algorithms being used by machine learning models closely relate to what method of learning that machine learning model is going to use.

In other words, different algorithms are used in supervised machine learning methods versus unsupervised, semi-supervised machine learning algorithms, and reinforcement machine learning algorithms. These algorithms will ultimately define what the computer is meant to do, how much it is meant to do, and what outputs it is expected to create in order for it to function properly. If a machine learning device does not produce the proper outcomes based on what the developer or programmer was looking for, one can conclude that they have created or inputted the algorithm in an incorrect manner. If this is the case, they must look through a series of complex coding to identify what the machine is doing, where it is essentially behaving "wrong," and what can be done to improve its behavior. Once the programmer has looked through the coding, they can improve the coding to ensure that the algorithm begins behaving in the proper manner, essentially meaning that the machine learning model will begin behaving properly, too.

When it comes to algorithms in machine learning models, they are always created using complex coding systems that define the rules being adhered to by that particular piece of technology. These rules define what pieces of information the technology should look for, how to authenticate and validate the quality of that information, and how to present it to the user. They also tend to define what types of inputs to look for, or other cues to look for to signal that something needs to be done. For example, developers might program a piece of technology with "If This, Then That" or IFTTT technology so that it behaves in a specific manner. In this case, anytime a certain trigger is pulled, a specific outcome is produced. For example, if you use a search engine and type something in the search bar, it automatically pulls up results for you based on what you have searched.

Likewise, if you include certain symbols such as quotations into the search bar, it adjusts how the search parameters work and ultimately changes the results you are likely to receive based on your search terms. All algorithms in machine learning technology will always be uploaded through a system of complex codes. These codes are often written into the technology or software and then stored on servers and then distributed to other devices on a chosen network, whether that is a closed or open network. It is very rare for the algorithm and the information relating to a software to be stored on the same platforms they are used on, as this would leave the software at risk of being infected by viruses or other malware that could disrupt the service. Instead, they tend to be stored on a remote server and are often backed up to offline devices to ensure that the original software itself is protected. This way, should anything ever happen to the machine learning system online, it could be restored by the offline backup and put back to normal in no time at all.

What is the Use of Machine Learning Algorithms?

The purpose of machine learning algorithms is ultimately to program the machines or software to do what they are meant to do. Without machine learning algorithms, the software has no way of knowing how it is supposed to behave or what it is supposed to do, which means that the user possibilities are not entirely limitless. In other words, because the machine has no way of knowing what to do, it ultimately can't do much.

With machine learning algorithms, machines can either work entirely based on what the user themselves are doing, or entirely unsupervised and on their own. This ultimately depends on what they were made to do and what the purpose of the machine itself is.

A search engine software, for example, will be automatically updated but will not perform any actions unless someone using the search engine inputs information to be searched. Alternatively, a bank server that is focused on tracking transactions and detecting fraud will continue to keep track of information so long as people are using their bank services, and it functions on its own entirely in the background.

Chapter 5: K Means Clustering Algorithm

T he K means clustering algorithm is one of the simplest and most popular forms of an unsupervised machine learning algorithm that exists. This particular algorithm makes it incredibly easy for developers to create, and use, machine learning technology. Because of how popular and simple this method is, it is one of the most commonly used algorithms for unsupervised machine learning methods out there. It also happens to be one of the most flexible algorithms that can create countless different outputs depending on the purpose of the machine and what the developers and programmers want it to do.

What Is the *K Means Clustering* Algorithm?

The K means clustering algorithm was designed to group similar data points together and then discover underlying patterns in those data points. The algorithm uses a fixed number of clusters in a dataset, which is represented by (k). In the case of algorithms and machine learning, clusters refer to collections of data points that are connected due to specific similarities. Which similarities the algorithm looks for depends on what the algorithm has programmed to do, or what the developer has asked that algorithm to do. This can also be interchanged depending on the commands used and the aspect of the algorithm being interacted with.

For example, let's say a large corporation was using the K means clustering algorithm about their customers so that they could improve their products and services and earn more sales. In this case, the exact same data about customers could trigger an algorithm to point out patterns about where those customers live, what age those customers are, or what products or services they are already purchasing depending on what the developer has asked the algorithm to do. When you are creating the K means cluster algorithm, you have to define what k means, or what target number will point to k.

Once you have defined that, *k* will point to a number of centroids in the dataset, or the imaginary or real location that is used to represent the center of a cluster of data.

How Does This Algorithm Work?

The K means algorithm processes learning data through mining data by first identifying an initial group of randomly selected centroids. These are then used as the beginner points for every cluster made. From there, the K means algorithm will perform repetitive calculations to optimize the positions of the centroids, ensuring that they are as accurate as possible. It will continue doing this until a specific set of parameters are met that indicate that it is time to stop.

The specific parameters that will stop a K means algorithm, ultimately meaning it has found it's "destination," are simple. There are two things that can happen that will stop the calculations from taking place and ultimately define the end destination of the K means algorithm. The process will stop when one of these two parameters is met, and does not require for both of them to be present in order to work.

The first parameter that could be met in order to stop the calculation and optimization of clusters is if the centroids have stabilized. This essentially means that there is no more change in their values because the process was successful and there was no need for it to continue. In other words, the calculations are no longer finding more optimal centroids, meaning that there is nothing more for it to do. In this case, it outputs its findings of the centroids for the user to then identify what those findings are and use them in whatever way they needed to. This particular parameter can only be met if the centroids have a specific, finite centroid that is exact and measurable. In this case, it can be located and presented to the user. The second parameter that the K means cluster algorithm could reach that would prevent it from conducting any further calculations is if the defined number of repetitions has been achieved.

In this parameter, the developer has to decide how many times the algorithm is going to perform the calculations to optimize its findings and produce the results.

The more times the calculation is done, the more accurate the centroid will be. The fewer times the calculation is done, the less accurate the centroid will be. This particular parameter is used when no clear centroid exists and so the programmer or developer wants to encourage the algorithm to locate the most accurate centroid possible. If the developer were to decide that they needed a more accurate centroid, they could increase the number of times the calculation was repeated to ensure that they had the best possible results. Based on the nature of the K means algorithm, those using this particular algorithm do not need to upload data into specific classifications but instead can use centroids to encourage the algorithm to identify these classifications on its own.

Since the algorithm is unsupervised, the goal is that it will classify the datasets into the best sets possible based on what you need the algorithm to do, ultimately allowing it to provide the most accurate results possible. The final pieces of information outputted by the K means algorithm are referred to as final classifications or clusters of data, which means that it is ultimately the most complete and accurate set of data based on what you have asked the algorithm to do. Ideally, it should take the initially anonymous data points and turn them into something that is complete with their own classifications and identities that represent patterns and trends within the data that was inputted in the first place.

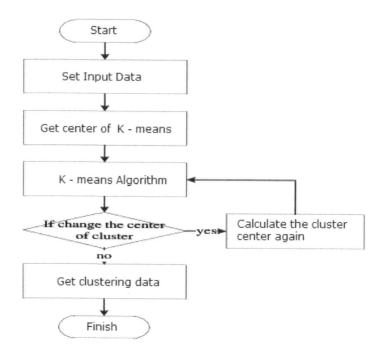

When Should This Algorithm be Used?

The K means clustering algorithm can be used in multiple different settings, ranging from behavioral segmentation to inventory categorization, and more. Because of how flexible this algorithm is, it can be applied to a variety of different uses, all of which can be incredibly helpful across various industries. The five most common areas that the K means cluster algorithm is used include: behavioral segmentation, inventory categorization, sorting sensor measurements, detecting bots or anomalies, and tracking and monitoring classification change. This can be beneficial to many industries, making it useful in all sorts of machine learning technologies and networks. To help you better understand these practical applications and uses, we are going to explore these five different areas of application in greater detail so that you can get a better idea of what the K means clustering algorithm actually does for them.

Behavioral Segmentation

Behavioral segmentation studies the behavior of different people. When it comes to the K means clustering algorithm, companies are able to get complete behavioral profiles on their customers that enable them to understand how they can better serve those customers. From an ethical point of view, this information can be used to shape a more enjoyable relationship between the customer and the business, ultimately creating more successful business, too. This can also be used to identify new products or services that could be introduced, or old ones that could be revamped, to improve a customer's experience with a given business.

In addition to behavioral segmentation supporting the segmentation of customers based on purchase history, it can also support businesses in segmenting things like activities on websites, applications, or even specific platforms. For example, if a company were to launch a new app to support customers in shopping with their brand, it could segment where the app was being used the most, how, by who, and when. Another way that behavioral segmentation has been used with the K means clustering algorithm is to define personas based on interests. In the analytical world, this is called *psychological profiling* and means that you use analytics to identify which types of people are most likely to behave in certain ways. Rather than attempting to come up with and confirm your theories through your own research, you could use the K means clustering algorithm to create clear and accurate psychological profiles. Through this, you could use these psychological profiles to identify which are most active in your business, and which could become more active in your business if they had the right products or services available to them. Beyond just business, these psychological profiles can also help identify information relevant to the educational system, or even the government. With them in hand, educational programs can identify high risk students and offer them more support, or the government could use these profiles to identify what types of organizations or support programs may be useful to their public.

Lastly, profiles can also be made based on activity monitoring, rather than interests. Often, true psychological profiles created through analytics will feature both interest monitoring and activity monitoring to create a clearer understanding as to who is being represented by the profile. In some cases, however, these two metrics may be looked at separately for different means.

For example, interest-based personas could be used to identify what types of products to advertise to certain people, whereas activity based monitoring could identify where to advertise those things to create the largest amount of interaction with that advertisement.

Inventory Categorization

When it comes to inventory categorization, larger corporations and those that have hundreds of thousands or even millions of products can benefit from learning how to categorize their products more effectively. Proper inventory categorization methods ensure that inventory stays organized, that companies know what is in stock and what is not, and that inventory is managed properly. For example, a proper management system can ensure that if a company has 10,000 units of a certain product, the units are evenly distributed across their 50 locations, rather than all sent to one or two single locations. With the K means clustering algorithm, the algorithm can categorize inventory based on sales activity, and based on manufacturing metrics. This means that the inventory can be categorized based on just about any set of predetermined categories the company may want to put in place. On a website, for example, the company can use the K means clustering method to organize their products based on best sellers, most relevant, top rated, or most cost effective. In their private inventory management systems, they may organize them based on their SKU, which would be a series of numbers used to identify what the product is and what category of products it belonged to. For example, the SKU might reflect that the product is a video game, or a small appliance.

By using these proper inventory category management systems, thousands of pieces of inventory can be uploaded and managed at the moment noticed using the K means clustering algorithm. For businesses, this can mean more effective inventory management for their employees, as well as easier shopping experiences for their customers. In both scenarios, the algorithm has effectively supported them by creating more success in their sales.

Sorting Sensor Measurements

There are multiple different types of sensors that may be monitored or tracked using the K means clustering algorithm. For example, it may be used to detect activity types in motion sensors, allowing the sensor to identify when something has come into the radar of the motion sensor. In some cases, it may be very basic and simply detect any motion. In other cases, it may detect certain amounts of motion, frequencies of motion, or types of motion and exclude other forms of motion. As a result, it is able to provide feedback on the specific type of motion and possibly even be used as the basis to build other more complex motion sensor-based projects off of. For example, the K means clustering algorithm might recognize a certain type of motion and then send off a signal to a security device to inform the owner of that device that something suspicious has been detected by the motion sensor. While the trigger and following behaviors would not be the responsibility of the K means clustering algorithm, the detection of the motion that initially indicated the trigger was met would be.

Another thing it can do is detect and group images.

Using proper algorithm measurements, the K means clustering algorithm can detect certain features in an image and present them upon request. For example, you would be able to upload 10,000 random pictures into the algorithm and it would group pictures together based on similar features. All images featuring the Eiffel Tower, for example, would be grouped together. Likewise, all images featuring people, or even a certain person, would be grouped together. In present day, this exact technology is recognized in modern smart phones where people can open their Photo Applications and type in a keyword, thus causing the phone to show any photographs they may have taken that featured that keyword. For example, if you were to open up your photo application and type in "Dog," if you had taken any photographs of a dog with your device, the device would show you all of those photographs.

In addition to being able to group photographs, the K means clustering algorithm can also group and separate audio. This means it can be used to separate audio tracks to draw out specific instruments or voices, or even categorize audio tracks based on certain types of sounds that are present in that audio track.

This is particularly helpful, for example, in cases where investigators may be trying to understand what someone is saying but is incapable of hearing their voice due to background noise in a certain audio tape. Using the K means clustering algorithm, they can separate the audio and remove background noise, making it easier for people to hear the actual voice being represented on that particular audio track. Another way that sorting sensor measurement is completed using the K means clustering algorithm is to identify groups in health monitoring. In this case, an individual might receive a series of different tests and measurements to track their health, and then they would go on to input that into the algorithm.

From there, the machine learning technology would be able to recognize normal patterns in their health, and identify any possible anomalies or differences in their health patterns. This way, they could accurately keep track of their health and quickly recognize anything was different from what it should be.

Detecting Bots or Anomalies

Aside from detecting anomalies in health, the K means clustering algorithm can also detect bots and anomalies in computers and software. This means that the algorithm can detect anytime bot activity is suspected in a certain application and can warn the application authorities of it, or shut down the activity if the device or software has been given the instruction to do so. A great example of this is commonly seen on social media, where many accounts will use bots to attempt to build followers and increase activity and engagement on their profiles. On the day of the influencer, this is seen as an opportunity to rapidly build your popularity and increase your engagement so that you are more likely to land brand deals and earn an income from your business. Typically, most social media platforms frown upon bot use however as it can dilute the quality of the platform and make the experience less enjoyable for other users. As a result, they tend to monitor for and ban anyone who has been suspected of using bots. In order to identify when and where bots are being used, rather than attempting to employ thousands of people to monitor the platform, they instead use the K means clustering algorithm to effectively remove, or suspend, the offending accounts.

Aside from detecting bots, the K means clustering algorithm has also been used to monitor activity on networks to make sure that nothing separate from the network itself has hacked the system in an unauthorized and unlawful manner. By setting up the algorithm to monitor activity, it is capable of recognizing anytime someone has attempted to hack into or attach itself to the network so that it can eliminate their advances. The algorithm is generally set up to automatically deny access for outliers so that their systems cannot be hacked or disrupted by those who are attempting to maliciously interrupt the network itself. This way, rather than having to manually protect their network there is a complex algorithm in place taking care of it.

Tracking and Monitoring Classification Change

Another way that the K means clustering algorithm can support developers and programmers is through detecting changes in where data is placed over time. For example, if a certain piece of data groups effectively with one classification, but over time groups more effectively with another classification, this can be monitored through the K means clustering algorithm. An example of this would be if, say, a certain demographic was largely buying name brand from a store but then began buying less known but more eco-friendly brands over time, this would be detected by the algorithm. In this particular instance, this change would represent the fact that more people preferred eco-friendly brands, and would indicate to that company that they should focus on purchasing and selling more eco-friendly brands in the future.

This particular tracking and monitoring of data changing from one classification to another can serve in many ways when it comes to tracking data. It can help track the evolution and change of people, or certain experiences, creating a more rounded understanding of various classifications for humans.

In this case, you would be able to effectively create an understanding of your customers and use this knowledge to create more meaningful programs, products, services, offerings, marketing, or other developments for those individuals.

Beyond tracking evolution, this particular area of the K means clustering algorithm can also help track devolution, or areas where regression or negative changes have developed in a system. For example, let's say you are tracking the wellbeing of a community, if you recognized that a certain group of society was beginning to experience a negative impact from the present societal structure, you could use this to help with advancements. This could, say, lead to the development of new social programs that would support the society in a more meaningful manner, helping everyone have access to equal rights and support from that particular segment of society.

Chapter 6: Artificial Neural Networks

Artificial neural networks are also known as connectionist systems, and they are a form of computing systems that are inspired by biological neural networks, such as the ones found in humans and other animal species. With that being said, they are not identical to biological neural networks because a biological neural network is more complex in nature, and would be incredibly difficult to reproduce in the form of coding or computing technology.

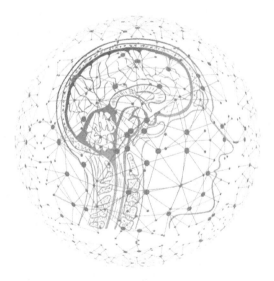

The purpose of the artificial neural network is to "learn" how to perform tasks by using examples as a means to "understand" how a task should be completed.

Typically, the artificial neural network is not actually programmed with task-specific rules, but instead is shown examples of what it is expected to do and then, based on how it is developed and programmed, learns how to do these tasks on its own.

Artificial neural networks became incredibly popular in the mid-1900s and were developed upon over time by computer scientists who were fascinated by how these artificial neural networks could allow computers to learn and function. They became the basis for many different advanced computing technologies at the time, and served a massive purpose in helping to increase the capacity of computers, mainly through the tasks that could be accomplished through a computer device. Over the years, the artificial neural network has been improved upon over and over again, until the point where they are now some of the most powerful forms of computer there is out there. As a result of all of this development, artificial neural networks have rapidly approached human-like capacities ranging from handwriting recognition to learning about languages and other tasks that are often reserved for human practice.

Artificial neural networks are likely to be the basis for any form of artificial intelligence that represents the form of robots that people frequently think about when they consider a robotic "species." For example, a robot that had human-like qualities both in appearance and in functionality. If a robot ever were to be developed in this capacity, it is likely that it would be programmed with the support of artificial neural networks.

What Are *Artificial Neural Networks?*

As previously mentioned, artificial neural networks are a computerized model of biological neural networks, although they do not quite look the same or behave entirely the same. In a sense, artificial neural networks are a more devolved version of the biological neural network that makes your, and my, brain work. The development of the artificial neural network has allowed for it to "learn" on its own, based on a series of information or examples that have been fed to it. For example, an artificial neural network could engage in image recognition and begin to identify a common thing in the image, such as "cat."

This could be trained to the artificial neural network by uploading a series of images and labeling them as either "cat" or "no cat." The artificial neural network would then be able to identify what the cats actually were based on all of the examples in the pictures.

Through that, they would be able to identify cats in the future. When this is accomplished, the neural network has no prior knowledge of what cats are, meaning that they have no idea that cats have fur, tails, whiskers, or faces that look like cats. In other words, the device has no means of identifying what a cat is, other than by processing all of the example images and formulating its own consensus. When the artificial neural network is properly developed, it creates the proper consensus in virtually all circumstances, making it an incredibly advanced and impressive algorithm.

The purpose of the artificial neural network is to solve problems using the exact same methods that the human brain would.

With that being said, over time the focus of the development was largely based on advancing these artificial neural networks to be able to perform very specific tasks, like engaging in computer vision or speech recognition, or even filtering social networks or playing video games. Some have even been developed to engage in medical diagnosis, or to paint pictures. As a result, they have deviated further away from true biological neural networks and into ones that are specialized to perform specific tasks with incredible accuracy.

How Does They Work?

An artificial neural network is developed with a collection of connected units, or nodes, which are correctly referred to as artificial neurons. Despite having the same term as biological neurons, and being loosely developed based off of biological neurons, these neurons do not behave the same way that a biological neuron does. Instead, they carry certain pieces of information and then connect to other neurons in a way to formulate entire behaviors. In a biological brain, these connections would be called synapses, and this is essentially the same thing that the artificial neurons do. In the artificial neuron network, the nodes are designed to transmit information between each other based on what that information is and what it means. Through a complex algorithm, this then becomes an "understanding" of the information being fed to the system, which results in human-like thoughts and behavioral patterns.

With that being said, most artificial neural networks are incapable of passing true emotion or sentient energy back and forth through their nodes, which means that they will behave differently from how a human would actually behave. Artificial neurons in the artificial neural network are each coded with real numbers, rather than biological information. Through that, they also have what have known edges, which is where they connect with each other and transmit information back and forth between other artificial neurons. Neurons and their edges have what are known as weights, which are specific numerical values that measure the capacity of that neuron. Over the learning process, these weights adjust to reflect increased information being learned through the network. Each neuron will have a threshold, and if that threshold is met it will no longer be able to engage in the learning process. If this occurs, the artificial neural network will then begin to attempt to work together with other artificial neurons to complete the same task. If it runs out of other artificial neurons to connect with, the process stops and the machine has "reached capacity." Another form of artificial neuron thresholds is represented by neurons being coded to only receive certain forms of information. By only being able to receive certain forms of information, the artificial neural network is able to organize which nodes are involved in various tasks, allowing it to keep itself organized and functional.

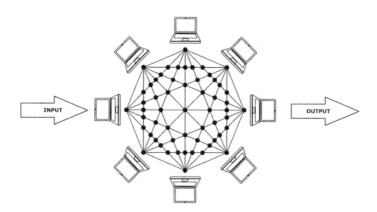

At this point, there are many different types of artificial neural networks that are being used for different reasons. The simplest forms of artificial neural networks use more static components, such as having a limited number of units, layers, unit weights, and topology. Other more dynamic artificial neural networks allow for these areas to develop in a more intentional capacity so that they can evolve through the learning process and become more complex. The latter form of an artificial neural network is more complicated and takes significantly longer to design, however it does make the learning process shorter as the device is already smarter from square one. As a result, it is able to learn faster and perform its intended functions with greater ease. The former variety of artificial neural networks is less complicated and is much easier to build, however it also takes significantly longer to train it anything, meaning that the learning process can be lengthy and even delayed in some cases.

In addition to the complexity of the machine varying, there are also varying degrees of supervision involved in artificial neural networks. Because of how complex they are and what they are capable of accomplishing, they have largely been developed with more supervision being required by the operator to ensure that learning is being done in the proper intended manner. This way, the machine learns what it is meant to learn and functions as it should, and it is not capable of doing anything it was not designed to do. In other artificial neural networks, however, they have been completely designed to run independently so that they do not require any significant human intervention. In these particular artificial neural networks, just about anything goes and they can be used in any number of ways.

When Should They be Used?

When it comes to artificial neural networks, a lot of people argue the ethics around them. This is particularly common in people who do not clearly understand how they are used, or those who are afraid that they will be built into machines that are capable of learning how to turn against mankind and become dangerous, essentially. Naturally, these types of fears and concerns are valid but should not be worried about too much as modern artificial intelligence and artificial neural networks are far from being able to do anything significant on their own.

73

Although they are incredibly powerful and functioning "brains," most lack proper bodies or other extremities to be able to actually perform anything. At this point, there is still a long way to go before we have completely functional artificial neural networks that feature both the smarts of present-day networks and the capacity of a robot with properly mobile and functioning extremities. With that being said, artificial neural networks are still being used in a massive way in today's world. Since their conception, they have been a focal point for many computer scientists and researchers, and as such there have been many tasks that have been able to be performed by these unique and diverse networks. In fact, you might be surprised to realize just how far this technology has already come, and what it is capable of achieving. The current areas where artificial neural networks are being used the most include: identification and process control, general game playing, various forms of recognition, 3D reconstruction, diagnosis, finances, and filtering.

Identification and Process Control

Identification and control, and process control, is an incredible feature of the artificial neural networks. Certain developments have led to these networks being able to essentially recognize specific systems and begin to actually control those systems purposefully. A great example of this is with vehicle control, where vehicles are able to become self-driving, or are able to monitor certain "behaviors" and support the driver accordingly. For example, these days many modern vehicles are able to apply the brakes before the driver were to hit something, such as a pedestrian or an unexpected obstacle in the road. While these systems are still largely debated and are still in the process of being developed to become more effective and efficient, they are starting to make their way into circulation to be used by cars in a more broad manner.

General Game Playing

Game playing has been completed by artificial neural networks in many ways, too. This goes for both physical forms of game play, and virtual forms of game play.

To date, machines have been trained to play games like chess or checkers flawlessly, often beating their opponents by a landslide, or serving as a formidable and strong opponent that poses a real challenge for the individual playing against the network. These designs have been made to either interpret knowledge and request the support of a human to move the piece for them, or with a robotic arm that allows the artificial network to both make decisions about game play and then complete the move on their own.

Outside of actual real world game play, artificial neural networks have also been used to help design digital game play systems, too. These artificial neural networks are able to be hooked up to a game playing device and are able to play digital games, such as on X Box or PlayStation by essentially "watching" the screen and playing just as a real human player would. In both cases, these artificial neural networks have proven to be incredibly quick at learning about new techniques and practices so that they can effectively play the games that they have been developed to play. The more effective a machine is developed, the more success it has in playing the game, too, which results in even more success down the line since it is essentially learning as it goes. Eventually, these machines can become so powerful that they are nearly impossible for any average human to beat in the games that they were designed to play.

Various Forms of Recognition

Artificial neural networks are incredibly skilled when it comes to varying forms of recognition. From recognizing faces and voices, to recognizing gestures and even handwriting, they are incredibly powerful. Some have even been designed to recognize what text says and then act based on the text that it has "read." In addition to these forms of recognition, they can also recognize various patterns, either in codes, data, or even in signals being gestured to the device. For example, if a specific sequence of signals were given to a trained machine, it would be able to perform specific tasks based on what those signals were developed to mean for that device. Recognition helps these devices in becoming aware of and informing other complex parts of their systems to complete certain functions.

Through this recognition it can begin to classify pieces of information within its own system and then use that information to inform other parts of the technology to complete certain tasks. At this rate, however, the artificial neural networks' involvement would be exclusive to the "thinking" or the receiving information, classifying it, and then outputting specific signals through the rest of the artificial neural network. Any tasks that were completed afterward, such as triggering movement in a robotic extremity, would be part of a different programming feature that was triggered into action based on what the artificial neural network "said."

3D Reconstruction

3D reconstruction means that a computer can capture the shape and appearance of real objects and then, if it wants, change the shape in time so that it can be "reconstructed." The purpose of this is typical to improve the structure of something, such as when it comes to design or even with medical imaging. Based on the advancements of artificial neural networks, these systems are actually able to aid the process 3D reconstruction massively. As a result, they are known as being fundamental in the process of 3D reconstruction.

Diagnosis

Based on how they work, artificial neural networks have the capacity to engage in medical diagnosis. Through this, the ethical standards say that these devices can be used to formulate a diagnosis, but humans must validate that diagnosis using manual tests to ensure that the device was correct and the diagnosis is accurate. With that being said, artificial neural networks have been used to diagnose varying types of cancers, ranging from lung cancer to prostate cancer, and it can even distinguish cancerous cells from healthy or typical cells.

Finances

In finances, various computer scientists have been developing artificial neural networks that can engage in tasks such as automated trading systems. This is how various high tech traders are able to engage in consistent trades, even if they are not actively engaging in any trading activity themselves. As a result, they are able to essentially earn passive money through the stock market, or other trading platforms, without any human intervention. As well, when cryptocurrency was first introduced, many computer scientists formed artificial neural networks to mine for the cryptocurrency so that they could begin to collect these currencies. As a result, they were able to take part in one of the world's first cryptocurrency experiments, and many of them made massive money doing it.

Filtering

Artificial neural networks are frequently used in social networks and emails as a way to conduct spam filtering, amongst other forms of filtering. Based on how they are developed, these networks are able to identify varying forms of information from what is being uploaded to social networks, or sent out via. emails, and classify accordingly. When it comes to email spam filtering, this is done in a relatively simple manner. The artificial neural network merely "reads" the emails and determines what is spam, and what is not spam. Of course, humans can always override the reading and change an email's label if they find that the filter did not function appropriately, or that an email made it into the wrong label. For social networks, the functionality of this is more complex. Rather than simply deeming what is spam and what is not, these artificial neural networks can do a lot. They can detect and take down photos featuring certain types of graphics that are not permitted on social networks, such as nudity or violence. They can also apply filters over particularly graphic and possibly offensive images to ensure that people are not automatically being exposed to photographs that may be too graphic or violent for them to see. As well, they can recognize when someone may be posting something that indicates that they or someone else is in danger and it can offer support measures to assist them in hopefully protecting themselves and getting out of danger. These filters can also do basic spam filtering to prevent spam from making it onto the platforms, or identify and remove bots to ensure that they are not taking over networks.

Artificial neural networks are clearly incredibly advanced forms of technology that can help take machine learning to a whole new level. Many people think that the future of artificial neural networks lies in developing complete robots that are far more advanced and complex than existing ones. For example, developing an entire robotic species that ultimately functions and behaves on its own. Of course, there are many ethical considerations we have to take into account, and other things that need to be addressed before this happens. However, the reality of a world where robots are far more prominent in our society is likely not as far off as many people think, and they could be used to bring about a revolution that completely changes life as we know it.

Chapter 7: Decision Trees

Decision trees are a form of visualization algorithm. What this means is that they take certain pieces of information and organize them in specific classifications, completing their intended functions as necessary. However, the process used by the algorithm is visually displayed in a way that makes it easy for the human mind to follow along and witness what was completed during the algorithm process. What ends up happening is we are shown statistical data in a way that makes sense, that shows us how certain conclusions were drawn, and that helps us use these conclusions to formulate decisions or make new plans or strategies going forward. That is exactly the goal of decision trees, with the entire focus largely being around how decisions were made and what was considered in the process of the decision being made.

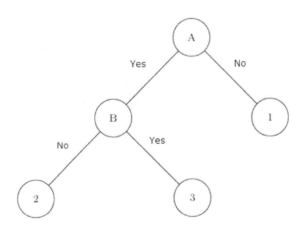

Decision trees largely show like a flow-chart, although they are an official form of machine learning algorithm that serves a very specific purpose when it comes to how and why they are used in various machine learning technology.

In this chapter we are going to discover exactly what a decision tree is, how it works, and when it is used so that you can understand this unique decision making algorithm and what benefit it serves in machine learning. Because of how niche it is, it is one that definitely serves a strong, and very specific purpose.

What Are *Decision Trees*?

Decision trees are a tool that uses a tree shaped graph to support individuals or organizations in making decisions. Using a decision tree you can identify possible consequences of your decision, as well as chance event outcomes, utility, and even resource costs. When it comes to making large decisions in big corporations especially, decision trees are an excellent way to identify exact areas where growth will prove to be most valuable and where companies will be able to get the most benefit from growth. However, they can also be used in many other ways. The decision tree is always shown in a flowchart style structure which shows the individual running the decision what things have been considered, what the possible outcomes are, as well as what the probable outcomes are. These flowcharts are made based on the fact that life is a complex thing and there is no way to guarantee what is going to happen, or how it is going to happen.

With that being said, using laws of probability and various calculations, the decision tree algorithm can identify what is most likely to happen given a certain set of circumstances, or certain situations. When you look at a decision tree, each branch of the tree represents a specific outcome of the test. Then, each leaf node, or "end" of the branch represents a class label. In order for a class label to be reached, a decision must move from the root node (the initial decision) through the branches (possible outcomes) and into the leaf nodes (final outcomes.) This process takes place through various classification rules that determine what will likely happen and how this information would be most accurately categorized on the decision tree. Everything is based on an algorithm and calculations that measure probability to ensure that the tree is as close to accurate as possible. Barring an incredibly unexpected and untraceable external event that could completely change the decision being made, this tree is typically incredibly accurate and can reliably be followed by those watching it.

When it comes to machine learning algorithms, the decision tree is one of the most popular supervised algorithms that is used. These algorithms can support predictive models with high accuracy, and can make it easy to stabilize and interpret results to ensure that you are taking appropriate action based on the decision you have made, or need to make. Unlike linear models that point down one clear path toward a specific outcome, decision trees represent all possible outcomes and are incredibly adaptable. Through this, virtually any kind of problem can be solved using a decision tree, as they can be used to show you so much information. As well, if you find that part way through the process you need to change direction, you can refer back to your decision tree to identify how you could change direction and what the probable outcome of a changed direction would be. The algorithm within decision trees that results in them being non-linear and exhaustive is called "Classification and Regression Trees" or CART. This particular algorithm is used in decision trees, as well as other non-linear models that are used by machine learning algorithms. This can include regression trees, a random forest which we will talk about later, gradient boosting, and of course decision trees.

How Do *Decision Trees* Work?

Decision trees are commonly used in solving data science problems, such as what should be done to resolve certain troubles that a scientist is facing. This could include anything from identifying possible outcomes of certain medical treatments, to identifying possible outcomes of certain marketing strategies or even initiatives that organizations or governments might take to attempt to improve the state of something. Decision trees are said to be far more effective than any other decision making a process out there because they can calculate massive amounts of big data and turn up complete, accurate results that let people or organizations know how to proceed.

Decision trees are something that we can do in our own brains, to one degree or another. When we are completing a decision tree in our minds, we are essentially looking at a problem and considering all of the possible solutions and what those solutions would entail.

You have likely done this yourself, and some people even find themselves doing it to the point where it almost becomes obsessive because they are trying to make sure that they make the right decision. With that being said, the trouble of a mental decision tree is that you are not able to actually represent that tree in a visual manner that shows you what truly is likely to happen, and what the possible outcomes would be. Furthermore, your brain is ridden with biases and limitations that prevent it from being able to truly recognize every single possible outcome, as well as the probability of those outcomes coming to fruition. With a decision tree, the information is carefully calculated using a specific algorithm that essentially guarantees that the information is sound and true. This way, you can feel confident that the results you gain from the decision tree are likely to be accurate and that you can safely follow them and expect that the probable outcome you anticipated based on the results of the tree will, in fact, be the actual result you experience, too. On the decision tree, there are seven things you need to know about. These include: the root node, splitting, the decision node, the leaf node, pruning, branches, and parent and child nodes. Each of these nodes represents a specific part of the tree, and learning how they work will inform you as to how the algorithm reads and presents information, and how you can read the decision tree to make your conclusions and choices going forward.

The Root Node

The root node is the initial node at the very top of the decision tree. This node represents the entire population of the tree under it, meaning that this is ultimately the first layer of knowledge being fed into the tree. Typically, the root node represents the primary decision that the person needs to make, and the topic of that particular decision.

Splitting

Splitting is the term used to describe the process of one node splitting into two or more nodes. As the tree drops down into further classifications of information, ultimately leading it to a decision, it splits up nodes into several smaller nodes that represent different pieces of information. All of these pieces of information will, in one way or another, be relevant to the topic and the decision being made.

The Decision Node

Decision nodes are any nodes that have nodes splitting off of them. These represent a new decision that needs to be made in order for different outcomes to be created. These decisions are sub-decisions of the primary decision, but they all lead toward an outcome that is relevant to the primary decision that needs to be made. For example, let's say the primary decision is: "Should I eat a sandwich for dinner?" this would become a decision node when the node split and two smaller nodes were made that said "Yes" or "No." If those smaller nodes were to break out into more smaller nodes through the splitting process, they would become decision nodes, too.

The Leaf Node

Leaf nodes are nodes where they do not split off. These are the "final outcome" of a decision tree, and represent what would happen if you made all of the decisions up until that point based off of the tree. These show you, ultimately, what to expect if you act based on the trees algorithm and what it has suggested for you to do.

If you find yourself at a leaf node, you can consider your decision and all subsequent decisions complete, and that particular experience would then be brought to closure since no further decisions or actions could possibly be taken.

Pruning

Pruning occurs when people choose to remove sub-nodes of a decision node. Sometimes, the decision nodes will represent something that the person or organization making the decision would never do. Sometimes these may be irrelevant, unreasonable, impossible, or unethical and so right from the start the individual or organization knows that they will not be taking action based on those decisions. In order to clean up the tree and make it more readable, and useful, they will do what is called "pruning." This essentially means that they remove the decision nodes so that only decisions they would reasonably take are reflected on the tree. In a sense, you can see this as being the opposite of splitting.

Branches

Branches are subsections of the entire tree. So, let's say that your primary decision splits off into four decisions, each of which splits off into several smaller decisions. Those four decisions would then become "branches" as they represent different completely different subsections based on an action that you could take, and the possible outcomes that you would face if you took those actions.

Parent and Child Nodes

Parent and child nodes are simply a way of representing larger decision nodes versus smaller decision nodes. The parent node is one that is higher up on the tree, directly above the smaller node in question. The child node, then, is the one lower down on the tree, directly below the larger node in question. Child nodes can go down several "generations," but in order to be related to the parent node, they must directly draw back to that specific decision at some point when you are drawing your way back up the tree.

How the Tree Works

When the algorithm is processed and information, such as the primary decision, is inputted into the algorithm, the decision tree goes on to fill out all of the nodes and branches based on the information you have inputted into the system. This is all automatically done through the algorithm based on any information you have fed the system at the time of creating your tree. If you have any situations, circumstances, or other things to factor in or consider, you would want to write those down in your algorithm to ensure that they are accounted for upon the creation of the tree. Once the tree was created, you could look through the decisions and prune the tree to remove any decisions that you absolutely know you would not make. For example, if they require you to do something impossible, unreasonable, irrelevant, or unethical, you could prune those branches away so that the tree more clearly represented things that you would actually do.

How the Tree is Read

After the decision tree is complete, you would look through the tree starting at the root decision. Then, you would look at your desired outcome. From there, you would draw your way from the root to the desired decision and identify what choices would need to be made and considerations would need to be factored in for you to be able to reach your ideal outcome. If you find that the method is something you would not, or could not, do you can always read the tree differently. In this case, rather than reading from the bottom up, you could read from the top down. Reading from the top down would require you to look at your initial decision, and ultimately pick your path down the tree based on what is most likely, or most possible. As a result, you would find your way to your probable outcome based on the decisions that you have made. After you have successfully read the decision tree, you need to turn your findings into a strategy or a plan for how you will proceed and create your desired outcome. All of your decisions in your strategy or plan should be based on the findings of the decision tree so that you are able to create the outcome you desire to create. This way, you are more likely to have the desired outcome, and you are able to take the clearest path possible. Ideally, you should look at the path that is going to get you to where you want to go with the least amount of steps. This expedites your results and ensures that you are not wasting time, energy, or resources on different steps that are not relevant for you to be able to create your desired outcome. The more direct your path to your desired outcome is, the more success you will likely have with the decision and the tree you have made.

When Should *Decision Trees* be Used?

Decision trees are frequently used in business decisions, government decisions, educational decisions, and other decisions within large organizations. It can also be used in data sciences, specifically around computer programming, to identify what possible functions a programmed device could feature. In each area of application, the use of the decision tree is the same and the benefit is the same, however the way that it is created and the information it features will vary from tree to tree. Let's take a deeper look at how they can be applied to give you an understanding as to what a decision tree can do in practical application.

Business Decisions

Decision trees are frequently used in business decisions, especially within larger organizations where there are so many moving parts and so many pieces of data and information to consider. Typically, decision trees will be used to help businesses create certain decisions in terms of marketing, product development, or expansion, to identify areas where they can increase business productivity and, therefore, increase revenue, too. The goal is always to identify expected and unexpected means of growth so that companies are more likely to take the best route toward growth possible. Naturally, growth and increased revenue is always the goal with businesses. When using decision trees, businesses can factor in everything from income, budgets, customer relationships and retention, new customer acquisition, employees, and even external factors like economics and location when it comes to making decisions.

By being able to introduce so many different focuses on the classification system, businesses can get accurate representations of what ideas would be best for them based off of the decisions shown in the decision tree.

Government Decisions

In government, decision trees can be used as a means to determine how a government can improve areas of their society while being able to reasonably consider factors such as the people they are leading, their budget, and the resources they have to help them. As a result, they can find rational, reasonable, and effective solutions to problems like funding, providing enough resources for their public, and more. When used effectively, a government can use decision trees to make the best choices for their people so that they can become effective and meaningful leaders.

Educational Decisions

In educational programs, decision trees can be used to determine how budgets will be spent, what types of information should be included in curriculums, and what new resources or services could be offered to support student learning.

Through factoring in things such as budget, students, learning comprehension, faculty, and resources, education boards can discover ways to overcome challenges being presented to their school system and improve results for their staff and students.

Programming Decisions

In programming, decision trees can be used to help programmers identify what route would be the most effective and direct way for them to program a certain piece of technology. When it comes to programming and developing new technology, creating the most direct route to your goal is important as it ensures that your goal is met and that there are not so many things that could go wrong with the goal you have. The more effectively you can choose the right algorithm or programming measure, the more effective you will be in creating a clear cut path toward your goal and programming your device effectively. This way, there is no "filler" code that could increase risk by presenting the opportunity for the code to break or malfunction, possibly rendering the entire coding network useless for that particular device.

Decision trees definitely have a strong capacity to support people in the technology industry, as well as in data sciences, when it comes to making rational and sound decisions.

By using decision trees, individuals and organizations can ensure that they have exhausted all of their possibilities and that through that they are taking the best possible steps forward to reach their goals and resolve any possible problems that have risen along the way.

Chapter 8: Naïve Bayes Classifier Algorithm

The naïve Bayes classifier is an algorithm that is considered to be incredibly basic and that, like the decision tree, has a very niche focus on what it is meant to do when it comes to machine learning. This particular algorithm uses simple probabilistic classifiers to perform functions such as filtering spam versus legitimate content, or other similar functions.

When it comes to the naïve Bayes classifier, there is actually not one single algorithm used to train classifiers, but instead a family of algorithms that are used. This group of algorithms is based on a common principle: that all naïve Bayes classifiers are independent of the value of any other feature in the model. An easy way to understand this would be to look at this example: let's say fruit is considered a grape if it is green, round, and about 1" in diameter. A naïve Bayes classifier would consider each of these features to independently contribute to the probability of this fruit is a grape, regardless of any correlations that might exist between the three features described. So, even if there were a plausible correlation that confirmed the findings, it would not be considered in the naïve Bayes classifier algorithms.

The naïve Bayes classifier is trained as a supervised learning algorithm, because it requires a human to input parameters that allow it to identify the probability of something. Without a human being able to input these independent values, the classifier has no way of receiving knowledge and therefore no way of functioning.

This particular algorithm cannot be trained to identify knowledge based on examples, so it has no way of becoming an unsupervised algorithm at this point in time. Furthermore, it has no purpose of becoming an unsupervised algorithm, since other algorithms would likely be more effective in an unsupervised setting, such as artificial neural networks. In this chapter, we are going to dig deeper into what the naïve Bayes classifier really is, how it works, and when and why someone would use it. Despite how niche it is, this particular algorithm does have very useful applications making it incredibly effective in the right setting.

What Is the *Naïve Bayes Classifier* Algorithm?

Classifiers in general are machine learning models that are used to discriminate different objects based on certain features in the object. This way, they can classify, or separate, those objects based on a specific set of similarities and group them together for greater purposes, such as formulating statistics or probabilities. The naïve Bayes classifier is no different, being that it is also a probabilistic machine learning model that is used to classify different objects. The naïve Bayes classifier differs only in the fact that it uses the Bayes Theorem to work, over any other model that may be presented.

How Does This Algorithm Work?

Not unlike other classifiers, the naïve Bayes classifier is a probabilistic machine learning model that can be used to classify things. This essentially means that, once it is programmed, it will organize things into specific categories and groups for the user depending on what they needed things to be categorized for. In order for this classifier to work, it requires the Bayes Theorem calculation.

This particular calculation is as follows:

$$P(A|B) = \frac{P(B|A)P(A)}{P(B)}$$

In this particular theorem, you can discover the probability of **A** happening based on the fact that **B** occurred. In other words, **A** cannot happen if **B** does not happen first. In the Bayes Theorem case, **A** represents the hypothesis and **B** represents the evidence. The theorem will first read the evidence (**B**) in order to produce a hypothesis (**A**).

In this particular theorem, it is assumed that the predictors and features are independent, which means that the presence of one does not affect the other. For example, in a spam filter in an email program, features such as: swear words, certain phishing words, and certain email handles could all be considered spam. However, all three would not need to be present for the email to be classified as spam.

So long as one of the three was identified in the email being sent, it would be considered spam even if the other two were not represented in it. Technically, there are different types of naïve Bayes classifiers. This is because naïve Bayes classifiers are more of a family of algorithms, rather than a single algorithm. Each type of naïve Bayes classifier will perform a different function and be used in a different setting and, depending on what is being done, a person may need to use two or more naïve Bayes classifier algorithms in order to complete their required task. The different types of the naïve Bayes classifiers include: the multinomial naïve Bayes, the Bernoulli naïve Bayes, and the Gaussian naïve Bayes.

Multinomial Naïve Bayes

The multinomial naïve Bayes is primarily used for document classification problems. For example, it can identify whether a document belongs to a specific category based on the factors relevant to that unique document. If it were, let's say, a news article, the multinomial naïve Bayes could accurately determine whether that article was best represented by sports, technology, politics, or otherwise. In this particular naïve Bayes classifier, the decision is made based on the frequency of certain types of language being used in a document.

Bernoulli Naïve Bayes

The Bernoulli naïve Bayes classifier is similar to the multinomial naïve Bayes classifier, except that the predictors are Boolean variables. This means that the parameters used to predict the class variable may only be a "yes" or a "no."

For example, the parameter might be, does the word "*soccer*" exist in the text? If the answer is yes, it would be classified under one category. If it was no, it would be classified under a different category.

Gaussian Naïve Bayes

The gaussian naïve Bayes classifier is an algorithm that is used to identify a continuous value that is not discrete. In this case, the values are present but there is no clear classifier that determines how much those particular values are present, so the gaussian naïve Bayes classifier uses a certain set of parameters to essentially measure those values and classify the represented asset accordingly.

When Should This Algorithm be Used?

The naïve Bayes classifiers are a very niche type of classifier that is best used in specific settings, too. The two most common applications of the naïve Bayes algorithm in today's world include sorting documents in large filing systems, and sorting out spam and priority filters in various internet mailing applications, such as emails or social media messenger applications.

Filing Documents

When it comes to filing documents, the naïve Bayes classifier can be used to essentially determine which categories a document fits best under so that they can be organized accordingly. For businesses that use a lot of online documentation applications and that store multiple files in the online space, such as on cloud storage, the naïve Bayes algorithm can automatically store their files based on certain classifiers.

The goal of the naïve Bayes algorithm would be for the classifiers to effectively store documents in a logical, meaningful, and useful manner that supports them in being found at a later date. If they are filed properly, they will be organized and easy to identify. A great example of large online filing networks would be news outlets. Some news outlets may manually sort their articles on their website, whereas others may employ the use of a naïve Bayes algorithm to ensure that their articles are being sorted and organized properly. In these cases, they will likely create a clause that states that the file can be saved in a preselected number of archives and folders so that it can be found more effectively. This way, it is properly stored and it is more likely to be found by interested readers.

Spam and Priority Filters

Another common way the naïve Bayes classifier is used is when it comes to spam and priority filters. Spam filters are the most common and longest standing filters out there when it comes to the computer, as they have been used to sort and file spam email messages and other spam content in separate folders away from primary folders.

This way, users are less likely to see spam content and will not have to filter through all of that content. In other words, it ensures that they are likely to see what matters and that they are unlikely to see anything else that may be sent to them by spam folks. More recently, companies like Google have included additional filters in their platforms like Gmail. These additional filters help to prioritize or organize content that is being emailed to people so that people are easily able to sort through their mail without manually having to do it themselves. These different filters are generally: personal, promotional, and social. By organizing content accordingly, users are able to easily sort through their emails without having to manually change the labels of different emails in order to do so. For many, this has made navigating email much easier and less overwhelming, since many tend to have a large amount of promotional or social media related emails being sent to their inboxes on a regular basis. This way, their personal or more important messages are not being buried under these less important and often less looked at messages.

Chapter 9: Random Forests

Random forests are another form of a classification system, similar to the naïve Bayes classification system, but structured more like the decision tree model. When you are using this classification system, information will continue to be classified but will help you come up with answers to the decisions that you may have to make. When it comes to big data sets, this can be helpful in identifying plausible solutions for overcoming challenges or reaching certain goals with the use of those data sets. When you look at the random forest algorithm, it looks as though you see multiple smaller decision trees lumped together into one larger tree. They are almost exactly the same in appearance, however the way they are established, the information they contain, and the purpose of these forests is somewhat different from a standard decision tree algorithm.

What Are *Random Forests*?

Random forests are a type of tree learning method that can be used by machine learning technology to complete certain decision-making tasks. A random forest is a form of standard data mining protocol that is able to scale and transform features of values. With that being said, random forests are more finicky than decision trees as they can include irrelevant and random values that may make the outcome less favorable than what the individual was looking for.

If the tree is developed properly, however, the tree will be more effective at producing accurate and meaningful results that can then be used for a number of different features. The thing to be most cautious about when it comes to random forests is trees that are grown very deep, or ones where every possible sub-decision is recognized and included in the model. In many cases, a lot of these decisions become irrelevant and are not useful in detecting what the likely outcome would be because they lead too far away from the initial decision and the initial goal.

By identifying this information and pruning it, however, one can use a random forest to create decision trees that are effective in helping them reach their goals and make the stronger decision based on the data sets they are working with.

The fundamental concept behind the random forest network is that crowds present a large amount of wisdom. In other words, the more knowledge you have, the more knowledge you have. By creating several decision trees and grouping them together in a random forest, data can be presented in massive amounts of different ways, leading researchers or data scientists through different possible outcomes and showing them things that are worth noting. Typically, the decision trees in the random forest are uncorrelated, which is why the algorithm got the term "random forest" in the first place. These uncorrelated trees provide information that outperforms any individual decision tree by giving researchers plenty to think about, factor in, and use toward making their final decisions. As a result, they are able to get as close to accurate as possible when it comes to deciding the proper way to proceed with a given problem that they are trying to solve, or goal they are trying to achieve.

How Do *Random Forests* Work?

The low or limited correlation between decision trees in the random forest is key to making this particular algorithm work. A great metaphor to relate this to in order to help you understand how random forests work and protect the results of their findings is through considering an investment portfolio. In the finance industry, traders will invest in multiple different stocks as a way to refrain from putting all of their eggs in one basket, so to speak. This way, if one of their investments does not work as planned and they lose money on it, they still have several other investments earning them money and their money is essentially protected. In this case, the protection is achieved by distributing the funds around to make sure that they are not all at risk of one single threat. When it comes to random forest trees, the same concept is applied. By using multiple different decision trees, the random forest is able to draw multiple conclusions and use them in a way to ensure that the decisions being made are protected by the other decisions around it. In other words, one flawed decision tree is unlikely to destroy an entire decision if there are three others that have offset the flaw.

96

The more decision trees you make that can help you come up with your decision, the more success you are going to have in offsetting the risk of something being wrong so that your findings are more accurate. The trees essentially protect each other from their individual errors, so long as they are not constantly moving in the same direction, or overlapping in input too much. In order to create a random forest, a person needs: some actual signal in their features so that the models they build are using those features. This way, they do better at random guessing. And, predictions and errors made by the individual trees that have low correlations to each other.

So, if a random forest is generated and the majority of the trees say the same general thing in terms of their predictions and errors, chances are the trees are too similar to effectively execute the purpose of the random forest. However, if you can see how the results all work together to produce a greater concept, then you have likely executed the random forest perfectly and you will find yourself getting everything that you need out of this particular algorithm. During the training process, random forests need to learn from a random sample of data points. This means that these samples are not correlating too significantly in any way. They are generally drawn with replacement, which is known as bootstrapping. This essentially means that the samples are going to be used multiple times in a single tree sometimes due to the nature of what they are and how they fit into the decision making process. In this case, although one single tree will have a high variance from other trees in the forest, all of the trees will have a low variance when you consider the forest as a whole. This randomization ensures that the trees are different enough to support the algorithm, but not so different that they are no longer relevant to the decision that the individual is attempting to make.

When the time to test comes, the random forest predictions are made by averaging the predictions of each of the decision trees in the random forest. The average of the predictions is then known as *bagging*, which essentially means that they are putting all of the information together in a way that creates one final outcome. Another more technical term for bagging is *bootstrap aggregate*. When it comes to random forests, you can assume that a massive amount of data can rapidly be accumulated if things are not put within certain parameters. After all, using an entire forest of decision trees can lead to nearly endless possibilities and therefore more data than anyone wants, or needs, to use.

Rather than having excessive trees that ultimately take away from the quality of the forest, scientists ensure that each tree is only able to create so many subsets. This way, it can consider a limited number of features and come up with a limited number of decisions, based on what the scientist or programmer has outlined. This prevents the trees from becoming overpopulated, and maintains the high diversity between trees to avoid massive overlap which can lead to muddied results. Typically, each tree will be limited to four subsets, although that may be increased or decreased depending on the unique set of circumstances and what the programmer needs from that tree. Aside from these additional rules and features of the random forest concept, random forests are still very much like decision trees. After all, this particular algorithm is made up of several decision trees. This means that, aside from bagging, the trees are all read in the same manner and the outcome is still the same. The only difference is that the reading of a random forest is done when you take the averages of all of the results, rather than having one simple and straightforward result delivered to you through one single decision tree.

When Should *Random Forests* be Used?

Based on the nature of random forests, they are used in virtually any situation where a decision tree might be used. They are especially helpful when there is an enormous amount of data in question that needs to be represented by the tree and, while the data does correlate in some ways, it may not correlate in all ways. By having a random forest, you can represent all of your data and still come up with plausible solutions for any problems you may be facing when it comes to data or data sciences.

Because of how interchangeable the two tend to be, you might think there is ultimately no reason for a decision tree and that people should exclusively use random forests instead. Naturally, it would make sense to lean toward using the algorithm that provides the most accuracy and the best results, and can reflect greater amounts of data, right? Technically, yes. However, there are some cases where using a random forest would be far too excessive for a situation, just like there are some cases where using a single decision tree would just not make sense. A great way to see this would be to use a boat as a reference.

You would not want to navigate a river in a yacht any more than you would want to navigate the ocean in a kayak, right? The same goes for decision trees and random forests.

When you have a limited amount of data and the results of the algorithm are important but not critical, a decision tree is ideal. These trees do not require massive amounts of data, nor do they take as much time to program and run as a random forest would. As a result, they tend to serve as a much more effective solution for less intense, or less sensitive areas of programming where a decision is made but there are no terrible risks or threats that will arise if absolute accuracy is not achieved. A great example of the application of a decision tree specifically would be in business, when businesses are looking for a solution in a certain marketing strategy or a new way to reach their customers. In these unique circumstances, the information is important but there is nothing sensitive about it, and being slightly off in the results would not be detrimental to the success of the company. Instead, it would simply provide more data for them to run again in the future when they were ready to create a new strategy for further implementation and growth.

Random forests, on the other hand, are far more high tech and are ideal to use in sensitive situations or situations where there needs to be a high level of accuracy in a large amount of data. If, for example, you were running data about a government organization or an entire population, a random forest would be more accurate as it holds enough space to run that massive amount of data. As well, the accuracy of it would be more effective for these scenarios as the data tends to be more sensitive and the results need to be more accurate to avoid possible challenges in the outcomes. Aside from areas with sensitive information, or with sensitive nature, random forests should also be used if there are massive amounts of data.

For example, a massive corporation like Wal-Mart or Target would be unlikely to benefit from a simple decision tree because there is far too much information within their businesses to effectively run it through a decision tree for adequate results. Likewise, a bank, a charitable organization, a government organization, or any other company or organization with high levels of data would not benefit from having all of that information stored in a single small decision tree. Not only are these trees less accurate, but they also do not have the capacity to store as much information as an entire random forest would.

For that reason, a random forest is ideal in the case of large amounts of data needing to be processed, too.

So, to summarize, you should use a decision tree if you do not require extremely accurate results *and* you do not have massive amounts of data to run. Alternatively, you should use a random forest when you need extremely accurate results *or* you have massive amounts of data to process and you need an algorithm large enough to allow you to effectively process it all.

Chapter 10: Apriori Algorithm

The Apriori algorithm is a unique algorithm that was introduced in 1994 by R. Agrawal and R. Srikant. These two scientists developed an algorithm that is capable of identifying prior knowledge and using it to identify itemset properties in datasets using the Boolean association rule. This particular algorithm is used in data mining as a way to find out certain correlations and connections in items using previous information.

There are many practical ways that the Apriori algorithm has been used in the modern world, especially in business where this particular algorithm has supported corporations in skyrocketing their sales by identifying like items and pairing them together for discounts. The way that this algorithm has been used is often a joke amongst computer scientists and is known as the "diaper beer parable" which you will learn more about later in this very chapter.

In order to help you better understand the algorithm that is associated with the "diaper beer parable" we are going to look into what the Apriori algorithm is, how it works, and when or why it would be used. This way, you have a better understanding of this particular algorithm that has been incredibly effective in helping draw patterns and trends in item sets and datasets for large organizations.

What Is the *Apriori* Algorithm?

The Apriori algorithm has a very specific function, and that is to identify relevant association rules and frequent item sets in data. In other words, it is used to identify how two different items might correlate with each other, what connections can be drawn between these items, and what these connections mean. This is where the diaper beer parable comes from. Back in the day, someone working at Wal-Mart decided to look back through sales data to identify what types of items people commonly bought together.

This way, they could leverage these items to increase sales by advertising sales of one item around the other item, when the two items were frequently bought together. A great example of this would be with jam and bread. Frequently, those who bought jam were also buying bread at the same time, so they would advertise bread near the jam, and jam near the bread. This would happen both physically in the store, and in flyers that were being promoted to their customers. In a sense, this was a way for Wal-Mart to upsell their customers so that they could maximize their earnings. While looking through the sales records, what the gentleman found was intriguing. Customers would typically buy diapers and beer at the same time. Although these two products have seemingly zero correlation, the data was undeniable: the two were paired together an incredible amount and therefore he was able to leverage one to encourage the purchase of the other. Thus, the diaper beer parable was discovered. This particular example showcases exactly how the Apriori algorithm works, too. The algorithm looks through data and identifies seemingly random pairs that have distinct and undeniable correlations.

This data mining allows new understandings of data to be reached so that new developments can be discovered. In the case of Wal-Mart and other corporations, this has led to massive increases in sales due to a better understanding of what customers are typically buying together and how products can be better marketed to encourage their purchase together. In other areas, this important correlation can also help data scientists, researchers, and other relevant individuals identify the relations between two seemingly random items in a data set so that this knowledge can be used to improve various other applications.

How Does This Algorithm Work?

The Apriori algorithm works using association rules. Association rule learning is a well-explored method of machine learning that is designed to help determine relations amongst variables in massive sets of data. Ideally, users should be able to upload massive amounts of data and the algorithm will run through it all and make these correlations and provide them at the end as an "answer" to the data that has been run. This way, the individual or organization can see these distinct correlations.

When the Apriori algorithm has been programmed, it works as follows. First, the user uploads a dataset into the algorithm in a way that isolates that dataset as a single group. For example, in a retail company a single receipt with a unique ID would represent one dataset. Every item that is a part of that dataset is then considered an item. So, for example, bread, butter, and eggs would all count as different items.

These would all be grouped together in the algorithm through the dataset, but the algorithm would begin to recognize the same items amongst all of the datasets. So, if the next receipt included eggs, potatoes, and milk, the algorithm would recognize these as two different datasets *and* recognize that both datasets included eggs. While this example only contains two receipts, the true Apriori algorithm would feature hundreds, thousands, hundreds of thousands, or even millions of individual datasets that each featured their own unique items. These could represent retail items, demographics, monetary values, or any other number of data depending on what the individual using the algorithm is attempting to discover. Ideally, in order to get a strong and accurate representation of their findings, the individual using the Apriori algorithm should have, or have access to, large amounts of data to ensure that their findings are accurate.

Using too small of an amount of data could lead to the findings not being accurate because it may be more up to chance than anything else. Once the massive amount of data has been inputted, the algorithm is designed to require a certain level of parables to occur before it recognizes it as a plausible pair. For example, 1/10 instances of a parable would not be recognized at all by the Apriori algorithm, but 4/10 or higher instances of a parable might be recognized, depending on how that unique software was programmed by the developer. The benefit of the Apriori algorithm is that it can pair together multiple different items and recognize the connection between groups of items, too. For example, it may recognize that people who buy bras and underwear are also likely to buy socks, or people who are religious and in the middle class are more likely to attend church on a consistent basis. This way, it can make extremely accurate findings based on the information being uploaded into the system.

After it has found these groups of relevant items, the Apriori algorithm moves into what is called confidence. This means that the algorithm must have confidence in a rule to confirm that said rule is likely going to be accurate and that the findings of the algorithm are accurate, too. In order to reflect confidence, the algorithm will showcase the exact statistics relating to the associations or parables it has made. Often, this is shown as a percentage so that the user can see an exact percentage of how frequently those items were paired together, allowing them to get a better understanding of how relevant these parables are. If the percentage is low, chances are the parable is random and does not mean much in the way of how people are actually shopping. If, however, the percentage is fairly high, chances are the parable is not all that random and if it is exploited they can actually increase the percentage. Typically, this exploitation is only done to improve desirable results, and is never used in an unethical manner to avoid causing unethical interference into people's lives. For example, a retailer might pair two items together to improve sales numbers, but a government is unlikely to use their findings of people who are religious and middle class to increase the number of churchgoers in their riding.

When Should This Algorithm be Used?

The Apriori algorithm is actually used in many ways in our current world as it has the capacity to shine a light into certain pairings that would otherwise be unknown to the people looking into this data. Using this algorithm, organizations are able to create more relevant and enjoyable experiences for the people they represent or support.

The algorithm can give them a better understanding of who they are supporting, and what those individuals need, want, or care about. Currently, the Apriori algorithm is frequently used in marketing and commerce, however it is also used in statistical analysis companies where they are trying to gain a better understanding of the statistics they are researching. National statistical organizations, for example, who keep track of certain public statistics will regularly use the Apriori algorithm to ensure that they have accurately drawn conclusions in all their findings. It is also used in companies that are responsible for taking care of electric motors, which tends to be surprising to many people.

Marketing

In marketing, the Apriori algorithm is used to support people in the same way that it helped the man at Wal-Mart increase sales in diapers and beer. By allowing marketers to identify correlations between two item sets, they are able to identify new methods for marketing to the people that they are selling to. On social media, the Apriori algorithm is used to show users advertisements that are relevant to their interests. For example, if the Apriori algorithm finds that people who regularly search dogs and horses tend to also buy buffalo plaid shirts, it could advertise buffalo plaid shirts that individual. The more these correlations are found, the more relevant targeted advertising becomes and, therefore, the more likely people are to act on that advertising and actually pay the company. For social media networks, this means companies are more likely to keep advertising through them, which ensures that their revenue stays up or even increases over time.

In email marketing, the Apriori algorithm can help companies identify what their subscribers tend to read about the most so that they can start to write targeted emails that are more likely to get opened and clicked on. This way, they are more likely to have an impact on their email marketing efforts and, therefore, they are more likely to earn money this way. When it comes to offline marketing, the Apriori algorithm is used in exactly the same way that the Wal-Mart guy used it. Marketers look through sales statistics and use them to identify ways that they can improve their sales strategies by finding offline marketing methods that reflect their findings. For example, grouping similar items together in flyers, or on instore posters where certain products are being promoted.

Commerce

In commerce, the Apriori algorithm is frequently used as a way to identify opportunities for growth, or new products or services that could be added or developed to help improve revenue in a business. For example, if it was discovered that two items were frequently bought together with a specific product, and that this occurrence was high, that company could develop more products in that particular area and focus on improving that particular service.

This way, the people who are already purchasing these products and services together are more likely to purchase even more based on the developments within the business.

Statistical Analysis Companies

Statistical analysis companies are necessary for helping us keep track of historical statistical data so that we can understand the state and evolution of our own society. These companies frequently store data reflecting demographics, health analysis, ecosystems, and more.

By preserving this data, they are then able to ensure that it is available when the data is needed at future dates. For example, when new research studies are being completed, researchers can look back at this historical data to create the foundation of their research, and to validate why they have come to this conclusion. They can also use this data to start creating theories that they can begin to follow. Often, this data will serve in many ways throughout the research process to help the researchers understand more about the specific area they are researching. Because of how these statistical companies work, the Apriori algorithm is highly useful to them. Using the algorithm, they can take their existing raw statistics and data and run it through the system to find out even more information, effectively creating even more statistics or data for people to use. For example, they might run information that shows that the middle class millennials are less likely to purchase a home by 30 years old than the middle class baby boomers, or other similar findings. Through the development of their statistics, these companies are able to create a better understanding of the landscape of our society now, and in the historical past. As a result, future researchers are able to fall back on this knowledge to create clear paths from how we have evolved or advanced through the years.

Mechanics

In mechanics, the Apriori algorithm is frequently used as a way to ensure that mechanics have effectively looked over every aspect of an engine and ensured its safety. It can also be used to troubleshoot engines when something is going wrong and the mechanic cannot find the answer.

Using the Apriori algorithm, if the mechanic can identify one clear issue, they can look at the data to identify what that issue tends to be associated with. This way, if it is something that they could not draw a conclusion to using common sense, the conclusion is drawn using the Apriori algorithm. Then, rather than cars being deemed irreparable or problems deemed unresolvable, the mechanic can go ahead and identify what needs to be addressed. In addition to helping mechanics fix engines, it can also help them identify common problems in certain engine types. Through that, they can stay informed as to what to look out for, and also inform people who own the vehicle attached to that engine as to what they should look out for, too. In situations where the instances are high and the findings are dangerous, they can also issue safety recalls ensuring that no one is left driving an unfit or unsafe vehicle.

Service Engineers

In addition to engines, the Apriori algorithm can be applied in the exact same manner for other service engineers, and even IT agents or individuals who are responsible for building and fixing things. Using the Apriori algorithm, engineers can educate themselves on problems to look out for, as well as things to consider when it comes to building or repairing different pieces of technology. If they find that the correlations are often catastrophic or dangerous, they can also begin to identify new ways to overcome those problems to ensure that they are no longer causing issues for the individuals who own the technology. Or, they can prevent the technology from being mass produced until it has been fixed and is fit to go out.

Chapter 11: Linear and Logistic Regression

Linear and logistic regression are similar, but they are not entirely the same. In this chapter, we are going to explore what linear and logistic regression are, how they work, and why they are used. It is important to understand that both linear and logistic regression can be used in similar settings, however in some linear regression will make more sense, whereas in others, logistic regression will make more sense. The key difference is how many possible values exist in the regression that is being completed. Linear regression has an infinite number of possible values, whereas logistic regression has a limited number of possible values. As a result, both are somewhat different and are shown slightly differently on graphs, too. Linear regression tends to be shown as a single solid line that is straight and gradually increases, whereas logistic regression tends to be shown as a curved line that increases based on the values being represented by the graph.

Using one graph in place of the other would be a mistake as it would essentially "break" the output number. In both linear and logic regression, the output should never be negative or greater than one. If these two scenarios were to occur, the result would be wrong which would mean that you were not receiving accurate or sound information from your regression. For this reason, it is important that you use the right regression algorithm for the right purpose, to avoid having your values turned up wrong or inconclusive.

Exploring how each algorithm works, when to use it, and what it's purpose is in the first place is an important element of understanding the value of this particular algorithm. Once again, this particular algorithm is one of the most basic machine learning algorithms, and it is used across many different areas in machine learning. For that reason, it is important that you take the time to educate yourself on how it works and put it to work accordingly.

What is *Linear Regression?*

Linear regression is a form of predictive analysis that measures probabilities to identify the likelihood of something happening. The idea of regression is for this particular algorithm to examine two things: the quality of certain predictor variables, and the significance of certain predictor variables. First and foremost, the predictor variables need to be able to effectively predict the outcome variable, otherwise they are not going to be effective in helping you with your predictions and probabilities. Second, you need to know that the variables you are using are significant predictors of the outcome variable, as well as how they impact the outcome variable. If you do not know these two pieces of information, you will not have an effective linear regression algorithm.

With these two pieces of information in tow, the linear regression algorithm is able to explain the relationship between one dependent variable and one or more independent variables, ultimately leading to the development of a probability measure. This way, you can start to see the likelihood of something happening, and how the dependent variables support or lead to the independent variables taking place.

Linear regression algorithms can be amongst some of the more challenging algorithms to learn about because they do tend to include so many variables, and the variables need to be qualified in order to make sure that they are good enough to use with the particular calculations you are running through the algorithm. If these variables are low quality or ineffective, they are not going to be able to help you create the outcome you desire, or the results of your linear regression algorithm may be inconclusive or inaccurate. Based on the number of variables that can be included in linear regression, it is understandable that there are also multiple different ways that this algorithm can be used to understand the variables and create your calculations. In fact, there are six different types of linear regression algorithms that can be used to help seek your probability answers, depending on what types of information you have available to run through the algorithm. These six linear regression types include: simple linear regression, multiple linear regression, logistic regression, ordinal regression, multinomial regression, and discriminant analysis.

While we will talk more in depth about logistic regression later in this chapter, due to it being a significant form of linear regression, let's take a moment to explore each of the other types of linear regression, too. Aside from simple linear regression, the other four types of linear regression tend to be more complex, but are still useful algorithms to know about.

Multiple Linear Regression

Multiple linear regression essentially means that multiple independent variables are being assessed in the algorithm. As with all forms of linear regression, multiple linear regression only takes into account one dependent variable.

Multiple linear regression is the easiest next step up from simple linear regression, which is a form of linear regression that only measures one dependent variable, and one independent variable. For both simple linear regression and multiple linear regression, the independent variable must be either an interval, ratio, or dichotomous and the dependent variable needs to be either an interval or ratio.

Ordinal Regression

Ordinal regression is a form of linear regression that involves just one dependent variable, and one or more independent variables. With that being said, the dependent variable should be ordinal, and the independent variable(s) should be nominal or dichotomous in nature. Ordinal regression can feature any number of independent variables, depending on what data is being run through the algorithm.

Multinominal Regression

Multinominal regression is another form of regression that features one or more independent variables, and one dependent variable. In the case of multinominal regression, the dependent variable must always be nominal. The independent variables can be either interval, ratio, or dichotomous.

Discriminant Analysis

Lastly, discriminant analysis is a form of linear regression that features one dependent variable, and one or more independent variables.

For discriminant analysis, the dependent variable should be nominal, and the independent variable should be either an interval or ratio. When a researcher is choosing which type of linear regression they are going to use, they start by determining model fitting. This essentially means that they take a look at what data they have and what their goals are, and they determine which method is going to best serve them in achieving those goals. By fitting the method to their data, they are able to get the best results that lead to them experiencing more accuracy and success in their research using linear regression.

How Does *Linear Regression* Work?

For the purpose of this explanation, we are going to discuss simple linear regression, which features one dependent variable and just one independent variable. With that being said, all additional forms of linear regression work in this exact same manner, and they can be used to perform the necessary functions based on what you are looking for in your data, and what type of data you have. The purpose of linear regression is to model the relationship between one or more variables, so that is exactly what you are going to do with linear regression. Each linear regression model is trained with formulas that indicate what the model is supposed to do. This way, the model knows what variables it is looking at and what relationships it is looking for. The goal of training the model and using it is to see the relationship between independent variables and dependent variables. For example, features versus labels. Once a linear regression model is trained, a user can begin inputting data into the system that will ultimately be run through the algorithm and represented in a series of relationships and values. These relationships and values will determine probabilities and predictive scenarios based on the relationship something shares with something else. This is a great way to reinforce assumptions or identify areas where the independent variables are more likely to support the dependent variable, so that the user can identify the best possible way to move forward.

Unlike decision trees or other tree based learning algorithms, linear regression will not give you a series of different outcomes or draw you down a path of identifying what you could possibly do. Instead, a linear regression algorithm will identify the probability of something happening based on you pre-emptively identifying what that something is and then inputting it into the algorithm. This way, you can reinforce whether or not that will actually be true or whether it will work or not, and you can move forward from there. In other words, if you do not already have a theory and some data surrounding that theory, you are unlikely to see any benefit in using a linear regression model.

When Should *Linear Regression* be Used?

A linear regression model should be used when you already have a basic understanding as to what needs to be done and what can be done to reach a certain goal. Once you have this basic understanding, you can input this information into a linear regression model using a dependent variable and then one or more independent variables in the form of nominals, ratios, intervals, or dichotomy.

Then, the algorithm will run through the information you have to create conclusive results that determine whether or not a certain outcome is likely to be achieved. If you do not already have a basic idea of what goes together, however, you will likely want to run your data through other algorithms first to begin to create a theory or a hypothesis. From there, you can then take your findings and run it through a linear regression algorithm to identify the best possible route, and how good that route actually is. In other words, this is a great way to discover which theory is correct and to which degree that theory is correct. In real life, linear regression can be used on things like budgeting, agriculture, ordering retail suppliers, and many other things. Essentially, anything you can use linear regression charts on anything that features two unique variables on a graph.

Budgeting

In budgeting, you can use linear regression to help you identify how much money you should expect to spend on something based on what you have experienced in the past, and what you need to do in the future. For example, let's say you are driving a car and that car requires gas in order to be able to go anywhere. If you were using linear regression, you could track how much money you put into your tank each time you fill up, and how far you drive before filling up again. In this case, you would start to be able to identify how many miles you get per gallon, and how frequently you need to put gas in your car. With this knowledge, your gas (dependent variable) is being measured against your miles driven (independent variable.) You, then, must identify how much the dependent variable relates to the independent variable, or how much gas you need to purchase in order to make it a certain distance.

With the answer to this equation in mind, you could then identify how many miles you needed to drive, and multiply that by the dollar value you came up with your linear regression chart. Through that, you would know how much money you need to budget for gas in order to reach a certain distance in your travels.

Agriculture

In agriculture, linear regression can help farmers identify what types of variables are going to affect things such as their crops. For example, let's say a farmer was looking into their crop yield and wanted to know how much certain independent variables affected his crop yield. In this case, he could run an analysis where he identifies how much these independent variables have affected crop yield in the past to get an understanding of what is likely to affect his crop yield. He might test against amount of rainfall, amount of sunshine, pesticides used, farming practices used, and other independent variables to see how much these independent variables have affected his crop yield. As a result, he would be able to get an accurate understanding as to what would affect his yield, and possibly be able to create a plan to offset anything that may negatively impact his yield.

Retail – Ordering

In retail, linear regression can be used to help companies identify how much products they should be ordering with each order. They would be able to measure the number of products sold against how long it took for those products to sell. In this case, the dependent variable would be the passing of a set period of time (the time between orders) and the independent variable would be the number of products sold in that timeframe. Through this algorithm, the retailer could identify how many products were consistently being sold in that time period so that they could identify how many products they needed to order. This way, they order enough to keep up with supply and demand, but not so much that they find themselves buried in excess products that their customers are not purchasing.

What is *Logistical Regression?*

Logistical regression is a form of linear regression, but it is different in that there are a fixed number of probabilities that can be measured by the logistic regression algorithm. This limited number of probabilities is based on the variables being inputted and the number of existing probabilities relating to these variables. Logistic regression should always be used when the dependent variable is measured in the algorithm is dichotomous, or binary. This means that it is represented in a series of 1's and 0's. Logistic regression specifically is used to explain the relationship between one binary dependent variable and one or more nominal, ordinal, interval, or ratio-level independent variables. Based on the nature of this particular form of linear regression, this algorithm can be more challenging to read than other linear regression algorithms. As a result, some people may prefer to use a tool like the Intellectus Statistics tool to help them interpret the output in plain English. Without it, one must have a solid understanding of coding and binary language to understand exactly what the algorithm is trying to tell them.

Logistic regression is used to estimate the parameters of a logistic model, much in the same way that other forms of linear regression are used. The purpose is to identify the probability of a specific outcome.

Again, like other forms of linear regression, it will not perform statistical classification, nor will it point toward multiple different outcomes. The sole purpose of logistic regression is to validate the strength of a relationship between a dependent and independent variable to see how likely it is that one will affect the other. Typically, the individual running this system already knows that one will affect the other, which is why they are running the two variables together through the algorithm in the first place.

How Does *Logistic Regression* Work?

Logistic regression works by taking into account the dependent and independent variables that are at play in any given scenario. The entire practice is performed exactly as simple linear regression is performed, however the goals will ultimately be different. As well, the types of variables being used are different, particularly with the fact that the dependent variable is going to be dichotomous, or binary. Once the dichotomous dependent variable has been observed, the individual running the logistic regression model needs to identify what their independent variables are. From there, they can turn those independent variables into ratios, nominals, ordinals, or intervals so that they can be run through the algorithm properly. Assuming that everything has been inputted properly, the entire process of logistic regression will be exactly the same.

You will be placing your probability on a graph with your dependent variable on the left side and your independent variable on the bottom of your graph, and mapping out your data points on a chart. Or, more specifically, the machine learning model will be doing this for you based on the information you have inputted into the system. From there, it will plot out the average path of probability, showing you what is likely to be true. Unlike plain linear regression models, the logistic regression model can be shown with a curved line.

With that being said, the line should always be curving up and to the right, starting at the bottom left side of the graph. If it is curving in any other direction, the algorithm has not been effective and it needs to be retrained or the information inputted needs to be reviewed to ensure that it is being run properly.

When Should *Logistic Regression* be Used?

Logistic regression is mostly used in machine learning technology that is related to medical and social fields. A great example of it being actively used is represented in the Trauma and Injury Severity Score (TRISS) which is typically used to predict the likelihood of mortality in a patient who has been significantly injured. Using logistic regression, they can predict the likelihood of whether or not someone is going to die based on the trauma or injuries they have sustained, across other independent variables that may be highlighted in their unique case. Another way that the medical field uses logistic regression is to identify the likelihood of someone developing something like diabetes, coronary heart disease, or another illness based on the observed characteristics of the patient, such as their age, weight, sex, and results on varying tests they may have taken.

In these applications, logistic regression is incredibly useful in helping doctors identify what measures need to be taken to help a patient, and to what degree those measures need to be taken. In other words, they are incredibly useful in helping doctors essentially choose a diagnostic path for a patient depending on what sort of health issues they are presently facing.

In socioeconomics, the logistic regression model can be used to identify the likelihood of people needing to join the labor force, being able to own a home, being able to manage a mortgage, or various other things that may be relevant to a person's lifestyle. Through taking a dependent, such as what they are looking into a person's likelihood of experiencing, and applying independent variables such as their demographic classification, the logistic regression algorithm can identify probabilities.

117

Conclusion

Congratulations on completing *Machine Learning for Beginners!* This book was written to be a helpful guide for anyone curious about learning more about machine learning and its many applications. From covering topics ranging from what machine learning is and how it is used, to discovering what types of algorithms and complex systems are run through machine learning devices, I hope you are starting to feel confident in your understanding of machine learning.

When most people think of machine learning, they either have no idea what it is, or they automatically think about artificial intelligence in the form of a robotic species that rivals humans. While these fascinating subspecies may one day exist as the result of machine learning developments, right now the primary focus is on how machine learning programs can become excellent at very specific tasks. Most machine learning technology is developed in such a way that it is excellent at performing one or, at most, two tasks. By focusing entire technology on one single task, they can ensure that it runs that task perfectly, and that it does not get confused between the tasks that it is trying to accomplish. While simple computing software like the one that runs your computer can easily run multiple programs at once with little chance of crashing, the technology that is used to run machine learning technology is far more complex. As researchers study it, they strive to keep the algorithms mostly separate, or specifically focused on completing just one goal, on minimizing room for error.

It is likely that as we become more familiar with machine learning technology and more educated in the algorithms, we will start to see more and more machines completing multiple tasks, rather than just one. At this point, that is the long term goal for many scientists who want to see these machines becoming more effecient, and requiring less hardware. After all, the hardware used to run some of these machines is not always the greenest technology, so the fewer hardware casings that technology needs to be stored in, the less of a footprint the technology sector will have on the planet. I hope that in reading this book you have begun to feel confident in your understanding of machine learning.

This topic is incredibly complex and diving into any one special area of it in a single book would be nearly impossible. Even computer scientists spend years studying multiple texts and research papers, trying to learn more about these machine learning programs and how they work. With that being said, *Machine Learning for Beginners* sought to put together the most important knowledge that any beginner should have to ensure that you had access to the best and most important knowledge for you.

As you move forward from this book, I hope that you will take the time to continue following the machine learning industry, or even consider dipping your own toes into it. Machine learning is not like traditional computer science fields that are focused on human created and managed algorithms, but instead it is focused on learning how to develop machines that can perform various functions on their own. With the proper training models and algorithms installed into these pieces of technology, these systems are already capable of performing incredible tasks. It will be interesting to see where machine learning goes in the next few years, and decades, as computer scientists continue to explore this uncharted territory.

Already, anyone who has used any form of technology, or who has gone to a doctor or government office where technology was used has benefitted from the existence of machine learning protocol. This means that literally everyone in the modern world has, in one way or another, been impacted by it. This particular form of science sprung up in the mid-1900s and has rapidly grown in popularity and served to provide us with the basis of what might be the earliest stages of the machine learning revolution, or whatever future historians may call it. With the evolution and implementation of machine learning technology, life as we know it may change completely. We could likely see changes ranging from reduced need for people in the labor force, to better transportation technologies, and even better medical and screening technologies. It is likely that, in time, no sector of our modern world will be without incredibly advanced, high powered machine learning technology that will change the way that the entire sector is run.

In the meantime, it will likely take time for this revolution to happen, as we are unlikely to see machine learning advance to the point where it would be ethical to overhaul most existing systems with it any time soon.

Before that can happen, we will need to further develop the technology to make sure that it is reliable, accurate, and ethical in every single scenario. This way, when it begins to be used in areas with more sensitive data, such as government records, health records, bank records, or educational records, we can feel confident that it is going to function properly.

After all, we do not want sensitive records or documents leaking into the wrong hands and causing massive destruction to our society. Which, as dramatic as it might sound, is entirely possible and could be a complete catastrophe.

Before you go, I want to ask you one simple favor. If you enjoyed reading *Machine Learning for Beginners: A Complete and Phased Beginner's Guide to Learning and Understanding Machine Learning and Artificial Intelligence* and feel that it helped you understand machine learning more effectively, I ask that you please take the time to leave a review on Amazon Kindle. Your honest feedback and support would be greatly appreciated.

Thank you, and have fun exploring the world of machine learning! The possibilities truly are endless!

Artificial Intelligence for Business Applications

Use Artificial Intelligence for Scaling Up Your Business Using AI Marketing Tools

By: Ethem Mining

Introduction

The book, *Artificial Intelligence for Business Applications,* focuses on ways in which this technology can help in business growth. The tools discussed in the book deal with marketing. Going through the book, one gets to understand what artificial intelligence is and how it started. One will get to see the changes the technology has gone through over time. Going through the book, one will learn of the opportunities that artificial intelligence technology brings in the world of business and economies. Apart from growth, the book covers the areas of innovation and productivity. In the book, the reader gets information on the challenges of artificial intelligence. How one can apply the varied applications in this type of technology is discussed. The book covers the topic of how one can get new customers using the tools. Combining the human element with this technology is addressed. It discusses the effect of artificial intelligence on market research, human resource, and the sales process.

One will find specifics on various artificial intelligence technologies. These include discussions on chatbots and autoresponders. The book gives a roadmap to follow when making a choice on which technology to use. A reader will find practical tips on how to promote their technology of choice. How one can connect the technologies with email is discussed.

The book shares practical tips on how to introduce artificial intelligence into a business setup. The author gives pointers on using the tool of strategy in achieving the incorporation of the technologies in an organization.

Chapter 1: What is Artificial Intelligence?

Artificial intelligence is a combination of computer development and human intelligence. Some refer to it as machine intelligence. Here, the machine carries out tasks attributed to humans. The computer systems within the device are responsible for the actions. The ability of the gadgets to carry out the acts without human intelligence makes them intelligent. AI is the abbreviation of artificial intelligence. It focuses on becoming a copy of the human brain. The use of robots to replace the human interface across industries exemplifies AI in the world today. Artificial intelligence applications are many transversing industries. AI utilizes the power of algorithms.

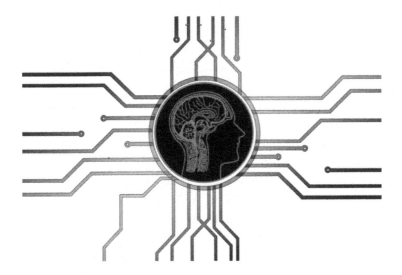

The specific tasks attributed to artificial intelligence include decision making, speech recognition, translation, and visual perception. Planning and forecasting are areas that can utilize AI. There are machine intelligent gadgets that can perform tasks based on previous experience. The actions that the devices carry out range from simple to complex ones.

Some robots can multi-task. AI products can now navigate, transcribe, and speak. There are artificially intelligent devices that can recognize emotions either in speech or in what they visually perceive. In the medical field, there are smart devices for diagnosis. The tasks are applicable in many areas, including agriculture, science, and travel.

The tasks attributed to artificial intelligence that involves decision making base themselves on learning, reasoning, and self-correction. Businesses can take advantage of the decision-making ability to determine their way forward. AI allows organizations to process large amounts of data in short periods, therefore, making the decision-making process faster. The decisions made by the devices are considered to be intelligent. The machines base their choices on data. The gadgets learn through inputs. The inputs create experiences for the devices which, allows them to solve problems. These experiences can be considered to be the neural networks of the machines. With regard to speech recognition, the machines having artificial intelligence convert spoken phrases and words into formats that they can read. The conversion process allows for identification. For the conversion to be effective, the devices should be able to overcome challenges such as accents associated with speech. The use of slang presents another hurdle. The gadget should be able to recognize voices. Speech recognition belongs to the field of computational linguistics. Here, the ability of a machine to predict and utilize input data comes into play. There are transcription services that rely on this type of artificial intelligence. Voice recognition plus AI gives speech recognition. Depending on the context within which translation occurs, it can be said to be dependent on the speech and voice recognition capabilities of machines. Artificial intelligence can be used to augment the speed and quality of translations carried out by humans. The best machine translators have learned from humans. AI machines are facing challenges when it comes to translating the cultural and emotional aspects of speech. They also face hurdles when it comes to tone, which can change the meaning of a word or phrase. For translation to be effective, AI must link with machine neural network technology. The visual perception of machines is dependent on how closely they can replicate human visual perception. The better the replication, the more accurate the machine visual perception is. The visual perception achieved affects the intelligence of the machines to a great extent. Machine visual perception helps them make decisions.

The ability to see involves the machine understanding what an image is. Visual perception involves deep learning. The stages of machine visual perception are the early stage, intermediate stage, and the high-level stage. The levels are hierarchal. For the device's visual understanding ability to be effective, it has to be active as opposed to passive in nature.

There are similarities and differences between human and machine intelligence. Most machines are programmed to focus on specific duties, whereas humans can perform a myriad of tasks concurrently. Some devices, like humans, have been shown to have a bias. Lately, a bias factor is added during programming to take care of the bias in machines. Both can be considered to be having neural networks with humans having millions of neurons. These networks help in decision-making.

There are tasks that devices can perform faster with a higher level of precision than humans. Human intelligence is considered to be faster as compared to that of machines. To understand AI, we will look at how it evolved. Here, we will look at how it started, the developments over time, and where it is today. Doing this will give a better appreciation of what it is. We will then expound on the value of machine intelligence, particularly within the business and economic situations. The book will cover the typology of AI applications. Here, we will delve into how each of them works. We will expound on their differences and similarities. The types discussed are dependent on the type of classification used. Within the chapter, there are discussions on examples of artificial intelligence.

Artificial Intelligence Evolution

To understand the evolution of artificial intelligence, one must understand that AI bases itself on the premise that the human thought process can be mechanized. This kind of thinking goes back to the first millennium. The Chinese and Greeks are thought to have formalized this kind of thinking. Myths and rumors abound during this time of beings from out of the earth that exhibit intelligence. Some societies refer to these beings as aliens. The actual origin of artificial intelligence is unknown.

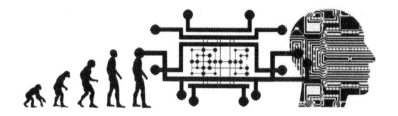

Machines that think first came into light in the 1950s. A Briton by the name Turing created a device that copied human thinking. He published a paper on the same. In the 1800s, there was postulation that machines could think like humans. Alan Turing was part of scientists who believed in devices that could exhibit a copy of human intelligence. He based his creation on the field of mathematics. Claude Shannon was also a scientist who contributed to the subject in the 1950s. The 1950s can, therefore, be seen to be the era where artificial intelligence moved from imagination to reality.

Turing, unfortunately, did not get to see his thoughts accepted into mainstream science. Incorporation of his thought process on machines happened in the mid-1950s. By the year 1959, an AI laboratory was established, referred to as MIT. MIT is an abbreviation for the Massachusetts Institute of Technology. By the 1980s, artificially intelligent machines in the form of personal computers were now available to the common man. Artificial intelligence in the 1990s brings gaming, self-driving cars, and domesticated robots. The 2000s showcase the commercialization of AI devices in industries like marketing and toy manufacture. AI devices are pitted against humans in the 2010s with robots surpassing humans in performance.

AI origins link to current developments through the Turing test. The test determines whether a machine can think or not. The commonality between the events is data. Currently, studies that are trying to mimic the human brain in both function and structure are ongoing. This kind of learning is known as deep learning. Applications include the prediction of texts and words in messaging or emailing.

The focus on further developing facial recognition machines is increasing. Businesses are embracing the use of this technology in workplaces. Organizations in the security industry are already utilizing this technology.

Current developments have brought to the fore concerns on ethics in terms of privacy. Those developing applications that use AI now have to contend with the laws that are coming up regarding this. Chip manufacturers are working on making AI-based features better. Cloud providers are increasing in size as more businesses take advantage of the services they offer. Organizations are using machine learning to make their marketing more effective. Some AI devices are in use both in military and civilian life. Drones are examples of such machines. Common gadgets in everyday life, like toothbrushes, are now using AI. Current strides made in the field of artificial intelligence are dependent on the ability of devices to learn by themselves.

This type of learning allows gadgets to forecast behavior. Search engines utilize the feature to predict what one is looking for as they type in words. Entertainment organizations currently suggest programs for one to watch using the predictive aspect of artificial intelligence. Applications are now available that can correct mistakes one makes as one is carrying out a task. Medically the machines are quicker than humans in reading biopsies. The advantage of this type of AI is that programming is not required.

The role of the developers instead is to ensure that the learning bases itself on correct perceptions. Some claim that by the year 2050, AI will be smarter than the intelligence of humans on all levels. There are claims that machines will be able to carry out tasks better than humans. The devices will be able to be autonomous. Their day to day decisions will be independent of humanity. In the future, artificially intelligent machines may replace the human face across industries. AI devices in the future should be able to analyze more information from pictures. Newer software reliant on artificial intelligence will be created to achieve this feat. The field of automated research will, in the coming days, improve on its use of artificial intelligence. The practice of individualized healthcare with the foundation of the genome is a feature to be seen in the future. Banking institutions will invest more in chips that are AI-enabled. These chips will be optimized. In the future, various AI systems will be learning from each other.

As the machines will do this, so will artificial intelligence be able to read and predict global trends. Some companies are working on creating AI machines that will be able to make appointments.

The Value of Artificial Intelligence

One cannot overstate the value of artificial intelligence in the marketplace. Currently, the use of artificial intelligence in core business functions is still low. Organizations that use AI in their day to day operations have found it to be transformational. Artificial intelligence does have its limits. The value derived from AI is dependent on how a company can use it.

The impact of the technology is expected to be in trillions of US dollars. This effect is industry dependent. AI also has the potential to create novel industries. Consumer-based industries being in a position to collect data from individuals have benefitted from artificial intelligence. The data, in combination with artificial intelligence, allows the businesses within the industry to offer personalized service. Organizations through artificial intelligence are now able to personalize promotional messages. Some are now able to customize prices to individual clients. With regard to the personalization of services offered, organizations should take into consideration related laws. Consumer-based industries that have been able to take advantage of AI include those involved in marketing and sales. They do use artificial intelligence in the management of customer service.

Manufacturing industries have also benefitted from the use of artificial intelligence. Here, the use of AI has reduced production costs. Artificial intelligence in manufacturing is being used to improve efficiency. Organizations are using AI to increase the accuracy of their production process. Production is being carried out by businesses at speeds higher than ever before. Manufacturers have now improved their capacity for product manufacture through the use of artificial intelligence. The industry has been able to improve the safety levels of those working within them using the power of AI. Artificial intelligence has also helped in the production of a better quality of products.

In the supply chain industry, the beneficiaries of artificial intelligence have been the businesses that deal with consumer goods. They are experiencing increased accuracy as regards their ability to predict. Artificial intelligence has allowed organizations to focus on drivers of trends. Earlier on predictions had been based on previous outcomes. The effect of AI on supply chain businesses is the reduction of costs related to inventory.

The impact is an increase in revenue. There are businesses in the industry that use AI to make decisions. The decisions made can lead to a reduction in operational costs for such organizations.

Industries dealing with risks like the banking sector are using artificial intelligence to tackle this challenge. They use AI to determine loan underwriting. Artificial intelligence is in use to detect fraud. There is an improvement in performance by the businesses that are using AI. Financial institutions like credit unions use AI to determine how much risk they are willing to take. AI, in this case, helps businesses to make decisions based on the data they have. Artificial intelligence can help organizations in coming up with a risk strategy. AI also helps organizations improve their efficiency regarding the costs of operation.

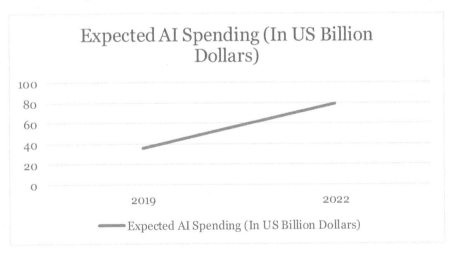

Expected AI Spending (In US Billion Dollars)

Within the service operation industry, artificial intelligence is for operating specific tasks as opposed to its use in a multi-dimensional setting. The actions can include predicting when servers are likely to crash.

When determining the artificial intelligence tool to use in organizations, one should think of the purpose of it.

Doing so will, over time, lead to shifting the thought process of such tools from the operational context to one of design. The design element should consider the ability of the AI tool to continuously collect data for it to be effective in the industry. In the field of product development, the design aspects are benefiting from artificial intelligence. The design of the products can be of new items or as an improvement of those already in existence. AI is involved in the automation of the testing process of the products. The role of artificial intelligence in product development has its basis on data. Businesses that choose AI to develop products have been able to break down barriers to production. With all the advancements in artificial intelligence, the uptake of the technology in product development is still low. The role of ethics in product development is a hurdle. The strategy-based industry is using artificial intelligence to expand their businesses. AI use in such scenarios depends on an organization. Different companies utilize AI in varied ways to achieve their overall strategy. The underlying tool that artificial intelligence uses in the industry is data. Countries are coming up with AI-based strategies with objectives driving the direction of the use of AI in the field. Some businesses input artificial intelligence in their overall strategic plans as a tool in the promotion of their organizational strategies. The plans identify artificially intelligent assets. The result is the production of products and services that are intelligent.

Typology of Artificial Intelligence Applications

The classification of artificial intelligence applications is in two ways. One method focuses on how well an application can replicate humans. The classes of applications in this method include reactive machines, those with limited memory, those under mind theory, and those that are self-aware.

The alternative classification method focuses on the intelligence capabilities of the applications. The classes here are ANI (Artificial Narrow Intelligence), AGI (Artificial General Intelligence), and ASI (Artificial Super Intelligence).

In the former classification method, the older models are less capable. The latter method showcases artificial intelligence capabilities that can cut across the ages of the AI models.

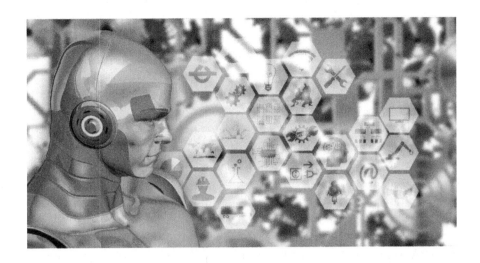

Reactive machines are those that lack memory. These are the oldest type of AI machines. They only respond based on stimuli, which makes them limited in capability. The stimulus they react to can be varied. These machines replicate humans in how they respond. Their lack of memory causes them to be non-learning. The improvement witnessed in these AI machines is not memory-based. The stimulus they respond to can only be of limited combinations. The ability to replicate human responses in previous years within the gaming industry is an example of how the machines work.

Limited memory machines, as indicated by their name, have memory capabilities. These capabilities, though, are limited in nature. The capacity gives them the potential to learn. The learning leads to an improvement in response. The functioning of these machines is memory-based, which allows them to be reactive. Here, the memory in use bases itself on historical data. The data previously collected undergoes conversion into a reference model. The model becomes the basis for decision making by the artificial intelligence machines. Deep-learning devices are examples of AI tools that belong to this category.

The other category in the first way of classification is mind theory machines. These are still in the concept stage or are a work in progress. The devices are expected to have the ability to understand and to identify needs exhibited by other intelligent models. Various companies are working to innovate machines that fall into this category. The overall goal of innovation in this category is to create devices that have a better understanding than humans. The pinnacle in innovation in this class will be to come up with machines that have their belief systems. Some scientists believe that devices will be able to show emotion.

The self-aware category is currently at a stage of hypothesis within the artificial intelligence industry. The belief is that the class will come into existence in the coming decades, if not centuries. This category personifies the ultimate goal of AI innovation. The aim is to come up with machines that replicate the ability of humans to be self-aware. Also, they will be able to exhibit human levels of intelligence if not superior. The devices are expected to not only understand emotions but also to evoke them. The aim is to create machines that can have independent desires.

ANI (Artificial Narrow Intelligence) machines belong to the alternate classification of artificial intelligence. Such devices currently exist. The complexity showcased by these machines is varied, ranging from simple ones to those that are complex. ANI devices have human-like capabilities. They exhibit autonomy as they carry out specific tasks. The capabilities of the AI devices categorized under ANI are dependent on programming. The dependence causes their competencies to be narrow. With regard to the former classification, ANI encompasses both reactive and limited memory machines. Deep learning and machine learning are part of the ANI capabilities. Some refer to ANI as weak AI. AGI (Artificial General Intelligence) devices show learning abilities. The machines, unlike ANI devices, can perceive. They exhibit understanding capabilities. Their functionality levels will be equal to that of humans and can act independently. They can have multiple competencies through the formation of connections across varied domains. These machines will have the added value of reducing training time. Such artificial intelligence does not currently exist but is a goal of AI. The focus of AGI is to replicate human cognitive abilities in machines. Artificial General Intelligence is also known as strong AI.

Strong AI based on cognitive capabilities will be able to find solutions to tasks that are not familiar to AGI software. The achievement of Artificial Super Intelligence is the pinnacle of AI. ASI is a future goal where AI software will be better than humans. Their memory will be more than that of humans. The software will process data faster than humans. The speed of data processing will mean faster decision making. Some believe that such software will threaten the existence of humanity. The software will threaten human culture. Super intelligent software will not suffer the limitation of the cognitive part of humans. This level of innovation will be the height of human creation.

Examples of Artificial Intelligence

Artificial intelligence is in use all around us, yet we may not notice it. Our lives are affected by AI, whether we are aware of it or not. We may interact with AI machines through voice options and those that do not depend on voice. Various industries are incorporating AI into their businesses. Organizations of different sizes are using the software. The goal of AI use is to improve the quality of the lives of humans. The future will have artificial intelligence ingrained in more facets of life. Business management is running through AI. Organizations are using AI as a competitive edge in the marketplace. Automatic responders work on AI software with process automation, as seen with telecommunication companies and email responses. The responses can be said to act as virtual assistants.

The automatic replies reduce associated costs for organizations. Some companies manage their customer service using AI automated responses. Organizations can forecast using AI software whose prediction as it does not rely on previous inputs but drivers of processes. In this manner, businesses get better management. Customers can receive support online from institutions through AI. Within the e-commerce industry, AI drives the use of smart searches. As one searches for an item, suggestions come up that have their basis as AI. Depending on the level of AI, businesses can personalize experiences for customers of their e-commerce platforms. An organization can use AI as a tool of prediction on expected purchases from potential clients.

137

For e-commerce, the ability to detect and prevent fraud is a role charged to AI. While taking into account related regulations, businesses are using AI to achieve dynamic price enhancement. These AI tools are assisting companies in improving their sales levels. E-commerce is in use in organizations of different sizes.

The marketing industry is one that is incorporating AI in a number of its processes. It is using AI to make recommendations to potential clients, as seen with the use of beacons that transmit recommended offers to people as they pass near brick and mortar stores. Within social media, the industry is using AI to market on the newsfeed of those on the platforms. AI is in use by marketers for ad targeting. There are AI tools that can segment customers, therefore, allowing for ad optimization. Marketing companies are sifting through customer sentiments on their promotions via the use of AI. With the advent of global security challenges, companies within the security industry are turning to AI for surveillance purposes. The world is witnessing the use of drones that have a basis on artificial intelligence to target areas of security risk.

Telecommunication companies are using voice recognition AI-driven tools to assist clients in protecting their communication devices. We now have phones are requiring or offering fingerprint AI technology as a security feature. Companies are producing machines that can scan the eye as a security feature. AI dependent software is in development to protect against attacks in cyberspace. The transport industry is using AI software in the form of drones that are reaching far-flung areas in record time. There are countries using drones to transport products that are for urgent use, for example, pharmaceuticals. The industry, in combination with security, is sending vehicles that are not controlled by humans. Some cities are using artificial intelligence to manage the movement of cars.

Applications like Uber and Lyft are examples of how AI is causing a change in the transport industry. Self-driven vehicles are now in use and are under further development by various companies. The human resource industry is not remaining behind in using AI. The industry is at the receiving end of AI development as some feel the tools developed are taking the place of humans. The field is at a crossroads as regards using AI. On the one hand, it is increasing efficiency while on the other hand, it may mean laying off workers.

There is software that is being used to sift through the resumes that companies are receiving. AI software is now available that human resource managers can use to facilitate mentoring. Some companies are using the tools as a provision of continual learning platforms. Healthcare companies are reaping benefits from the field of artificial intelligence. The area of pathology is seeing AI-based tools that are assisting in the reading of biopsies. When linked with administrative components, healthcare companies are using AI to help medical workers provide individualized care to patients.

There are surgical robots that some hospitals are incorporating in management regimens. Some are showing higher levels of accuracy in comparison to humans. The focus in the healthcare industry is to provide more time for medical workers to interact with patients as opposed to working on administrative issues. The pharmaceutical industry is using AI software to come up with newer and better medicines.

Chapter 2: Artificial Intelligence: Promises and Challenges

As with all innovation, artificial intelligence comes with its challenges and opportunities. One comes across these aspects of artificial intelligence as they interact with the software in various forms in the goings-on of daily life. Individuals and organizations can choose to take advantage of the opportunities that artificial intelligence presents. The challenges should not be a reason to discourage the use of artificial intelligence. As with other human innovations, the focus instead should be on continuously improving the same. The occurrence of the opportunities and challenges can be due to the one interacting with them.

The promises and challenges that artificial intelligence is presenting are sometimes industry-specific. The artificial intelligence software may work well in one industry as opposed to another.

The occurrence may be due to the kind of input that a specific field gives to the artificial intelligence software. What may be an opportunity in one industry may turn out to be a challenge in another. The focus here should be on whether the promise or challenge cuts across industries or is limited to a particular field.

Customer-centric industries may, for example, be able to get access to more data than those that are not.

Artificial intelligence, though considered as being independent of machines, can be affected by the human element. For the artificial intelligence software that relies on input from humanity, the biasedness within individuals may affect how it works. The artificial intelligence software that relies on historical data assumes that the data earlier present is accurate. The effect of the human element can present as a challenge. Artificial intelligence software that is dependent on programming by people has its limitations as being defined by those who created it. The knowledge humans have limits or create opportunities in artificial intelligence.

The field of artificial intelligence is one that embraces innovation, yet this characteristic can be a source of a challenge as it is of opportunity. There are scenarios where improvements in historical artificial intelligence software lead to unprecedented development. The changes can cause unexpected negative occurrences. Innovation in planes is, in some cases, leading to crashes of airplanes. Though new artificial intelligence software undergoes tests before releasing into the marketplace, some effects present when used on a massive scale. Some innovations do get new uses once released into the general population. Artificial intelligence software concerning both promises and challenges has to contend with the political aspect of human life. There are innovations within the artificial intelligence space that do not attract political goodwill.

These innovations are being shut down from a global perspective, with these occurrences presenting a challenge to those interested in developing artificial intelligence software. Political goodwill can be a source of opportunity for those working on artificial intelligence software seen to be helpful to society. Countries are using artificial intelligence to determine their stand globally on an economic scale.

Promises

The opportunities artificial intelligence portends are massive. As we interact with AI software in our daily lives, we realize the benefits they bring. The benefits cut across various aspects of our lives. Some AI tools are so much a part of our lives that ignoring them would be to our detriment. The benefits are changing our world as we know it. Those who are undermining the potential of artificial intelligence are doing a disservice to themselves. There is an expectation that in the future, artificial intelligence software will improve on its intelligence aspect. Socially, AI is proving to be full of promise. The use of AI is supporting sustainability, for example, in the use of software that is creating social communication channels that are low in cost. The reduction in cost creates easily sustainable communication models that are helping in building the social fabric of humanity. These AI-based channels are acting as a medium through, which, various cultures are interacting, allowing for an appreciation of vast human social structures. Social media systems based on AI are changing the way humans are interacting with one another. Some contend that the channels are creating a basis for the realization of a global culture.

The promise of AI is affecting the political or governance aspects of human life positively. Candidates who previously had the right ideology but were limited by, for example, the cost of reaching their intended audience can now ride on AI channels. Such channels are providing affordable ways of reaching out to populations. There are cases where their use has led to political upsets that are considered to be positive. Some individuals in the political space are using AI to solve social concerns. Those passionate about the environment are reaping the fruits of AI. AI-backed communication systems are reducing the need to use paper. Using AI in this manner is saving trees. The field of meteorology is using AI to predict weather patterns. The prediction is allowing for preparation in case of weather forecasts that are heading in the wrong direction. Such data from AI systems are in use for saving lives. Transport companies are relying on the weather warnings to determine how safe it is to embark on travel. There are global standards of weather patterns that airlines can fly in. AI is showing promise in the education sector with learning accessibility rising due to its use. E-learning is an example of how AI is changing how humanity is educating itself. It is creating opportunities for learning in sectors that are becoming available due to the advent of AI.

The possibilities include the fields of data research and data mining. Global standards on education are increasingly becoming popular as AI is connecting the world. There is an increase in the number of individuals receiving education powered by AI software. AI is making education affordable and convenient.

Benefits for Business

The benefits that businesses are deriving from AI is immense. From machine learning software to deep learning tools, the opportunities the field of AI is presenting to the world of business is vast. Organizations are using AI to build a competitive edge within the marketplace. The importance is visible in highly competitive industries. For companies to benefit from AI, they have to invest in data mining software as data drives AI. Latter AI software combines data with algorithms to produce analytical models that businesses are using to make decisions. In highly competitive industries, efficiency is improved using AI. The automation of processes allows for better customer experience for business clients. The automation may include AI software that can give insight on ways to improve operations. The knowledge from the comprehension assists companies to work on their operational weaknesses. Cloud computing, as an example, uses AI to negate the disadvantages of servers being present on business sites. There is AI software that helps businesses reduce their costs of operation. AI is helping organizations operationally by reducing human workload, therefore, allowing people to focus on core business operations. The sales and marketing aspects of businesses are transforming by the advent of AI use. Individualized customer marketing is, now a reality. Targeted ads on websites and search engines are now part and parcel of today's marketing program for businesses. On the sales front, AI-backed CRM (Customer Relationship Management) software is commonplace as concerns working the sales process. These tools allow for aggregation of large amounts of data giving insights that were not previously available. Companies are using AI-based beacons to personalize shopping experiences from pricing to offers. Marketing ads are now a staple on social media platforms.

The human resource aspect of businesses is benefitting from AI in a variety of ways. The development of AI is creating opportunities for businesses to access the global workforce at the touch of a button.

Organizations are seeing a surge in the availability of freelance workers willing to work remotely for industries able to take advantage of the opportunity. The ability to work remotely can be a competitive edge for businesses and can be a way to reduce human resource costs, given the varied pay structures on a global scale. Businesses are transforming how they interact with customers using AI-backed systems. Some companies have incorporated AI tools like chatbots as part of their customer care strategy. Studies are showing that the use of automated customer care tools is improving levels of customer engagement. Moreover, it can augment the human aspect of customer service with people taking over from the AI systems when the task is beyond the abilities of the AI software. AI systems are in use for follow up purposes on customers by businesses for cases that require feedback by the company to the client.

Benefits for Economies

Economies with a global outlook are now using AI to advance their interests in the world stage. Some are choosing to be the hub of specialization in the field of AI or AI-backed industries. Countries are investing in AI-based military hardware as a way of protecting their economic interests. For economies, the marketplace has increased as the world connects via AI-backed systems. Countries can trade conveniently at the touch of a button.

Increased competition between economies is leading to better product quality for customers. Wealth generation is happening at a rate never seen before through the use of AI. Economies are investing in IT systems that are backed by AI to improve the efficiency with which they are generating wealth. Industries that are supporting AI are springing up changing economies worldwide. Global wealth is favoring economies embracing the use of AI. Countries are making economic decisions from data collected through AI-backed IT software. The use of AI in the IT industry is giving a chance to economies that are lacking traditional resources to generate wealth based on human resource AI skills. Economies are leveraging on this opportunity that AI is presenting. Virtual economies are now a reality with AI playing a role in their growth. AI-backed systems are introducing digital currencies as an alternative to traditional monies in economies.

Though still being worked on, there are those expecting the future economy to be cashless. AI systems like blockchain are expected to be the backbone of the digital currencies. Social media companies are looking to take advantage of these developments. Economies, where the companies are based, are growing at an unprecedented rate. Virtual jobs are now a part of any economy that is growing.

Some economies are transforming by using AI-backed manufacturing processes which are leading to a shift in where companies are choosing to base their production facilities. Economies are growing in size by investing in AI-focused systems, leading to a reduction in costs of manufacture, therefore, being competitive in the global marketplace. Cost reduction is in both labor and capital aspects. Industries incorporating AI into their manufacturing processes are seeing positive changes on a large scale.

Manufacturers are increasing their efficiency by using AI automated systems. Countries are changing the source of their economic strength by investing in AI-backed manufacturing industries. AI is proving to be an integral part of the healthcare system with its use in the diagnostic stage of treatment. The healthcare segment of clinical research is benefitting from AI-backed systems with economies transforming their workforce with interventions generated from such investigations. Some countries that were losing their workforce at a younger age are using AI to improve the length of life. Economies are growing by generating new ways of treating diseases, transforming some countries into medical hubs. As people travel to these economies for healthcare, they pump money into the sectors.

Contribution to Productivity, Growth, and Innovation

AI is contributing to the growth, innovation, and productivity of economies and businesses. The AI model in use is the one determining the extent of the contribution. The effect of AI on growth, innovation, and productivity is expected to increase as AI incorporation increases.

Businesses and economies should be aware of the factors that could slow down this contribution and take steps to minimize them.

It is best to consider AI as an augmenting factor to labor and capital, which are traditionally factors increasing productivity, growth, and innovation. In terms of growth, AI is contributing to economies with some showing accelerated growth levels.

Some countries are changing their economic prospects by working on becoming a hub, for example, for manufacturing by using AI to reduce their costs of production.

The result is they are increasing their global competitiveness. Businesses are increasing their capacities by investing in AI tools that are increasing their efficiency levels. The economies investing in AI tools are witnessing a growth of opportunities as their capacity increases. Businesses and economies are seeing a growth of jobs associated with AI. The contribution of AI to innovation is undisputable within the field of healthcare. Here, AI development is augmenting humans as they seek better healthcare outcomes. From diagnostic tools supported by AI to those assisting in surgical procedures, AI is driving innovation in the medical arena. Innovation in Information Technology is increasing as the demand for improvement in AI is being pursued. Countries are innovating new ways of improving their military capability using the power of AI, for example, by using drones instead of humans. Industrial growth due to AI is now a reality as businesses supporting AI are increasing.

AI is contributing to productivity by increasing efficiency levels. The speed at which processes can be carried out using AI is at times higher than that of humans. AI can carry out tasks with increased accuracy even at higher speeds, through automation. The combination of AI abilities is leading to increased output levels. There is an increase in production volumes in economies and businesses that are investing in AI. AI augmenting humans in work is leading to increased productivity levels as humans are focusing on core tasks. Individuals experience freedom from mundane tasks as they can focus on those requiring creativity.

Businesses and economies can ignore AI to their detriment as it is becoming a part of daily life. Entities using AI are expected to have a competitive edge in the market as consumers get a better experience from them.

In a global marketplace, AI can help organizations reach far-flung regions at a minimal cost. Businesses can use AI to improve service or product offerings. The effectiveness of AI for organizations will depend on its use. Capital owners are at an advantage concerning benefitting from AI.

Challenges

No human invention is perfect, and AI is no exception. Businesses and economies should be aware of the issues associated with AI and put into place systems that negate the hurdles or turn them into strengths. It is better to face the negatives than ignore them and suffer down the line. Being aware of the challenges puts businesses and economies in a better position to navigate the world of AI. The awareness may become a driver of future innovation through a goal of improving on weaknesses of AI. Acceptance of the issues allows entities to know their limitations in advance. Businesses are at risk of losing customer loyalty due to the use of AI if clients feel interaction with an entity lacks a human element. The social aspect of human interactions is critical. Potential clients may feel a business is choosing machines over humans, for example, if jobs are lost. The message an organization may portray by incorporating AI may be ill-received by the public.

Customers may feel profit is the focus of a business as opposed to humans. The lack of cognitive ability by AI tools can portray a business as inhuman. Studies from various quarters portend that as AI becomes part of daily life, the result will be job losses. The reasoning is that AI has higher capabilities than humans in terms of, for example, speed and accuracy. Loss of jobs would lead to a breakdown in the social fabric as individuals look for means to survive. Stress levels are expected to increase with security challenges expanding. Individual levels of stress will increase as they look to adapt to changes in the marketplace. The reduced levels of human interaction are expected to increase the negative emotions experienced. The growth of fear is a challenge associated with the advent of AI. The emotion is leading to a reduction in productivity as individuals are battling with the idea that they could be redundant shortly as machines are looking to take over their jobs. Others are having to contend with changes in their job descriptions to keep their work opportunities alive.

Families are facing changes in job locations to stay in employment as companies are changing business strategies, for example, by changing manufacturing locations. Businesses are taking these actions in a bid to remain competitive. AI challenges include building trust, AI-human interface concerns, Information Technology infrastructure, and investments. These challenges affect how the general population is adapting to AI in their daily lives. The issues need addressing so that humanity can take advantage of the full potential of AI. Each of the challenging elements may require a different approach. The overall focus should be on how to turn the challenges into opportunities. The process would allow for continuous improvement within the field of AI. The issues will affect how economies choose to strategize for future generations.

Building Trust

Given the emotive issues raised concerning the effect of AI on the general population, building trust should be part of the agenda of future AI strategy. Issues of ethics, data protection, safety, and transparency are critical to consider. The approach to these concerns determines whether the trust is built or lost. Without confidence, the AI journey will attract more challenges from a variety of quarters, including the political class. The more the challenges, the slower the progress to full AI potential will be. Trust will make the transition to AI smoother.

An element that the AI industry is tackling to build trust is ethics. The hurdle is in creating agreeable boundaries that are acceptable to all stakeholders. Companies are updating and sharing privacy policies with potential customers. The goal of AI in the context of ethics is to come up with an acceptable global standard applicable worldwide. Such an achievement will standardize expectations from customers. Ethics, when appropriately applied, should not strangle AI but instead, promote it. Changes are coming up in ethical standards as issues are arising as AI is undergoing implementation on a much larger scale than ever before. Data protection is an element of trust-building when it comes to AI. Individuals want to know that their data is safe when they share the same.

There have been cases where hackers have gained access to data from companies without authorization. Such occurrences are breaking down trust towards the use of AI in daily life. AI tools dealing with sensitive areas like finance cannot afford to have laxity when it comes to data protection issues. The use of AI tools in the financial industry is facing data protection as a hurdle to building trust in potential clients.

The safety of individuals is an issue when looking at building trust in AI. There are AI tools that are in use as security measures. The challenge is in the boundary between using AI as security without creating the feeling of loss of privacy. When one senses that they are losing their privacy, they tend to shy away from using AI tools. AI tools should not be a source of a security risk as witnessed when an individual has their personal information shared due to a security breach. Businesses and economies need to embrace transparency to build trust with potential customers. Customers should not get a sense that they are not getting the full information on how their data is in use. There are cases of organizations getting exposed through cases where their affiliates are using the information they are sharing without customer approval. Entities need to share information and update if needed, on how they are using shared data. When potential customers consider an organization as transparent in their dealings, they tend to trust the entities. Organizations should aim to create the right balance of honesty in the eyes of the public.

Artificial Intelligence Human Interface

Humans possess the need to interact with other individuals regularly. This innate need is presenting a challenge to the AI field, for example, for AI tools that do not have a human interface. Some customers may feel offended at the lack of interaction with other humans when transacting with a business. Some report feeling as though they are just a number to the organization. In a world where competition is increasing, entities need to tackle this apparent business challenge.

Artificial Intelligence Human Interface is facing a challenge in the context of augmentation. There are AI tools, for example, in healthcare which are in use to assist in treatment processes. When something goes wrong during treatment, where does the blame lie? At what point is the responsibility of the individual and at what point is it a machine issue? Businesses that are incorporating AI tools in areas like customer service are facing the challenge of determining when to shift a conversation to include the human element. If not done correctly, incorporating AI tools may become a weakness for a business. The advantages of AI tools are not changing the way some individuals perceive the software. Some consider organizations that revert to AI tools without a human interface as untrustworthy. They are those who believe that virtual assistants are not knowledgeable about products and services as compared to individuals on location. The perception is presenting a challenge to organizations looking to scale using AI-backed services. Context is a factor that determines the quality of customer service and can be compromised. Some AI tools have their programming done in a limited manner, for example, in the variety or specificity of choices the software presents. Currently, AI tools do not have cognitive abilities, which are a factor in the challenges facing the AI-Human interface. AI tools programming is generally focusing on dealing with specific tasks.

When an AI tool is facing an option or input that is not part of its program, it gets challenged. The balance between taking advantage of the full potential of an AI tool and knowing when to introduce a human interface is a challenge for organizations. Businesses must determine what is delegatable to AI tools and where individuals will add value. Speed can be an element of the AI-Human interface challenge, for example, when an individual is in a faraway location from the AI tool in use.

There is the element of time in terms of how fast an individual can respond to a query forwarded through AI tools. The person on the other end may assume that they are in contact with a human and not a machine. Time zone differences may lead to a slowing down of responses. A business may receive negative reviews on their services due to this challenge.

Insufficient IT Infrastructure

The challenge of IT infrastructure insufficiency is one that can be solved. The underlying focus in dealing with this challenge is to find out where the source of lack is. It can be an issue of processing power, hardware, skill, and even support. Each of these sources will require different responses. Businesses should opt for solutions that will have the most impact in the case of competing interests for limited resources meant to deal with the concerns. Organizations should also consider the most affordable solutions. Approaching the challenges in such a manner may help a business sort out more than one source of the lack at any given time. Given the large volumes of data associated with better models of AI tools, businesses that choose to invest in the latest AI devices should prepare to have higher levels of processing power for the data.

Within the AI strategy of an organization, an entity may choose to focus on improving the processing power of its AI tools over time. The advent of cloud computing is proving to be a solution to this challenge. Some companies are utilizing the power of parallel processors. IT infrastructure can lack in terms of hardware. AI that is dependent on machine learning may require a company to have its machines at location. With AI being a dynamic field, what may be of use today may be unusable shortly. Companies may need to keep updating their AI tools, which may come at a cost that is unsustainable to the organization. Businesses may consider how long an AI tool they are to purchase will remain relevant. The versatility of such devices can help a company keep its costs low.

Without the right skill, the use of AI will be a challenge for businesses. Some AI-based devices are facing a limited market globally due to a lack of supportive skills needed for them to work effectively. Some companies are choosing to limit where their items are on sale to deal with this challenge. The available workforce may prove expensive to some organizations, which translates to investing in some AI tools untenable.

The gains from AI may be slowed down for organizations that are relying on skilled labor that is overburdened. In such cases, the investment in AI tools may prove to be a costly mistake. AI as a discipline is dependent on other skills for it to be effective in its goals. Lack of support from industries that complement IT infrastructure is proving to be a challenge for some organizations. An example is the lack of a reliable internet connection that may be a requirement for some AI tools to function. Several regions globally still lack, for example, fiber connections that are a requirement for processing high data volumes, which is a feature of newer models of AI tools. AI devices relying on other sources of data may work incorrectly when the providers of such information are missing.

Inadequate Investment for Implementation

Organizations should withhold investing in AI tools if the investment is inadequate for useful implementation. Businesses should consider all the elements required for AI implementation before starting the process. Some facets to consider for efficient AI implementation include the availability of human skill, hardware, supportive industries, and goodwill. An organization choosing to ignore any of the facets may end up with an incomplete project which may add unnecessary costs to the business.

For any AI tool, a business is looking to incorporate in its processes, the human skill element is critical. Companies should tackle this aspect in advance. If applicable, the level of knowledge and skill of staff needs confirmation before investing in AI tools. A plan on acquiring the skills can be part of the implementation strategy. Some companies are establishing modules for continuous training to keep the skill levels of staff up to date. Such a program is to ensure that the full potential of the AI investment is in reach. Organizations can use the power of Frequently Asked Questions (FAQs) to assist staff in handling challenges they are facing during AI implementation.

An efficient AI strategy takes into account all the components of hardware required to implement AI successfully.

During the planning phase, an organization should consider if all the hardware elements are easily accessible. Scenarios, where an AI tool is not functioning because an organization is waiting for the shipping of a piece of equipment, is common. Businesses end up losing opportunities due to such occurrences. Adequate investment in this context may mean having a spare piece of hardware at any time.

The successful implementation of AI can be dependent on supportive services and products. Businesses looking to implement AI should ensure such services exist and are readily available. It may be prudent to hold off instituting AI if there is no guarantee of support for the same. Going ahead with no backing may present a business challenge in the future. Lack of fiber installation can be why an organization cannot implement AI in some regions. The effect is the slowing down of benefits connected to such AI opportunities from reaching the firm.

Several organizations may forget to consider the political aspect of AI implementation. Companies need to invest in AI in regions where there is political goodwill for the same. A lack of political goodwill for AI projects can cost businesses. Politics can clash with AI implementation as people may feel that the incorporation of AI will take away their jobs. A prudent organization will look at the impact of the political climate concerning AI implementation before deciding to invest. Finding a balance between investing for the future and taking care of political interests can be the key for a company to survive in the marketplace.

Chapter 3: How Artificial Intelligence is Changing Business Processes

Business process as we know it is changing, thanks to the power of artificial intelligence. The rate at which AI is changing how business is processing information is dizzying. More organizations are taking advantage of the promises of artificial intelligence. The difference AI is making in such organizations is clear. Companies are increasing their levels of efficiency to never seen before standards using AI tools. Operations that were taking days to complete are now over in hours or less. Some AI tools can achieve speed without losing quality. Workers are getting much-needed support from AI tools leading to better outcomes.

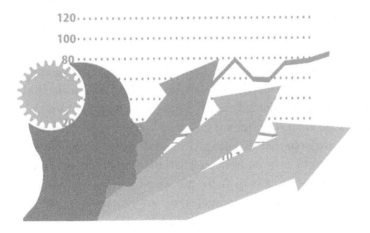

The more the AI tools get incorporated into business processes, the more innovations are increasing. Modifications of AI tools are occurring as their use is growing in businesses. The workforce is getting more creative to survive the onslaught by machines. They are also getting more time to create, as AI devices are taking over mundane tasks.

Artificial intelligence has brought the facet of convenience to business processes. Procedures previously taking hours to complete can now be finished in comparatively shorter periods, sometimes with the click of a button. Industries based on this factor brought in by AI are blossoming, for example, purely e-commerce based businesses. Businesses are now able to take advantage of growth opportunities that were not available before the advent of AI. Brick and mortar stores can run e-commerce shops in tandem. Businesses can reach customers that were previously unavailable to them at a minimal cost. The range of products companies can offer customers are also growing. AI is converting manual business processes into automated procedures. Companies are using this opportunity to stay ahead of the competition as automation is allowing them to reach more customers in shorter periods. Faster processing is attracting more clients to businesses. Automation is also lowering business costs. Businesses are now able to incorporate segmentation into their internal and external processes. The effect on marketing is companies having the ability to personalize product offerings. The use of beacons as a way of optimizing sales promotions is becoming more common among business marketing strategies. Businesses are adding value to products and services using AI-backed tools. Some products previously unavailable in digital forms are now in production in e-formats thanks to AI-driven possibilities. Examples include producing reading materials in digital formats as well as traditional hardcover types.

The overall effect is increasing value for businesses in terms of sales opportunities. The productivity from the AI-backed business process is growing faster than traditional models. Some tasks are processing at faster rates as machines are taking over mundane tasks. Increasing productivity is leading to cost savings for companies. Some AI-backed devices are allowing companies to function for longer hours. The creation of new jobs is occurring as AI is changing business processes. Jobs are paying more in some scenarios. Opportunities involving less mundane tasks are characterizing the AI-backed changes in business processes. The new opportunities require individuals to change their way of working. Cross-functional skills are a requirement in the jobs. AI is changing business processes including, customer acquisition, new customer service types, personal assistants in businesses, marketing research, human resource and hiring, and the sales process. The extent to which the methods are changing is proportional to the investment businesses are putting in concerning AI-backed tools.

New Customer Acquisition Process

The cost of acquiring a new customer for businesses is an element of company processes that adds to the cost of doing business. Getting a new client is more expensive than retaining one to companies. Regardless of the negatives, organizations must keep the process of acquiring customers active to avoid becoming redundant in the marketplace. Businesses are spending huge volumes keeping themselves in the mind of potential clients.

Budgets for such activities are consistently in renewal as organizations are trying to maintain their competitive edge. AI is changing the way companies are approaching the process of expanding their customer base. The advent of AI-backed e-commerce opportunities is providing new ways for businesses to acquire customers. E-commerce platforms are adding a convenience factor that brick and mortar concepts are unable to present to the market. Some organizations are choosing to combine both ideas for greater appeal. Some organizations attract customers looking to purchase online without visiting stores physically. Businesses are offering products and services to attract such customers, for example, free shipping. Customers can sign up for membership online to stores with the click of a button. Businesses are gaining customers who have never stepped into their stores physically.

AI through social media is giving businesses new tools with which they can reach new customers. From business pages to targeting ads, organizations can use varied ways to acquire new clients. The social media platforms are providing tools that allow personalization of business pages. Organizations can share information that is attractive to potential clients through such media. The modern customer is expecting that businesses have a social media site that they can reach them through if need be. Potential customers are raising queries through the social media news feed and expecting a rapid response from organizations. The effectiveness of social media platforms is no longer debatable. AI tools are providing opportunities for businesses to target with more accuracy potential customers. The effect is opportunities to personalize product and service offerings to new customers. Sites like Facebook and Instagram, are allowing for targeting based on varied criteria include geography, age, and interests.

Businesses can work on the timing of their acquisition messages for effectiveness. Since the targeting tools are using data and AI, the accuracy levels are making it easier for businesses to acquire new customers faster. Organizations are, therefore, spending less money on expanding their client base. AI is allowing companies to place targeted ads on websites that are appealing to the kind of clients they want to acquire. In the world of marketing, AI has created business opportunities to expand the market for businesses through the use of beacons. These devices can, through the help of AI, interact with potential customers passing near a brick and mortar store. The tools will send messages that are personalized by businesses encouraging customers to walk into the stores. Organizations are taking advantage of these tools to send individualized messages while taking advantage of proximity to the potential client as a means of acquiring new clients. The power of AI-backed search engines is a reality for the majority of the world's population. The company Google is one of the largest in the world, with the largest search engine. Businesses are using the platforms to reach out to new customers by aligning their websites and contents to be the digital place of choice for clients. Organizations are investing in keywords that are optimizing their sites for search engines to rank them higher than the competition. An industry based on search engine optimization is budding based on the opportunities the AI-backed systems are providing to businesses. AI-backed software is allowing businesses to acquire new customers on a global scale. Industries based on digital products and services can transact across borders. AI-backed payment systems are making the process easier, effectively expanding the potential client base for businesses that are embracing the tools.

AI-backed logistic tools are giving customers, real-time ability to track shipments, increasing trust levels between companies, and customers leading to the increasing willingness of clients to take risks concerning purchasing from faraway locations. The convenience associated with digital products shipping instantly via AI-backed tools is increasing the global reach for new customers for businesses.

New Type of Customer Services

AI is creating new types of customer services by providing opportunities within the marketplace that were unavailable in yesteryears. These services are gaining ground as they are less tedious than traditional services. The services do not have to contend with the challenges of geographical borders. The services are coming up as a result of innovation driven by AI. Some regions require less regulation, which is encouraging the fast growth rate witnessed in this sector. Some of the services are springing up in support of AI-backed systems. Such services include those that make sense only if backed by AI tools.

The digital payment industry is a service that is growing based on the premise of AI. Businesses relying on digital products are requiring means of payment. Companies working as escrows on online platforms give the much-needed trust factor for online transactions. The companies provide a medium through which both the buyer and the seller can get protection from fraudulent activities. These payment modes are also providing convenience as one can release or receive money at the click of a button. Without these services, businesses transacting online would be less efficient. The convenience factor the companies are having over brick and mortar stores would also reduce considerably.

Education traditionally is held in a physical location where students gather to listen to knowledge. AI is creating platforms that are in use in online classrooms. The advantages of this mode of education include increasing the global marketplace for education.

The diversity allows for increased multi-cultural understanding, which may lead to a more unified global society. The convenience element that this service offers cannot be understated. Online educational platforms are increasing access to education, which can be a media to achieve equality. Some platforms are giving options for potential students to personalize their educational journey. Digital TV service is running on AI-backed systems, and its growth is proportional to the availability of AI in different regions. This service is pushing out traditional forms of entertainment with its convenience factor. Some providers are allowing for more capacity per payment made with clients able to stream services on more than one device. Users can access providers on a global scale without limitations associated with traditional boundaries as providers can present offerings worldwide.

Competition within this service is stiff with providers changing how they provide entertainment to potential clients. AI support services must be in place for one to take advantage of these services. The industry of freelancing has its backbone as AI. Individuals are now able to work from remote locations while being as efficient, if not more, as being in a physical office. AI is allowing economies to work on a 24-hour basis through freelancing. Those from across the globe can work while others are resting using AI-backed tools. Teamwork is possible using AI without the hurdle of geographical boundaries. Companies have the opportunity to outsource tasks that not core to the business on a global scale. Outsourcing globally could mean saving costs for businesses. AI is responsible for the growth of online stores with Amazon proving its worth on a global scale. Brick and mortar stores are also able to take advantage of this AI-backed tool, therefore, taking advantage of the online marketplace. Sales are increasing for businesses using this platform. The stores can be set up conveniently with companies now available providing templates for online stores. The updating of store offerings is convenient with AI-backed tools. Dropshipping services through companies like Shopify are now available riding on AI. Such online stores require minimal investments, therefore, lowering operational costs.

Since AI is running on the web, services that support the web industry are coming up. AI support services like fiber-related companies are becoming commonplace across the globe. Independent businesses that traditionally would require large sums of investments like TV stations are coming up at a fraction of the cost.

Such companies are taking advantage of AI-backed organizations like YouTube. Here, they are building channels with some achieving high levels of views from minimal initial investments. Other services include creating digital products that are selling via online platforms. The products include digital games, stickers, and fliers. Graphic designers can now provide services online as opposed to the traditional methods of yesteryears.

Using a Virtual Personal Assistant in Your Business

Traditionally, a virtual personal assistant is an individual who is remotely connecting to the clients of a business. AI is changing the industry at dizzying speed. Machines are taking the place of humans in the field of virtual personal assistants. AI devices acting as personal assistants include chatbots and autoresponders. The devices are programmed to lead one through, for example, a series of questions to get a predetermined solution. Some can communicate in various languages expanding the options available to business customers.

The opportunities that AI is bringing to businesses that are opting to use virtual personal assistants include lowering costs of doing business. An organization using virtual personal assistants does not have to take into consideration labor laws associated with a human interface. Issues of overtime, medical leave, and union rights do not arise. AI-backed virtual personal assistants can work round the clock, unlike their human counterparts. The devices work remotely and require no direct supervision. Businesses can upgrade AI whenever it is feasible, ensuring they are up to speed with the standards in their industry. AI-backed virtual personal assistants can be programmed to deal with specific tasks.

As with all human developments, virtual personal assistants come with their challenges. Unlike humans, virtual personal assistants, even those associated with AI, lack cognitive capabilities. They are unable to connect emotionally with business clients, which can portray a business as having a cold persona. Depending on the industry an organization belongs to, it may be a source of negative feedback from potential clients. Politically there may be pushback on replacing humans with virtual personal assistants as economies struggle with unemployment rates.

Getting the right balance between machine and humans, for businesses looking to incorporate AI into their operations, is a common challenge. A strategic mindset should be in place when businesses are looking to incorporate AI-backed virtual personal assistants into their processes. The incorporation of the tools into the overall business strategic plan gives the best direction to follow. The business policy should allow for counter-checking on which virtual personal assistant would work best for overall organizational strategy. The goal of incorporating virtual personal assistants should be easing the movement of a business towards its end goal. AI-backed virtual personal assistants may provide a competitive strategic edge over other market players.

Companies providing AI-backed virtual personal assistants are many with providers located all over the world. Some virtual personal assistants do not need complex support systems. Some providers allow businesses to use them for free while some charge. Some social media platforms are allowing companies to personalize their own virtual personal assistants at no extra cost to the business. Businesses can create their own virtual personal assistants online like chatbots.

Organizations can consider choosing virtual personal assistants that come with the added benefit of machine learning. Companies should work with authentic sources of AI-backed virtual personal assistants to avoid unnecessary downtimes. When determining the virtual personal assistant to use, a business looks at the context of the industry. There are industries, for example, customer service, that are accepting of virtual personal assistants. Clients are on board with technology and are focused on the convenience factor. Other industries are not so liberal, for example, those where clients are looking for a human touch like healthcare, and counseling. In the latter scenario, potential clients may find it offensive working with virtual personal assistants. Businesses in sensitive industries should get the right balance between the use of virtual personal assistants, and delegation to the human workforce.

There are various industries where using a virtual personal assistant in business would be beneficial. Examples include the customer care industry where potential clients are more focused on finding a solution and hold liberal views when it comes to communication methods. Some service-based industries, like travel agencies, are incorporating virtual personal assistants with success.

162

There are virtual personal assistants now available for personal use. Some businesses within the manufacturing industry are using virtual personal assistants to automate processes as a means of freeing the workforce to focus on their core job description. Companies involved in retail marketing are also using virtual personal assistants.

How Artificial Intelligence Is Changing Marketing Research

Historically, marketing research involves sending the human workforce to chosen areas where they would ask questions to a predetermined sample population. The answers would give a glimpse of the opinion of the market towards a product or service. Data would come from the answers, and analysis would yield a conclusion. The whole process was tedious and would take months, even years, to conclude. The cost implication of the process was high in terms of money and time. The possibility of a research result, being redundant by the time it was submitted, was a possible reality. Artificial intelligence is changing marketing research by erasing some of the challenges previously experienced within the industry. Marketing research companies can now carry out work conveniently and can, therefore, interact with larger populations. The result is higher levels of accuracy. The convenience is breaking down barriers that had fewer people willing to take part in surveys. For the research done remotely, the privacy factor associated is giving researchers a larger pool of individuals willing to share their opinions on issues. The timing of responses is also now convenient with respondents choosing appropriate times of answering surveys. Artificial intelligence is giving marketing research companies opportunities to expand their reach of possible respondents. Through AI, market research is now possible on a global scale. Geographical barriers are a thing of the past for market research companies that are embracing the use of AI in their research processes. AI is tackling barriers like cultures that were a hindrance to marketing research. Examples include those that inhibit part of the population from giving their opinions on varied issues.

AI is allowing individuals to share their views without necessarily revealing who they are, which is allowing more people to speak. With AI, marketing research companies can segment their target population at a faster rate. At the click of a button, a company can determine the boundaries of the sample population. The limits to be defined can include geography, age, sex, gender, religion, and work. The potential of targeting accuracy is more with AI-backed marketing research tools. Targeting with AI gives results that are a better reflection of reality. Marketing research companies working on a global scale can determine the appropriate timing of the process per region.

The result may be an increase in the number of respondents per survey that is carried out. Artificial intelligence is allowing marketing research companies to carry out their processes online. The benefits of online platforms are numerous, including the opportunity for marketing research companies to tweak surveys as results are coming in. Marketing research companies can add or reduce the scope of their research as respondents are acting. There are marketing research companies that are creating applications that send out surveys as needed. A notification would pop up on the devices of potential respondents, giving them a chance to share their opinions conveniently. Online research is allowing companies to see results in real-time.

The advent of AI in marketing research has considerably reduced the turnaround time for results. Marketing research companies can see the results as they are trickling in from respondents. The speed is allowing for versatility with marketing research companies carrying out multiple types of research concurrently. The companies can serve many customers while using their resources efficiently. Businesses looking for quick turnaround times from market research companies are at an advantage. The quick turnaround time is proving beneficial to organizations as they can react to the market faster. Businesses can use AI marketing research as a tool to keep abreast of market changes.

AI-backed marketing research methods are devoid of human bias, which may lead to better results. AI is immune to biases that humans are prone to like gender, race, and religion. AI devices can be programmed to get rid of bias. A lack of bias may give new insights previously unseen. Businesses may end up seeing opportunities that were blocked by human biased results.

Unbiased insights can be for companies, a source of competitive advantage, growth opportunities, or new markets. AI-backed marketing research that bases itself on machine learning will lessen the bias further. Such results will give real-time changes in consumer opinions.

How Artificial Intelligence is Changing Human Resources and Hiring

Human resources is an industry as old as the advent of businesses. The focus of human resources is the people element of an organization. The people in a business can cause an organization to succeed or fail, which explains the importance of the human resources industry. The success of the human resource department directly reflects in the performance of a business.

The industry should, therefore, keep abreast of developments, which allow them to attract the best people for a business. A workforce can be the competitive edge for an organization. In many parts of the world, unemployment is rising. The human resources department of most organizations is receiving tons of resumes from applicants whenever they advertise for opportunities. Sifting through the documentation was a nightmare in yesteryears. The advent of AI use in human resources is automating this process. The availability of AI software to sift through resumes sent by applicants is reducing the administrative workload for human resources departments. AI is allowing the human resources industry to focus on the central tasks of interviewing the right applicants for vacant positions. AI resume processing is also allowing human resources to sift through more resumes than ever before. AI is making tremendous changes within the human resources industry with online platforms budding based on this industry.

Platforms like LinkedIn are allowing recruiters to reach potential team players via non-traditional methods. It is not uncommon to find human resource departments sifting through the social media platforms of applicants for a glimpse of who applicants are.

165

The job marketplace is expecting potential workers to have a presence on these platforms. Some vacancies are filling based on the profiles on these platforms. Connections among the workforce in these platforms are leading to opportunities in organizations. Some organizations are accepting online applications as the primary mode for filling vacancies. The convenience factor is driving this method of getting the best human resources available. Online applications are saving time with organizations that care about environmental issues opting for little to no paper trails in their human resources processes.

For organizations with large workforces, the power of online human resource tools is making interactions faster. One can log in to human resources portals and find solutions on a need-to basis. The online systems are making it easier for human resources departments to manage team workers. Diversity is an element that some organizations have a goal of achieving, which is being aided by AI use in human resources departments. Human resources departments can in real-time, tell if they are within their goal of equality within their workforce. AI is allowing human resources to reach more applicants, which can give companies a global outlook. Human resource departments working in regions demanding strict diversity requirements can keep abreast of these regulations using AI-backed resources. In such environments, adherence may determine the success of a business entity as there are opportunities organizations get based on the diversity of their workforce. Human resources being a competitive edge in the marketplace has AI to thank, for providing opportunities, for companies to outsource tasks as needed.

Smaller companies can get vital tasks sorted without the process of hiring an individual permanently. Many companies are opting to use freelancers for delegatable tasks. AI, in this way, has led to the growth of the freelance industry spanning a variety of jobs. Organizations can, through freelancing, attract highly skilled individuals for required periods whom they would ordinarily be unable to afford. The arrangement offers companies opportunities to leverage the available global workforce to minimize hiring costs. For the human resources industry, interviews are the tools through which they determine the success of an organization. Depending on the context, the interviewing process can be long-drawn and tiring. Human bias may also affect the effectiveness of the interviewing process.

Companies are using AI to negate the human bias component during the interview process. Some companies are choosing to hold interviews over online platforms. The AI-backed interview process is helping human resources sift through suitable candidates with some organizations meeting the top candidates for the final interview. The result is a standardized process that is giving companies a better chance to add the best possible available human resources to their team.

How Artificial Intelligence Is Changing the Sales Process

In yesteryears, the word sales would give a picture of an individual going house-to-house following up on sales prospects. It was a job not for the faint-hearted with rejections a staple of the work description. It required lots of traveling with long work hours expected from salespeople. For most businesses, the sales process is the driver of their existence. Without sales, businesses become extinct. The sales process is, therefore, a fundamental business process that organizations focus on regularly. Artificial intelligence is changing how organizations are approaching the sales process. Tools backed by AI are now a staple of the business sales process. The Customer Relationship Management (CRM) tool is an AI-backed software that organizations are incorporating to make their sales process more effective. The benefits of these tools include faster responses and better follow up to sales leads.

Teams can interact remotely, making better decisions for organizations. Companies are finding it easier to follow up with their sales personnel on the ground using the software. Organizations can access sales data on a real-time basis allowing faster reactions to the market dynamics. Organizations can now carry out a complete sales process online, for example, through e-commerce stores. Some businesses are purely online while others are taking advantage of the opportunities, and adding the e-commerce component to their brick and mortar stores. The effect is organizations can reach more customers at minimal cost, which translates to higher operational efficiency for businesses.

The advent of AI in the online space is allowing for the rise of new sales promotional methods like the use of online bidding. Companies can access the global market using online platforms, therefore, increasing their potential market share. Artificial intelligence in the sales process is giving rise to the use of applications (abbreviated as apps) in promoting sales. Many companies now have apps that potential clients can download onto their devices through which they can access varied services, including making orders. Such applications can give companies access to information on potential clients that they would have no other way of getting. With the data, companies can personalize the sales process to an individual level, which gives organizations greater accuracy of sales impact. Businesses can use the data as a competitive edge in the marketplace as they create products that will resonate with their potential clients. For businesses to succeed, they must make a profit enough to sustain the enterprise. Some companies allow for credit, whose basis is the belief that the buyer will be able to afford the payments in the future. Artificial Intelligence is providing tools for businesses to analyze, in advance, whether an individual can pay for their services or products in the future via their use in the credit report systems.

The systems have their basis as previous data, which is a component of artificial intelligence. Companies can use these systems to take calculated risks while taking advantage of opportunities. AI-backed tools are allowing organizations to be accurate in their targeting of sales prospects. For companies selling online, AI devices can give data based on defined algorithms by an organization. The result is minimal sales cost for the maximum impact attainable. The efficiency of the sales process and the coverage is increasing due to these AI-backed tools. The data generated from artificial intelligence is helping companies determine where to focus their sales energies on, for example, in terms of geography, interests, and competition. The data can reveal opportunities organizations previously unknown to companies. Companies are tweaking the sales process by using AI to lead their decision making. Data collected from artificial intelligence tools is devoid of human bias, which allows businesses to make objective decisions. Accessing the data can be in real-time, which can allow the synergy of the sales process and the dynamics in the marketplace, for example, tweaking of sales promotions as per market response. Companies using AI to make decisions can access new opportunities. They can compare data from other business aspects which can expose trends that can create new avenues and markets, through which, they can sell their products.

Chapter 4: Focus on Strategy and Evaluation

Businesses are opting to incorporate AI into their overall company strategy as a means of staying competitive within the marketplace. Some are going an extra step and creating a separate AI strategy. Businesses are using AI to create a competitive edge over other market players. In highly competitive industries, given the globalization of the market place, AI could be the tool that keeps a company afloat. Some companies are using AI to achieve their overall strategies. Strategies are data-dependent with AI being the link between the two components. History is not lacking examples of enterprises that have collapsed due to a lack of adopting AI into their processes.

Strategy as a process can be broken down into three steps that are planning, implementation, and evaluation. A business should consider these steps to achieve the full potential of AI utilization within a business setting. Plans should be in place evaluating the actual impact of AI use in a business relative to the expected projections. Going through the steps will allow a business to identify gaps and come up with solutions to address the discrepancies between reality and expectations. The steps should be in a constant state of action to make adjustments as quickly as possible.

Strategy First: Plan Your Strategy

Every business worth its salt has a strategy in place. It acts as a roadmap that helps a business focus on its overall vision. The end goal should be a success as pictured in the mind of the business owners. Writing the strategy is an element that helps solidify the map towards the end goal. The process of coming up with a roadmap can help a business deal with issues unthought of when the business vision was just an idea. Businesses should opt for the path that takes them fastest to their end goal while maintaining the integrity of their end goal. Artificial intelligence is versatile when it comes to strategy as it can be the strategy itself or a tool to achieve the same. Some businesses are using AI as a means to edge out the competition from the marketplace via, for example, utilizing AI to expand their customer base. Others are choosing to center their overall strategy on AI. The latter option portrays a company as adaptable to technological change. Each path has its benefits and challenges with the choice depending on what works best for a business entity.

Issues like adaptability by the potential clients of business to AI technology is a consideration when a company is determining which path to follow. Creating a strategy incorporating AI in whatever form is a process that requires a holistic approach. The expected end impact and its ripple effect on departments making up the business unit is a consideration. Each business unit can involve itself in this process of strategy creation. Having varied views allows for brainstorming that promotes creativity, an element of creating a unique product offering in industries facing high levels of competition. Any weaknesses noted during this period can be a chance for businesses to consider how to turn them into strengths for the business entity.

The creation part of a strategy requires decisions that are best to base on research. Here, artificial intelligence can play a vital role as it lacks the weakness of human bias that can lead to subjective decision-making processes. AI tools are in use by businesses to retrieve data that is assisting in decision making. Looking at data, particularly from different departments, can help in revealing opportunities aligned with the overall goal of the business that can end up being a new source of business for an organization. When coming up with a strategy, the sustainability question is an element that requires an answer. The business can focus on pursuing strategies that they can afford.

The use of data can help in determining what is within sustainable budgets and what is not viable at present. This process allows for the prioritization of strategic roadmaps within an organization. Companies making such decisions on data are less likely to run into accusations of subjectivity among team members. The effect is a synergistic push towards the goals of a business which may hasten the time taken to achieve the intended vision.

The launch of a strategic plan in a business setting should involve all relevant departments to promote a sense of synergy among team members. Business units should prepare for the launch in advance, allowing for changes where needed. When team members feel a part of the process, they are more likely to take ownership of delivering their portion of the roadmap to success. The launch is best done at the same time across all departments so that the impact concerning teething problems is identifiable simultaneously. This method allows for a faster turnaround time of sorting issues and portrays the company to business customers as unified. As the initial implementation of the strategic plan is going on, a team can be on stand-by to deal with arising issues over time. The stage of strategy implementation is critical as it beats logic for a business to spend time going through the initial steps of strategy without implementing it. Follow up at this stage is helping companies in determining the real effect of the AI tools introduced into the business processes. Resistance to change at this stage may occur as team members may feel the need to go back to traditional methods. As the strategic tools are in use for longer, the resistance to change will start declining. The benefits of AI to the business processes, particularly how it augments the function of team members is the key to fighting the resistance to change. Once the workforce can see how AI frees them to focus on their core tasks, they are likely to embrace its use. Businesses can address the fears of embracing AI by pointing to the benefits at an individual level. Connecting the benefits to what matters to each team member breaks down the resistance cycle initially expected. Evaluation as a step in developing strategy is assisting businesses in making adjustments required for transition into AI-backed processes.

Continual evaluating is encouraged for organizations not to lose focus on achieving their end goal. Any changes in the market affecting the roadmap is identifiable at this stage of strategy development. Some changes require businesses to change their roadmap and even their end goal.

Having a strategy in place is helping organizations in making changes in a dynamic marketplace, helping them avoid becoming obsolete. AI tools can keep information current helping enterprises survive any market onslaught. AI can be a determinant of whether the strategy of a business succeeds.

Evaluate Marketing Tools and Technologies

The AI tools and technologies available in the market are varied, with each offering different benefits. Businesses need to carry out an evaluation process to determine which devices will align well with their overall goals. Having AI that is not in tandem with the roadmap of an organization can lead to wastage of much-needed resources. The effect may be resistance by the workforce in the future as the business attempts to introduce other tools. The evaluation process should be systematic to ensure objectiveness. All stakeholders should play a part to gain their trust, which is critical during the transition process.

Businesses can research the available tools by evaluating the tools currently in use in the marketplace. Reviews from entities already integrating AI into their marketing can give a glimpse of how the tools are working on a day-to-day basis. Going this route allows businesses to choose AI marketing systems already in use. They can opt to incorporate better models of AI marketing tools than those in the market, giving them an edge over the competition. Taking risks on novel AI technologies can pay off if the impact is positive in the long run. Some businesses are becoming market leaders by opting for risk-taking on new AI marketing technologies.

When choosing AI marketing tools and technologies, businesses should opt for those that do not have a bias component or have a minimal bias.

The accuracy of the results can be affected by the same, which can result in businesses making decisions that can lead to losses. Marketing tools and technologies having an ability for deep learning are preferable. These require less programming and can give insights that are independent of human bias. Deep learning marketing tools and technologies can learn from previous experience as they can form artificial neural networks. Marketing tools and technologies having predictive ability allows businesses to react faster to a dynamic marketplace. In a highly competitive global market, such AI software can give companies a competitive edge. Consumers today are demanding and spoilt for choice, making reaction time a critical component of attracting much-needed market share. The predictive factor of the marketing tool in use should be adjustable with those able to predict from the point of drivers of changes being better than those giving predictions from previous inputs. AI marketing tools with machine learning ability are best.

Evaluation requires businesses to monitor the tools that are working well and the extent to which they are fulfilling company expectations. The analysis will allow a company to determine whether an investment in a marketing tool or technology was worthwhile. The report from the evaluation can indicate what areas the business needs to work on and which ones can they bank on to move towards their overall vision. The gaps noted can be filled in by the human workforce creating a synergistic process in the marketing departments. The monitoring should be continual for real-time adjusting. As with all human inventions, businesses will face challenges as they adapt to AI marketing tools and technologies.

Companies should not get discouraged by such scenarios but instead, use them as opportunities to improve on their transition to using AI marketing tools.

Choosing to forfeit transitioning to AI marketing tools and technologies can mean the demise of a business entity. Some companies have become obsolete based on not adjusting to the marketplace demands fast enough. The examples are many across many industries with household brands disappearing from the marketplace. Companies should strike a balance between investing in the right marketing tools and technologies and minimizing losses due to wrong investments. The best marketing tools and technologies for businesses are those aligned with their overall strategic plans. Companies can choose to make their decisions on the marketing devices to incorporate by basing it on whether it will support their strategic objectives. This method allows for objective assessments of available AI marketing tools in the marketplace. The process of choosing becomes clearer when requirements are unbiased. AI can assist in making decisions, particularly when combined with data. Focusing on strategic alignment as consideration for choosing which tool to invest in can remove biases from decision making. The best marketing tools and technologies lacking the characteristic of ease of use will create resistance from the workforce. A user-friendly interface can be the deciding factor in the adaptability rate in the business. Marketing technologies with unfriendly user interfaces can translate into added costs through the need for training periods that are longer. Staff may require additional time to understand how the tools will work and their roles in the marketing process. Businesses should look at interfaces from the point of the customer as well as that of the workforce. The interface can determine the reaction of the market to the tools a business chooses. Businesses should choose marketing tools and technologies that are in alignment with the skill set of the workforce.

Outsourcing of support can be an additional cost that enterprises can avoid if the skill set is available within the business. Companies can consider training their workforce in skills that will aid in the utilization of marketing tools and technologies. Companies should compare and decide if outsourcing or internal skill training is more plausible, particularly in the long run. Businesses should avoid being in situations where the marketing tools and technologies are not in use as they wait for support from external sources.

Chapter 5: The Future of Marketing: Predicting Consumer Behavior with Artificial Intelligence

Businesses are looking for ways to predict consumer behavior as a means of maintaining their competitive edge within the marketplace. AI tools classified as machine learning devices can, based on artificial neural networks, achieve this. Given the amount of data that businesses receive, companies need to make sense of the same in a manner that is beneficial to the business operation. The ability to predict consumer purchases may reduce the turnaround time for consumers to get their preferred products. Predictions anticipate client needs in advance, which may be a crucial differentiating factor for a business within the marketplace. Deep learning is a characteristic of AI tools that can predict.

The advantages for marketers in predicting consumer behavior are numerous, including preventing potential loss of sales. Predictions can give a business a sense of the right timing concerning stock replacement. Companies can, therefore, reduce costs associated with inventory, for example, by reducing the time stock spends on the shelf awaiting purchase. Marketers with predictive information can optimally target promotional messages to potential clients influencing their purchasing decisions.

For organizations able to combine data plus artificial intelligence, the opportunities for marketers are numerous. In the long run, the benefit of businesses preparing using AI may surpass the investment cost. Companies able to predict consumer behavior can leverage the same for their sales growth. Predictive data for business use is via varied sources including, social media platforms that potential clients use. The data reveal trends that may be useful to a business entity. When sourcing for data, businesses should ensure alignment with applicable regulations. Clients should not feel their privacy is not guaranteed. Such revelations may be to the detriment of the company as potential clients protest these actions by not purchasing from the affected companies. Consumer behavior data gives companies a glimpse of what is of value to clients.

AI tools can collect this data digitally, which removes the labor-intensive nature of traditional means of data collection. This method is less prone to human bias, which increases the accuracy levels of the data a business receives in this manner. The best AI tools focus on the drivers of consumer behavior as opposed to predictions based on previous inputs. Focusing on the drivers allows companies to be aware of the consumer choices, sometimes even before potential clients are aware that they need the products and services on offer. The consumer behavior data collection can be from personal devices.

Businesses looking to grow their market share should use predictive data by AI tools to align their marketing strategy. Decisions made using data is objective as it misses the weakness of human bias. Predictive information is useful for businesses to adjust their marketing goals in alignment with the dynamic nature of the marketplace. AI data provides information for marketing that would take longer if left to the human workforce. Given the complexity of what drives human behavior, AI can be the source of information businesses have been missing to move to the next level in the marketplace. Factors to consider when thinking of predicting consumer behavior include levels of prediction, big data and AI, and AI tools for predictive purposes. Each of these elements plays a critical role in predicting consumer behavior, which plays a role in effective marketing by business entities. Businesses should make choices based on their internal needs and how aligned the tools would be to their strategic intent. The consumer behavior of interest includes emotions that some consider as an element that determines human behavior.

AI is improving its capability to identify and predict human emotions, which gives the tools insights previously undiscovered.

Levels of Prediction

Prediction levels concerning consumer behavior depends on a variety of factors. These may include the ability of the AI tool, particularly its deep learning functionality level. AI tools that have deep learning capability are more likely to predict consumer behavior to a higher degree of accuracy. The deep learning functionality is dependent on the AI's ability to form artificial neural networks.

The data available to a business entity determines the levels to which AI can predict consumer behavior. Businesses that can access more data based on the industry they belong to like customer care companies and retail stores are at an advantage of predicting consumer behavior. The regulatory environment within which a business is determines what level of data access is legal. Highly regulated environments may limit to a great extent the kind of data companies are allowed to access from potential clients. The levels of prediction achieved of consumer behavior should tally with the strategic objectives of the company investing in AI tools. Unnecessary expenditures should be limited to functionalities relevant to a company's level of need for data. Businesses should focus on AI tools of prediction that are within their investment budget so that the company does not undergo unnecessary monetary stress. The long term effect of the purchase on the company's financials should be the standard for making the decision.mThe skill levels at the disposal of the company is a factor that will determine the levels of prediction the business can achieve in the long term. Training of in-house staff and outsourcing of relevant support tasks should be a consideration by businesses incorporating AI tools for prediction purposes. Human behavior is considered complex, and predicting the same is sometimes impossible, even with the best AI tools. Companies choosing to utilize AI tools to predict human behavior in their marketing exploits should be aware of the limitations of the technology.

The machine learning capabilities of AI tools determine the levels of predictions available to businesses choosing to use AI in predicting human behavior. AI tools that can collaborate with supportive technologies are better placed to predict consumer behavior.

Other tools that can support AI include those used for analytical purposes and the human component, the latter of which has strengths that AI is still lacking.

The levels of prediction of consumer behavior within the marketing context include intent analysis, category patterns, and future actions. Intent analysis, also known as emotional analysis, refers to the prediction of the emotions that underlie consumer behaviors or the intent behind their actions. Marketing that connects to the emotional state of consumers is likely to impact clients more than one that deals with non-emotional cues. The emotional connection allows business entities to garner a competitive edge within the marketplace. When companies connect emotionally with potential clients, they get their loyalty, which can assist a business increase its market share. Knowing the why behind a consumer's decision can help companies connect better with potential clients in the marketplace within which a company finds itself. Category patterns are all about segmentation, with this level of prediction allowing businesses to group potential customers that react similarly.

The ability of an AI tool to segment populations will allow for the creation of marketing promotions that have a personal feel to a segment of customers. Segment ads can give a feeling of belonging to potential clients, which may earn their loyalty in the long run. Segmentation allows for a better understanding of the categories identified by AI marketing tools as the segments undergo more study. Companies can avoid mistakes that may, for example, cause offense which may cost a business potential clients. AI tools that can predict future actions of consumers are valuable to businesses in the long run as the entities can prepare for client expectations in advance. This prediction level can be the key for organizations to influence the future behavior of consumers as they focus on the drivers of their actions. Predictive abilities by business through the use of AI tools can propel a company to an influencer position in the marketplace. The lessons this level of prediction can give to businesses can help in aligning strategies to consumer expectations.

The AI industry is focusing on creating tools with predicting levels of future actions, and the expectation of businesses will be more accurate reports. The goal of AI concerning future predictions is doing so in real-time so that organizations can keep up with changes in the marketplace as they occur. The effect will be a change in how marketing will look like in the future with businesses changing their sales techniques. Marketing tactics will also shift as more information on consumer behavior comes in a timely fashion to businesses. AI tools will be a critical component for marketers looking to connect organizations to potential clients within the marketplace.

Big Data and Artificial Intelligence

The backbone of artificial intelligence is big data, which gives AI the foundation on which, it develops artificial neural networks, that determine the levels to which, AI can predict the future. AI outperforms humans in processing large volumes of data that is an element of future predictions. AI tools can process information at a faster rate than humans and analyze the same with more precision than a human workforce. The processing of big data can lead to the revelation of patterns that can give insights to businesses on market dynamics that they can turn to opportunities.

The precision levels of predicting consumer behavior rise proportionally with the volumes of data available for analysis from varied inputs. Businesses can understand consumers better and can predict their future actions with more clarity than when the sample data is minimal. Combining the elements of large volumes of data and artificial intelligence tools with deep learning capabilities is the future of predicting consumer behavior. With the right amount of data combined with the right AI tool, businesses will be able to make predictions up to months in advance. Organizations can use the results to prepare for the needs of potential customers by, for example, purchasing adequate stock for their anticipated requirements.

Such data can help businesses minimize loss due to the stocking of obsolete products that will no longer meet the needs of the market in the days ahead.

Big data can realistically undergo processing via traditional methods due to the complexity and volume of the expected results. The data is dynamic as it is under continuous update as various sources act as inputs to the systems tracking consumer behavior even in real-time. Businesses are adopting big data and AI to keep ahead of the competition with organizations that delay risking becoming irrelevant in the marketplace.

Big data and AI can give businesses forecasts of up to a year from the present time, which gives companies requisite time to adjust to market changes. The predictions focus on the underlying drivers of decisions like human emotions and the causes of the intent behind consumer decisions. The sources of big data for a single business can run into the thousands, which give results that can be highly accurate. Organizations with access to such information can tailor their products almost to a real-time basis, sometimes turning into influencers of consumer decisions in the process.

Businesses can use the data and results from AI to become a part of the culture of consumers in the marketplace giving them a competitive edge over other market players. Big data is negating the function of focus groups as AI is allowing for the processing of large volumes of data. The unbiased nature of data fed into AI systems is allowing companies to make objective decisions faster with more assurance. AI outperforms the human workforce in analyzing big data as it can work with varied data types, whether structured or unstructured.

AI tools have algorithms by which they analyze big data into insights that businesses are using to take action in the marketplace. Source of big data for use by AI tools for turning into insights for business entities include social media platforms and trending news topics.

Big data and AI is in use by organizations to adjust their strategies in the marketplace as pieces of information come in from varied sources. Businesses that can anticipate how consumers will react to situations can tailor their brand to be part of the positive side of culture. AI via big data can act as a research laboratory for businesses looking to introduce new products and services into the marketplace. For AI with future action prediction ability, the opportunity to get a feel of how consumers will react can be priceless for a business as it enters new markets. The kinds of AI that can combine with big data include pure AI and pragmatic AI with the latter combine various technologies to give insights. The choice between the AI types is dependent on a business and its vision for the results of predicting consumer behavior. Organizations can enhance the experience of their consumers when they utilize AI to predict the future actions of their clients.

Big data and AI can give results that allow businesses to come up with products and services that potential customers can relate to easily. Relevance breeds loyalty in the marketplace, an ingredient that can propel once unknown brands to levels of influence above the competition. Segmentation through the identification of patterns from big data by AI allows businesses to present marketing promotions that are applicable at individual levels. Big data and AI can help companies provide support to their customers in real-time. The result is a positive experience for the customer who may share their view of the company, therefore possibly increasing the market influence of the brand.

Artificial Intelligence Tools for Prediction

Artificial intelligence tools come in many forms with the variety based on their functionality, particularly in terms of deep learning and machine learning abilities. Businesses should choose the AI tool in the context of their strategic intent as AI can help a business reach its overall vision faster.

The best kind of AI tool is one that can integrate with other systems already in use within the organization. This feature helps in the transition period reducing the possible issues that can arise during the implementation stage of AI tools. API.PI, Google Cloud, Infosys Nia, Microsoft Azure, Premonition, TensorFlow, and Wipro HOLMES. API.PI is an AI tool that allows businesses to customize the software to their brand while using natural language in its functionality. It combines its functionality with data from varied sources including encyclopedias, information on flight schedules and weather patterns. Businesses whose marketplace is driven by such data can utilize the AI tool to predict consumer behavior. The insights given will allow the organizations to be better prepare for the expectations of their clients. The AI Google cloud is a prediction tool that bases its functionality on machine learning capabilities allowing it to identify patterns in the data of a business. It can then predict the future, for example, categories based on real-time data giving suggestions to organizations on actions to take. Its machine learning capabilities can assist companies in detecting mails the entity can categorize as spam. The tool can work with varied computer languages, including Java and Python, which make it versatile. Businesses can, therefore, integrate it with their in-house tools, making it a preferable choice for organizations looking for a smooth transition into AI use.

Infosys Nia is an AI tool having capabilities to predict described as knowledge-based, which in combination with its machine learning capabilities can allow businesses to automate processes. Businesses using Infosys Nia can employ a culture of innovation, riding on the information presented by the tool, as it analyzes company data. Infosys Nia can solidify fragmented processes to give companies insights that may reveal new opportunities. Businesses can use the machine learning abilities of the tool to work on their systems continually which companies can use to stay competitive in the marketplace.

Azure by Microsoft, is an AI tool, with abilities to predict, that employs machine learning analysis, and is cloud-based, making it accessible, regardless of a company's geographical location. Azure presents analytical results in a simple way, which allows businesses to make decisions faster. Azure is a web service that can be mobile-enabled, with varied applications including business intelligence, digital marketing, and e-commerce. Microsoft Azure is suitable for businesses looking to gather information from different sources continually to stay relevant in the marketplace.

The predictive AI from Microsoft can work with different operating systems making it a viable option for businesses looking for AI tools that are versatile. Premonition is an AI tool that is specific to an industry that is the litigation industry where it gives information on attorneys and the cases they have handled. It uses algorithms, that are of interest to their clients, like how many cases an attorney has won, what rate an attorney charges, and what kind of cases they have presented. It is a database of litigations that are analyzed, continually giving clients real-time information that they can use to determine which attorney to work with on their cases. The information allows clients to question potential attorneys on whether they are the right fit.

TensorFlow is a predictive AI tool that helps businesses predict consumer behavior, which is a critical element of staying relevant in the marketplace. TensorFlow is an open-source program that focuses on creating machine learning models that businesses can use for prediction purposes. TensorFlow works through the numerical computation of data flow in the form of graphs with nodes and edges of the graphs having different meanings. Businesses can use TensorFlow to build neural networks based on data from different origins that organizations are using to analyze consumer behavior. The AI can translate languages using the neural networks formed through machine learning capabilities.

Wipro HOLMES is a predictive AI with a myriad of capabilities, including deep learning, processing of natural language, and semantic ontologies. These abilities help this particular AI possess cognitive characteristics that are critical in the development of robots, drones, and visual computing. Companies can use Wipro HOLMES to create virtual digital assistants that have cognitive abilities. The AI can automate processes, including the ones involving the cognitive characteristics. The result is businesses can continually improve on the quality of their artificial neural networks. The algorithms used in Wipro HOLMES include deep learning and genetic learning as components in developing its cognitive characteristics.

Chapter 6: Chatbots and Autoresponders

Artificial intelligence is changing the way businesses carry out tasks that they consider repetitive and mundane, with organizations looking for ways to automate these processes. The AI tools organizations are opting for are varied and depend on factors that may align with the size of the business. The benefits of the AI tools are many, with some needing little AI knowledge to incorporate into business processes.

One of the reasons why businesses opt for these AI tools is the ability for the devices to automate processes that take the human workforce from focusing on the core mandate of the organization. There are various AI tools that businesses can use, to computerize their recurring tasks, including chatbots, and autoresponders. The organizations make a choice depending on, which AI tool best suits their companies. Some companies choose AI tools as a way to reduce their reliance on human labor, for example, if the business relies on seasonal orders.

The AI tools used for automation do share similarities with some not being charged by the companies that develop them for use by those interested in utilizing them. The commonalities can translate to an identical range of advantages depending on how businesses choose to implement them.

The benefits for the AI tools chatbots and autoresponders may include the ability for businesses to increase the scale at which they can respond to potential customers. The organizations increase their efficiency levels by using the chatbots and autoresponders. Companies can integrate some chatbots and autoresponders into their social media platforms through which they interact with potential clients.

The processes that the AI tools chatbots and autoresponders can automate are varied, including interaction with customers on a real-time basis. Some are suitable for scenarios whereby the human workforce of a business is unable to respond immediately to customer inquiries.

Businesses are utilizing the AI tools in augmenting their marketing efforts within the marketplace as they form stronger bonds with their potential clients. Some companies are integrating the AI tools giving potential clients a better customer experience that is synergistic. The implementation of these AI tools by businesses can be a competitive edge in a marketplace that is digitally dynamic.

Chatbots

The abilities of chatbots vary depending on the creators with characteristics depending on the implementation within a business. They may have auditory and textual aspects with the specifics depending on the range that an organization may require for their processes. The focus of chatbots is to replicate humans in the actions they are in use in the marketplace. The Chatbot software can utilize natural language in performing their functions within business processes. Chatbots can interact and integrate with other applications that organizations are using within the marketplace.

186

Businesses are personalizing chatbots in their interactions with potential clients through this AI software platform to build their brands. Organizations are working with Chatbot creators that are allowing companies to create an identity that distinguishes them from the competition. Businesses should be aware that there are chatbots that do not have AI capabilities, which limits their range of actions. Chatbots perform actions by relying on algorithms that are preset depending on the specific requirements of a company. The requirements include the level of interaction that a business requires, from the Chatbot, for example, before a human interface takes over the conversation. The advantages of chatbots that businesses can take advantage of include their ability to work with autoresponders, which are part of the AI software devices. Some organizations have increased their sales by using chatbots in their interactions with potential clients looking for sales information. Chatbots are versatile in their use in business processes, with their ability to function across departments, for example, sales and marketing. Chatbots are convenient to use with businesses varying their functioning depending on the end goal.

Some companies are using chatbots to deal with FAQs (Frequently Asked Questions) interactively capturing the attention of their clients. As with all technology, there are challenges that businesses are facing with chatbots, including the software giving irrelevant answers to potential clients. Some companies are reporting chatbots that are giving incomplete answers to their customers, which may lead to loss of business. The question of monetization also comes into play, with some companies struggling to find ways of creating sales from the chatbots. Some chatbots tend to annoy clients with their programming giving a feel of talking to a machine vis a vis a human. Chatbots, although classified as AI, is not yet considered as passing the Turing test, which is a standard of determining whether a machine can think on its own.

What are Chatbots?

Chatbots are a type of artificial intelligence software that can be in use either in an auditory or textual context that automates the process of interaction. Depending on the Chatbot AI level, they can mimic to a great extent the actions of a human that one is interacting with, in a conversation.

The AI class within, which chatbots fall under, is conversational AI because they are in use, in the context of communication. The algorithms used in chatbots include pre-programmed user phrases either in the form of texts or sound. Chatbots come in many forms with their classification depending on their abilities. The main categorizations are AI and non-AI with the latter denoting those that do not have machine learning capabilities. The non-AI category of chatbots is sometimes referred to as scripted.

Another categorization model classifies chatbots based on whether they work alone or in combination with other software like messaging applications. There are chatbots known as menu-based which have a flowchart kind of design that leads one to various points depending on the questions asked. Some chatbots work across a variety of platforms, therefore, classified as multi-platform. The uses of chatbots vary with the most common application being the scaling of customized customer care within the setting of a business interacting with clients. Chatbots are also in use for gathering the information that organizations are looking for to enrich customer experiences. Some chatbots are in creation for entertainment purposes with users interacting with the AI software for recreational purposes. There are chatbots whose use is to assist individuals in performing tasks that they assign to them. Chatbots are in use to substitute how communication is occurring between businesses and clients with this AI software being more interactive than some traditional methods.

Chatbots are in use in a variety of industries, including e-commerce, where it is allowing potential customers to interact with the products and services on offer in the business. The marketing industry is using chatbots for a variety of promotional campaigns across different platforms. The sales industry is on board with using chatbots with the interaction with potential clients allowing for customization. The travel industry is using chatbots in booking for hotels and airline trips for potential customers and directing clients to partner stores. The healthcare industry is using chatbots to gather information from clients before connecting them to a human interface.

188

Tools and Platforms for Chatbots

The tools and platforms for chatbots come in many forms with varied benefits depending on their capabilities, giving businesses a choice. Organizations should choose the tools and platforms for their chatbots that most closely mirrors their path to achieving their strategic objectives. The tools and platforms are in use for building chatbots with some being easy to use, and others are more complex. Businesses are using the tools and platforms to create chatbots that are helping them maintain their competitive edge. They are also in use in creating chatbots for personal use.

There are tools and platforms for chatbots that require the creator to have coding skills, while others do not require the same. The platforms can be open source or can require payment for use by private entities. Some tools and platforms for chatbots include Chatfuel, Botsify, and Flow XO with each having varied benefits. Chatfuel can integrate with Facebook messenger and does not require the skill of coding with the platform offering an option for use at no charge. Paid versions in the platform give more information to a business with functionalities like data management.

The Flow XO platform for creating chatbots also boasts of one not requiring coding skills to use their tools and can be used in a variety of platforms. The ability for this tool to work across many platforms makes it versatile, which can give businesses convenience if they want to utilize across varied platforms. The platform allows for integration with other applications and is allowing incorporation into websites. The features allow for businesses to let their customers share their Chatbot with others, which can create a referral system for organizations. The platforms allow for one to create several chatbots, which creates more avenues for use by their potential clients.

Botsify is a tool and platform for chatbots that works across Facebook and on websites making it a multi-platform tool and, therefore, versatile. It can integrate with other applications that a business can use to communicate with their potential clients making its incorporation into company processes easier. This platform allows organizations to merge the technology of Chatbot with a human interface.

The integration may prove to be a competitive edge for a business in the marketplace as some clients may prefer talking to a fellow human. There is a free version available, and the platform can allow companies to create conversational forms.

Promote Your Chatbot

Businesses can promote their chatbots in many ways depending on the strategic objectives the organization is looking to achieve with the AI technology. Companies should prepare for the promotion of their chatbots in advance, taking into account the benefits that are important to their potential end-users. How the target consumer of a company will perceive their interaction with a Chatbot will determine the effectiveness of the AI software. The preparations should be extensive with businesses being ready to spend the required time to present a product worthy of their brand. Businesses can promote their chatbots by adding buttons on other platforms that they have a presence on, for example, on their websites. The buttons leading to their Chatbot experience should be in a visible place that potential clients are likely to see to increase users.

The chatbots for businesses should contain exclusive codes either as a messenger, QR Code, or a URL Code. The QR codes best function when organizations place them in non-clickable areas like in billboards and posters which allow potential clients to scan the codes.

Businesses should note that the messenger code is specific for the Facebook platform. Businesses can promote their chatbots through the use of plugins that can connect to the presence of the organization in other platforms, for example, on websites. The plugins will direct potential customers to the chatbots on the platforms where the Chatbot lies. One can take advantage of the opportunities presented by bot stores that work with a company to promote their Chatbot with businesses choosing the store that aligns with their strategic interests. Companies can create a story around the Chatbot to keep customers interested in using the AI-backed platform. Some businesses are creating landing pages for their chatbots as a way of explaining to potential customers how the Chatbot can assist them.

190

The landing page can be SEO (Search Engine Optimization) optimized to increase the reach of the business, encouraging more people to try out their Chatbot. Companies can use their social media pages to promote their chatbots, giving detailed explanations showing how easy it is to use the same. Potential customers may choose to give it a try when they see visuals on how to make use of it. The businesses can use the option of paid promotions to take advantage of the opportunities to create customized targeted messages.

Reduce Customer Service Workloads

The benefits of chatbots vary with one of the main advantages being to reduce customer service workloads as it automates business processes. In decreasing customer service workloads, businesses can reduce the costs related to interacting and following up with customers. Some sources say that chatbots can reduce customer service workloads by up to one third depending on how a business implements the AI software.

Chatbots reduce customer service workloads by streamlining the processes in the department. Companies can focus on delegating the customer service tasks that are administrative as they are usually repetitive and mundane. Reducing the customer service workload allows the human workforce of a business to focus on tasks that are too complex for the chatbots a company decides to use to automate their processes. The human workforce can then focus on creating engaging interactions with potential clients. Chatbots allow for scaling in terms of the amount of customer service workload a business can handle as they can serve multiple customers simultaneously. Chatbots reduce the customer service workload by allowing for the establishment of customer service for hours beyond the working hours. Businesses can achieve faster turnaround times by reducing customer service workloads. The techniques that businesses can employ in reducing customer service workloads include creating a Chatbot interface that gives clients links to FAQs (Frequently Asked Questions). These help in filtering repetitive inquiries that the business has solutions to that chatbots can handle.

For more engaging chatbots, entities can choose to use avatars and emoji that can create an emotional connection with potential clients. The chatbots should not overwhelm the customers as they may opt to walk away from the business or interact with the human workforce. The result is the chatbots will not have a maximum effect in reducing customer service workloads.Businesses should consider using chatbots in reducing customer service workload as an opportunity to enrich the customer experience with their brand. Companies are revolutionizing their customer service workload processes using this AI software that can multitask beyond the human levels. Chatbot integration with the customer care team is now possible in a seamless manner allowing for better performance. These tools are allowing businesses to be available in sorting out their customer needs all through the day and night. In this case, they act as a continuation of the customer care workforce after working hours.

Autoresponders

Autoresponders, just like chatbots, are in use by businesses to manage their customer service processes that they consider as routine and mundane. The autoresponders allow companies to free their human resources within the customer service department to focus on more complex tasks. Such tasks left for human resources may include objectives requiring the cognitive element of individuals that some machines lack. Companies are choosing autoresponders that can integrate with other applications that may already be in use in their business processes. They are also looking for autoresponders that allow for seamless human-interface incorporation.

The autoresponders are allowing companies to scale their capabilities within their customer service departments.

Autoresponders are achieving their tasks by automating, which is allowing for multitasking and scaling of customer service processes by businesses. Businesses are personalizing the automation process to reflect their chosen pathways towards their strategic objectives. The complexity of the automation processes can differ among organizations depending on the capabilities of the Autoresponder chosen. Autoresponders with machine learning capabilities can achieve higher levels of automation as they have a sense of cognitive abilities. Businesses need to determine the optimal level of automation they require taking into account the intricacies of their industries. Autoresponders can be in use by businesses to achieve segmentation or targeting of potential clients as they can be in use to focus on particular customer segments. Some organizations choose customer segments by allowing for signing up for autoresponders. Businesses should consider customer privacy policies when integrating autoresponders to avoid breaking regulatory requirements or create a negative experience for potential customers. Potential customers want to feel they are in charge of the communication process with businesses they choose to communicate with on various issues.

Companies can achieve segmentation by giving choices to potential customers on the type of autoresponders they prefer. Autoresponders are useful for processes that do involve FAQs (Frequently Asked Questions) as some businesses are incorporating them into the AI software.

These questions are generally repetitive and asked in similar forms by potential clients seeking answers for their inquiries from companies. Businesses can tailor FAQs as they communicate with their clients, making changes as required. FAQs assist businesses in reducing their customer service workload as clients can take advantage of the self-service aspect of the responses. Some autoresponders present FAQs in a flow chart system leading customers to the appropriate response in an interactive manner as opposed to the traditional search methods.

What is an Autoresponder?

Autoresponders are AI tools limited to the use of emails as the point of interaction with potential customers who reach out to the business. The response in the form of an email is in a standard format that is pre-programmed and usually does not require an answer. The complexity of autoresponders varies depending on the requirements of a business regarding interacting with potential clients. The initial point of contact with an Autoresponder can include when a potential client subscribes to receiving information from a company. Within the subscription process, businesses can share the cycle of email deliveries to expect with the potential client. Various types of autoresponders are available in the market with companies opting for those that align with their overall strategies.

Companies utilize strategic objectives as triggers setting off Autoresponder systems incorporated into their processes. Sequence emails are a type of Autoresponder where the sharing of particular topics or related topics is through sending emails at regular intervals. These work well in keeping subscribers engaged and can be used to lead them to affiliate websites. For businesses looking to convert interested customers, lead-generation autoresponders may be suitable. These give more information on the products of interest over a period to lead the client to purchase. The uses of autoresponders are as varied as the goals a business may have, including educating subscribers on topics of interest over a period.

Autoresponders are in use by companies looking to keep in contact with their subscribers by sharing engaging content at regular intervals. Some businesses use autoresponders as a pathway to promote their affiliate businesses or products to subscribers. Companies can use autoresponders to share the content of interest to subscribers using a sequence of preprogrammed emails. Companies can use autoresponders to gather input from subscribers, for example, by including survey links within the emails. Platforms providing autoresponders for personal and business purposes vary in both price and capabilities. The best autoresponders are those that mail delivery platforms do not classify as spam. Autoresponder platforms can be outsourced or set within the server of a company with the latter requiring technical skills. The word Autoresponder is interchangeable with email marketing as the AI software use is generally limited to interacting through emails. Apart from the timing factor, businesses incorporating autoresponders decide on how many emails to send per interaction with the customer.

How to Choose an Autoresponder

There are many options for businesses looking to incorporate autoresponders in their processes with the choices, including outsourcing and in house platforms. The Autoresponder chosen can add or take away from the journey of a business towards its strategic objectives. Companies should consider how the autoresponders align with their goals and their versatility in application. The market provides free and paid versions of autoresponders allowing businesses of different sizes to benefit from AI technology. Organizations should consider their sales cycle when deciding on the Autoresponder to utilize as the length should direct the frequency of sending the emails. An organization can consider many factors when choosing the Autoresponder to utilize, including the ease with which they can create an email. The ease of sending the emails is critical with those allowing for presetting of time of email release preferable as they are convenient to use. Autoresponders with tracking capabilities are useful for businesses in determining the effectiveness of the content they are sharing. The tracking results can be applicable in benchmarking how well customers are responding to sent emails. For companies using the emails to promote products and services, choosing autoresponders that provide inline promotional email templates can be preferable.

Another consideration is the number of emails the Autoresponder platform can allow a business to send over a period in the context of the sales cycle of the company. The autoresponders of choice should augment the goals of a company and not take away from it. Its ability to integrate with other applications in use by companies is critical in guaranteeing a smooth incorporation process.

The level of segmentation is another consideration for companies, particularly for organizations looking for highly targeted content sharing opportunities. When it comes to automation, businesses should choose autoresponders that limit the need for human action in terms of responding to subscriber options. Companies can look through reviews by other users to get a feel of what the perception is towards the service of autoresponders available in the marketplace. This action may save a business from investing in an Autoresponder that will disappoint, and that may erase gains in the market. Companies should choose autoresponders that have features important to them and not a myriad of features yet do not apply to their context. In most cases, how long a company that is providing Autoresponder platforms have been in the market is an indicator of their competence. Their interactions with companies handling emails will determine if mails get delegated as spam.

Enabling Autoresponders

Enabling of autoresponders is dependent on the platform a business chooses to utilize in integrated the AI technology into their processes. Autoresponder platforms offer various category capabilities to choose from, including intervals between emails to be sent and details on the text to be included. The periods between the emails are varied, with some platforms giving choices in hours and others down to minutes. In regards to timing, and depending on customer location, businesses can choose the delivery to align with the local times of the clients. Businesses will need to specify the triggers for the autoresponders taking into account the context of the focus of their strategic objectives.

The strategic goals should be the first step in determining to enable autoresponders as the effectiveness will depend on how aligned the expectations are to the capabilities of the AI technology. The objectives should be listed to ensure every possible aspect is covered.

All departments within a company setting should be part of the process. Businesses match Autoresponder capabilities, and strategic objectives, at this stage. Activation of Autoresponder features that match the strategic objectives is the next step with details like the timing of the intervals triggered. Businesses can define the cycle lengths between communication times and update the contact list of subscribers.

Segmenting of customer lists is possible depending on the capabilities of the Autoresponder platform the business is using to communicate. Filling of the details of the body of the email message, including using templates as provided by the Autoresponder platform, is possible. When defining cycle lengths, businesses can choose the particular days they want the communication forwarded. Tracking features are enabled once all the details are activated. Most Autoresponder platforms give detailed explanations on how to set up the AI software in a business context with some providing FAQs (Frequently Asked Questions). Businesses can utilize this portion to maximize the capabilities of the Autoresponder platform they decide to use. One can send a test email to have a feel of what the end customer will receive, which is a good practice to allow for any changes in advance. As customers interact with the Autoresponder platform of choice, businesses can be open to making changes in response to feedback from clients. The main focus is to be responsive to customers in a convenient manner to the company.

Autoresponder Email Message

Autoresponder email messages are communications sent automatically in response to an action by another party communicating with, for example, a business. The content of the Autoresponder email messages are pre-programmed and linked to specific triggers. Pre-programming allows businesses to homogenize their communication with potential clients with organizations using similar templates. The templates can contain different elements with various platforms offering free and paid versions. Autoresponder email messages may be a medium through which a potential customer interacts with a business for the first time.

Autoresponder email messages are also known as out of office messages as they are generally in use when one is unavailable in a professional context. Autoresponder email messages come with a variety of advantages, including reducing customer workload regarding tasks that are repetitive and mundane. Businesses using Autoresponder email messages can serve customers at a larger scale as compared to working with a human workforce. The result can be an increase in market share as the business can do more with fewer resources, freeing the human workforce to focus on core tasks. Autoresponder email messages also help companies portray a professional image to those interacting with them as it is considered a standard business practice. Autoresponder email messages come with challenges, including potential clients getting frustrated, for example, in contexts where they need an urgent response. Depending on how the Autoresponder email message is formatted, customers may find the response cold. Drafting an Autoresponder email message that fits across all contexts may be a challenge depending on the industry dynamics.

The benefits though outdo the negatives, including Autoresponder email messages acting as an automatic while you were away system of response. Autoresponder email messages can help in dealing with the feeling of frustration when one gets no response. When instituting Autoresponder email messages, one should remember to provide options on the way forward like alternative contacts. The Autoresponder email message body should be professional, taking into consideration the varied contexts it is meant to serve. Details like how long one is likely to be away can be part of the message body with the actual return date also inserted. Businesses can consider Autoresponder email message branding in maintaining a brand presence across their communication channels. Autoresponder email messages should be brief, with one placing reminders to activate them before being absent. The main goal of the Autoresponder email messages is to inform the communication partner of one's absence.

Automation Rules

The automation rules regarding Autoresponder email messages are specific to trigger matched responses to actions taken by the recipient. The parameters of the rules specified must be spelled out to direct the platforms on the email message to send from the pre-programmed bundle. The rules are specific to business processes with organizations taking into consideration their context. The specifics of the rules are dependent on the platform that businesses use to implement their Autoresponder email messages. The parameters help in handling multiple lists of contacts who should receive different messages depending on their actions.

Automation rules assist businesses in making the process of customer segmentation less manual, allowing them to handle clients at a larger scale. The segmentation should allow for shuffling of the pre-programmed emails sent when a business changes the triggers. The result is organizations can customize their Autoresponder email message body in alignment with changes in the marketplace. Companies should consider the email message body in the context of their overall strategic objectives taking advantage of the opportunity presented by subscribers. Businesses are using the Autoresponder email automation rules to include marketing messages that promote products and services to subscribers. The automation rules change depending on the industry with some specifying actions based on purchasing decisions and others on information requests.

An automation rule can specify an Autoresponder action when someone pays for an item where the message body can contain details of the transaction. For the latter case, businesses can use the rules to send information to clients at regular intervals. Companies should include options to unsubscribe within the body of the Autoresponder email message sent to clients. Some businesses opt to, for example, let a subscriber remove themselves from an email list while others want the subscriber to specify the particular emails they want stopping. The effect of automation rules depends on the complexity of business operations with the impact proportional to the number of email lists requiring managing. Some platforms classify the automation rules into when, if and then with the first parameter stating when the rules apply.

The second parameter will detail the criteria that need fulfilling for the sending of the Autoresponder email message. The platform should allow for capturing of data of triggers and actions occurring based on the automation rules set by the business.

Chapter 7: Scaling Up Your Business: Artificial Intelligence Marketing Platforms

Many artificial intelligence marketing platforms can help in scaling up businesses, including autoresponders, chatbots and business analytics. Each of the platforms come with various benefits which enable companies to move towards their strategic objectives at a faster rate. Benefits include saving time with AI supporting automation, which allows companies to achieve a quick turnaround time. The result is some companies can reduce costs previously associated with manual marketing efforts as scaling is possible with AI. Businesses employing AI in their marketing efforts can manage more activities that are personalized and specific to customer interests. The platforms are evening the marketplace with startups using AI to compete with established businesses.

Emails as a marketing platform that is AI-based is automated and allows for lead generation when businesses use the message body to, for example, share product availability. Having an email as an Autoresponder is improving the customer experience businesses are offering. Automated emails can serve more customers, as it diminishes the laboring requirements of the human workforce, writing an email per customer. Automated emails can contain links to Frequently Asked Questions (FAQs) to reduce the number of customer inquiries. The email message body can contain promotional messages or links to affiliated sites.

Chatbots are in use widely by companies as an AI marketing platform to scale the reach of business in various operations, including promoting deals. These improve customer service as the response is instant, and it covers the questions frequently asked by potential clients. The quick turnaround time exhibited by chatbots can be used by companies to gain a competitive edge in the marketplace. They are convenient to use as most have a flowchart interface that answers inquiries as an interactive session with potential customers. Chatbots are efficient as they are versatile with some working across various platforms available to businesses.

Other autoresponders include text messages connecting to actions taken by consumers as they interact with businesses, for example, after transactions. Texts can contribute to lead generation, with companies including links within the body of the message. Businesses using text messages as AI marketing platforms are serving more customers with less labor required of the human workforce. Companies are using texts to receive feedback from customers in real-time with organizations requesting ratings of services offered or products purchased. The businesses can achieve this through the use of two-way text messaging AI platforms.

Companies are including links to promotional activities in messages to customers as they look for opportunities to upsell. Businesses are using analytics powered by AI to gain a competitive edge in the marketplace with the tools analyzing data from customers. The analysis reports are in real-time for quicker turnaround time by businesses as they seek to align themselves to a dynamic market. These reports are allowing companies to make decisions that are of higher impact as they react faster to changes in the market place.

The predictive nature of AI marketing tools that can analyze is saving costs for businesses as they can reduce inventory costs. Insights by AI-powered business analytical tools are actionable. Businesses can use AI-powered marketing tools that can optimize content to allow for a higher impact in the marketplace at a lower cost. These tools are allowing companies to reach more individuals as scaling is possible, depending on the requirements by specific businesses. The content generated is being distributed by various platforms, including autoresponders, like emails that may require a subscription from interested customers. The AI platforms also act as a source of content for businesses to take advantage of while creating content. Companies can outsource managing content to AI-powered platforms that are helping organizations align messages shared with their strategic objectives. Social media channels are becoming the go-to AI-powered platform for businesses looking for an interactive experience for their customers. Here, companies are building brand loyalty as customers interact with them on a larger scale with a quick turnaround. Businesses on social media can deal with customer inquiries and concerns on a real-time basis, which may increase their market influence. Some social media platforms are providing organizations with opportunities to sell their products and services.

There are AI marketing tools that are facilitating businesses in marketing across various social media platforms at the same time. Beacons are AI-powered tools that have the unique capability of interacting with customers who are in close proximity to, for example, a brick and mortar store. Businesses stocking items that customers are buying based on impulse are taking advantage of the opportunity that these platforms are presenting.

Some are connecting with applications that are sending pop up notifications to clients who are passing nearby stores looking for customers. Companies are sending specific offers based on various factors like time of the day to, for example, invite passing customers for lunch offers. The beacons are also providing data for businesses that are aiding in decision making that is objective and is useful for future marketing activities.

Businesses are using digital ads as an AI marketing platform to reach customers in a dynamic way that aligns with the interests of the target clients. The ads have the capability of personalization as, for example, a potential customer is browsing through an affiliate website. Some AI marketing platforms are providing businesses with an opportunity to sponsor the ads to allow for the segmentation of customer groups. The result is a higher impact of the ads as compared to traditional ads achieved at a lower cost and a larger scale. Digital ads can work across platforms including mobile phones, laptops, and different websites, changing depending on pre-programmed triggers.

Many businesses now have apps that customers are using to interact with organizations in various capacities, including accessing promotional messages. The messages may come on screens as pop up notifications which, when clicked, give more information on marketing activities.

The advantage with apps is the amount of data that a business can gather from a customer who chooses to install the AI marketing platform. The companies can use the data to personalize marketing campaigns while gaining knowledge on the network of individuals connected to their primary customers.

Chapter 8: Artificial Intelligence Email Marketing

Artificial Intelligence (AI) email marketing is a part of digital marketing. It has the benefits of relying on machine learning, and deep learning depending on the complexity of the platform an organization is using to share the emails. The goal is sending emails to a potential customer that is personalized, allowing for the interaction to be human-like. AI email marketing is allowing businesses to scale their customer service operations at a reduced cost. Companies can use AI to limit the possibility of the categorization of their emails as spam.

The data from machine and deep learning is in use to align customer interests with business goals. AI email marketing can be used to approach potential customers directly, avoiding the cost of the middleman in marketing. The result is a better use of resources, which can mean an increase in the number of customers a business can serve at any one time. The automatic nature of AI comes with the convenience not associated with manual processing. AI email marketing is known to portray a business professionally with the marketplace expecting the responses as standard practice.

Features of AI email marketing may include efficient send time optimization and effective automation workflow. Each of these facets can assist a business in improving different aspects of their operations. Companies now have various platforms they can choose to institute AI email marketing at their convenience and with varied complexity.

The Convenience of Automation

The convenience of automation is one of the advantages of artificial intelligence (AI) email marketing. The automation capability is dependent on the deep learning and machine learning capabilities of the chosen platform. Businesses are reducing their workload using this capability. There are templates available across AI platforms that are increasing the convenience factor of email marketing. Automation can be specific to the subject lines of the emails. Others can automate the content in the form of templates that businesses are using to personalize emails sent to potential clients.

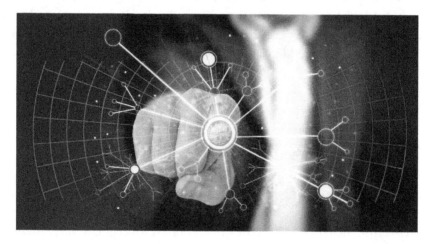

Personalization can be in different forms depending on the goals of the business. Some businesses are opting to personalize the emails by including the name of the intended recipient of the communication. A company can specify the time of receipt of the email. Depending on the platform in use for AI email marketing, a business can choose to align the affiliate links within the email message to the interests of the customer. Some are opting to include promotional messages within their emails. These can act as lead generation opportunities with the goal being to interact in a human-like manner with clients. The convenience of automation regarding AI email marketing is allowing for the capability of optimization. Data is driving the optimization with the platforms' sourcing for information based on machine learning and deep learning capabilities. Optimization can be of capacity in handling more customers. Segmenting of customers through AI-powered email marketing is contributing to optimization.

Businesses can take into account the effect of local timings when sending emails to potential clients. AI is helping in the optimization of personalization as one does not have to manually insert, for example, the name of the recipient per email sent. Optimization of content is now possible as businesses can link email triggers to customer moods. The convenience of automation regarding AI email marketing has the advantage of frequency setting. Businesses can set intervals at which potential clients are to receive their emails in bulk with little labor expended. Details like how many emails require sending at any one time are now possible. Businesses are setting these details in advance, allowing for aligning to strategic goals for periods at a time. The convenience of automation can take into account the dynamic nature of the marketplace. Some businesses are opting to align their frequency schedules with the actions of their consumers.

The goals of the convenience of automation regarding AI email marketing are varied. These may include conversion for businesses looking to move potential customers to make purchases or take action like subscribing to, for example, newsletters. Some companies are looking to minimize their manual workload. The convenience factor is increasing engagement for businesses looking for an interactive relationship with their clients. With convenience, some organizations want to increase sales. The increase in sales might translate to increased income for the businesses. Some want to serve their customers faster to gain a competitive edge. Some challenges come with the convenience of automation in AI email marketing. These may include, for example, the ability to align with the context in which customer segments are receiving the email. An email may have been pre-programmed when dynamics in the marketplace were different. Depending on the complexity of tasks required by a business regarding AI email marketing, the costs of the platforms may increase. The charges and impact should be balanced. With more companies providing platforms for AI email marketing, businesses may get confused about which one would best fit their dynamics. Organizations can use marketplace reviews as a filter.

Why Apply Artificial Intelligence to Email Marketing

The reasons why businesses should apply artificial intelligence (AI) to email marketing vary. The context of the industry within which the organization belongs can determine how applicable AI is to email marketing. Some industries are more conservative than others.

There are industries where AI in email marketing is a standard expectation by potential clients affecting their perception of businesses. AI in email marketing is allowing companies to track email metrics. The aspects may include time length before an email opening and the percentage of those opened. Some businesses are achieving an increasing return on investment (ROI) with AI email marketing. Personalization is achievable with AI email marketing with less manual labor. Businesses can choose to personalize the subject line for various reasons, like capturing the attention of potential clients. AI allows companies to automate the personalization of the addressee within the body of the email. The content of the email can be in alignment with the end goal of a company with tweaking done to fit the communication context. Information shared can be in alignment with client needs. The aligning has its basis as the data mining that is possible with AI-based email marketing.

Businesses are achieving a competitive edge in the marketplace using AI email marketing. The promotions within AI emails are allowing companies to predict the needs of potential customers with higher accuracy. These marketing communication channels can adapt to the dynamic nature of customers. Faster responses are now possible with AI email marketing, therefore, improving the customer experience. Conflict resolution is achievable quicker in case of miscommunication. The opportunity to include FAQs (Frequently Asked Questions) within email marketing is portraying businesses as responsive to potential clients. Interactive emails through AI technology can increase brand loyalty. Data generation in AI email marketing is from the capability of machine learning within the platforms. AI email marketing can take into account the dynamics of differences in global time.

During pre-programming, the timing of an AI email message can be in alignment with variances to the appropriate time of delivery. A business would not want an email with a morning greeting arriving in the evening. These tweaks can determine how potential customers perceive the image of a company.

The timing of an email can affect the impact of the information shared. Global timing is critical in the context of culture with marketing best if aligning with the expectations of potential customers.

AI email marketing can help businesses capture the attention of potential clients. First, businesses can align with client expectations within the industry regarding how responsive they are to potential customers. Automated emails due to AI give companies a professional outlook. AI email marketing is allowing businesses to have a trackable system of follow up for customers who reach out to them. Organizations can track multiple customer segments consecutively. AI email marketing is giving customers a choice to connect with businesses shortening the sales cycle as, for example, subscribing denotes interest from a potential customer.

With AI email marketing businesses can achieve segmentation of customer groups. Companies can use the segmentation to rethink the promotional messages within their AI email message templates. The segmentation is allowing companies to gain more insight into client groups. Some companies are manufacturing new products and services from data analysis of the customer segments, which in turn is increasing their market share in the marketplace. Segmentation can be in alignment with the culture and time zones. Businesses can add new segments according to the changing interests of their potential customers in real-time, depending on the capabilities of the AI platform in use.

Efficient Send Time Optimization

Businesses using artificial intelligence email marketing should consider the effect of time. Globally, the world has different time zones with some countries experiencing the same within their borders. An email, for example, sent in the afternoon in one state, though sent and received immediately may be at night in another region. The impact of the body of an email message is affected by these variations. An example is sending an email message that a business intends to send best wishes to a client on a particular holiday, yet it arrives a day later. The timing effect, in this case, negates the impact and intent.

Various platforms provide different methods of efficient send-time optimization. Businesses would want to choose platforms that allow for the segmentation of customers by time zones regardless of their locations worldwide. The platforms allowing for optimization up to the second component are preferable. Some time zones differ with days, some hours, and even down to minutes. When thinking of efficient send-time optimization, one should consider the challenges of time zones heading to weekends. AI technology is critical in achieving this capability across platforms in a convenient manner. This optimization allows businesses to achieve their goals. When establishing efficient send-time optimization, businesses should consider the location of the intended recipient. Issues like culture can determine the appropriate time for sending email to achieve the intended impact. Time zone consideration is a critical factor when looking for efficient send-time optimization for emails to recipients. The focus is on the time the recipient is to receive the communication. Businesses should choose the time that has the best impact concerning the intended message the company is looking to communicate.

The content of the email message can be an indicator of the optimum time of receipt. The benefits of efficient send-time optimization to businesses are many, including receiving customer responses in real-time. Near-instant responding can help companies in adjusting to the dynamic nature of the marketplace. Quick turnaround time is known as a loyalty-building quality among customers. Some businesses are opting to outsource this element of email marketing. The optimization is creating an opportunity for organizations to improve their marketing strategies. Data from efficient send time optimization responses can give new insights to businesses. Some businesses have created new product and service offerings from the analysis of such data. When factoring in time zones, companies should consider downtimes and use the same to their advantage. The process of achieving efficient send-time optimization has its challenges. Businesses must wade through the myriad of platforms claiming to offer artificial email marketing tools that can attain the goal. Companies can opt to rely on reviews from the marketplace. The challenge comes in for a new provider with apparently unique possibilities which may determine whether a company moves to the top of the market. The choice may involve a risk that may lead to a loss for a business.

When choosing AI tools for achieving efficient send-time optimization, companies should consider whether the cost of implementation is worthwhile.

Businesses have no choice but to adapt to efficient send-time optimization to keep up with dynamic marketplaces. Customers are demanding faster and more accurate customer service experiences. Companies that are not aligning with customer interests are losing market share. Some businesses that were once market leaders no longer exist due to their slow reaction to market demands.

Customers are expecting personalization of experience even to individual levels. Efficient send -time optimization is a tool that businesses can use to differentiate themselves in the marketplace. The capabilities of AI platforms in achieving the same is increasing.

Effective Email Automation Workflow

Having effective email automation comes with benefits that businesses can utilize. It allows for convenient work processes that can give companies a competitive edge within the marketplace. Clients have a positive perception towards organizations with an email automation workflow that is effective. Such an organization has an increased capacity. Customers consider such organizations as responsive. Effective email automation portrays synergy within business processes to the benefit of the customer. Businesses can use the automation workflow to meet customer needs in real-time. Effective email automation workflow has its base as an AI. The AI activates the automation process. An effective workflow focuses on following up on the details that the business is using as triggers for the automation process. The result is the human workforce can focus on core business processes. There are visual workflows. Companies use the optical element to have an overview of the workflow at a glance. The email automation workflow builders are allowing businesses to see both the email automation and flow in tandem. There are a variety of platforms currently providing these builders. Access for interested companies is possible. The builders make the automation process simple. The advantage is they save time for businesses looking for a convenient way of achieving effective email automation workflows.

It is possible to achieve an effective email automation workflow. Businesses can opt for platforms that are providing visual builders over the traditional manual approach. Integration into the AI system of the triggers for realizing an effective email automation workflow is possible. New triggers can be identified by AI systems increasing workflow effectiveness. Businesses can use the new triggers to communicate better with potential clients. Nurturing of leads is possible. This capability is allowing companies to keep pace with the changes within the marketplace. Visual elements in building effective email automation workflows work well for those who are visual learners. Coming up with an effective workflow can be taxing. Those who are not optical learners may not appreciate visual workflows. Some platforms providing email automation workflows may not be versatile enough to integrate with other applications in use by businesses. As with all software, AI-based systems are prone to hackers. Some AI software may be susceptible to computer bugs. Some individuals may negate the advantage of automation by over detailing email automation workflows. Some AI systems in use to back the email automation workflows may be costly vis a vis the expected impact.

Businesses should institute email automation workflows. Customers today are more demanding of quality services which may entail responding to potential clients. Companies that choose to ignore the demands of potential clients may lose their share in the marketplace. An organization can no longer afford to react slowly to customer inquiries.

The result would be negative news. Customers today can spread a negative experience at a faster rate than in yesteryears. Email automation workflows are allowing businesses to take care of all critical tasks in the process of communicating with potential clients.

There are various platforms providing email automation workflows. Businesses should opt for those that are in alignment with their strategic objectives. The implementation of the workflows using platforms that are in alignment with the strategic goals will have a better impact in the marketplace. Businesses can opt for platforms that have good reviews. Experience can be a critical factor in providing the right support in case the company faces any challenge integrating the email automation workflow. The cost versus ROI (Return on Investment) should be a consideration. The user interface should be easy to use for a smoother integration process.

Chapter 9: Exploit Artificial Intelligence of Big Companies

Exploiting the artificial intelligence of big companies can be the foundation upon which a business builds its presence in the marketplace. Some companies have experience in the AI industry spanning decades and are improving their platforms continuously in a bid to grow their market share. These companies offer opportunities to smaller establishments to ride on their achievements as they move towards their strategic objectives. Small companies can choose a big organization aligning with their interests.

The advantages of exploiting AI of big companies are many, including the opportunity to create a competitive edge in the marketplace. These companies already are attracting brand loyalty and in extension can cause their clients to trust a small business seen to be sharing their AI system. When using the AI of big companies, small businesses may not have to worry about cybersecurity as much. The big companies are continuously looking for ways to protect their systems, therefore, having better protection than small businesses.

Big companies that have AI that small businesses can exploit are many with their platforms having different benefits that may assist small businesses. Some of the companies include Amazon, Apple, and Facebook. Another big company having AI that other organizations can exploit to their benefit is Google which has many AI products currently in the market. Each of the big companies produces AI platforms that are helping them in achieving their strategic objectives.

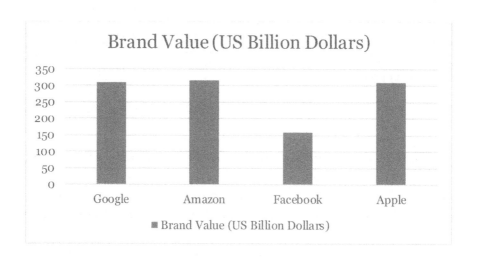

Google's Artificial Intelligence Activities

The artificial intelligence activities of Google are many with the company investing in continuously improving their AI capabilities which are in use across many businesses. These include Google Ads, Google Maps, and Google search engine, which companies are using worldwide. Each of these Google tools is providing varied benefits to those exploiting their capabilities within their contexts. Google's AI platforms are generally accessible online with different tools geared towards specific population segments. The abilities of Google AI-based activities depend on the generation and analysis of data. Machine learning and deep learning are capabilities of these AI platforms with new versions periodically released.

Google Ads is an AI activity for marketing and information purposes with the platform allowing businesses to create personalized ads.

The delivery of these ads is dynamic with potential clients seeing them when they align with their changing interests. As potential customers are browsing through websites in affiliation with the Google company, they come across ads relevant to them. Currently, the AI capabilities regarding Google Ads are allowing for a suggestion of how to create ads making the process more convenient.

The creative ad capability is allowing Google Ads to act as dynamic templates that businesses can exploit to further their interests. Google Teachable machine is an AI that is for the student population, making it a platform that can expand the opportunity for businesses in the education industry. Companies looking to explore opportunities in understanding the concept of machine learning can find this AI useful. The teaching process has not integrated coding, which makes it easier to use for those inexperienced in computer languages. One uses a camera to aid the machine in learning with the lessons' facilitation being online-based. The platform is combining the advantages of AI and machine learning.

The Google Search engine may be the most recognizable AI from the company with businesses using the tool to source for information. The search engine uses algorithms that trigger answers to searches that come up when users type in keywords when looking for information. This AI platform can specify search results based on the location of the one typing the keyword giving greater information accuracy to businesses. Language-based results are possible, which creates a better customer experience for potential clients. Google search engine is now allowing users to translate pages that can create a connection with potential clients as they feel a part of the company. Google Maps is an AI in use by businesses to augment their operations, for example, by the taxi-hailing apps available in the market.

The drivers can use the AI to determine their location and the directions to where they intend to go, including tips like the shortest route. Google Maps are helping brick and mortar stores showcase their position, which may lead to an increase in walk-in clients. Companies can use Google Maps to increase customer interactivity by establishing tracking maps allowing customers to see the workflow of their transaction. Regarding the AI technology by Google in use in search engines, businesses can use voice options to triggers searches to topics relevant to the organization. The Google AI of choice for companies can focus on needs the company is looking to fulfill both within and without the business entity. Businesses can employ varied Google AI platforms, consecutively. The Google AI possibilities are allowing for integrations with existing applications in use within organizations. There are specific Google AI applications geared towards assisting businesses to increase efficiency in various processes. The processes the AI tools may cover include marketing, sales, and operations.

Facebook's Artificial Intelligence Activities

The AI activities of Facebook can be thought to revolve around the underlying social nature of Facebook, taking into account the social changes. Businesses can use Facebook AI to track and report the dynamic changes within the society that may affect their operations. The follow up is via deep learning and machine learning with the details being of the highest quality. Facebook is generating purely social AIs that businesses can take advantage of the opportunities it presents. Facebook's AI activities involve more than one billion people giving their data a high level of data, and therefore higher levels of accuracy.

Facebook AI activities include analytics which businesses can use in understanding the interests of their clients and aligning their product and service offerings to their needs.

The analytics Facebook shares are specific and dynamic as the data in use is continuously updated as people are interacting within their platform. Businesses can determine the parameters that they want to see, for example, filtered through location, age, and distance. Organizations are using the data from Facebook analytics to create new product and service offerings. The use can propel a business to a position of influence within the marketplace. Chatbots are now available within Facebook for both personal and business pages with the latter helping organizations take advantage of the benefits of the AI tool. These are for messaging clients in a timely fashion using the automatic nature of AI-powered chatbots. The chatbots are in use by businesses for different purposes, for example, gathering of customer information. Chatbots by Facebook are in use by companies to upsell and market promotions to their potential client bases using the platform. Businesses are including links within the chatbots. These are leading customers to their websites, hoping to turn them from interested customers to actual clients. Sponsored ads by Facebook is another form of AI businesses can take advantage of within the platform. These require payment by the organization after a set period. Companies are using ads to reach their intended target clients. The timing of the sponsored ads is possible, allowing a business to personalize their customer experience, which can be a source of the competitive edge in the marketplace. The types of ads companies can create through Facebook are different, including videos, and photos which can help a business reach visual customers.

Facebook shares data on how the promotions are performing and allow changing of the content of the ads as they are running. Facebook AI activities include running of survey questions within a user's newsfeed. The surveys are generally short containing one or two inquiries that require a click response which encourages a higher rate of customer action. Businesses can use this feature to get feedback from their potential customers regarding product and service offerings. The survey feature offers convenience as companies can create their own from their Facebook business pages. Businesses can create surveys in different forms, including poll questions. They can be versatile in terms of visual presentation, for example, including videos and pictures. Facebook AI allows for third party integration of applications making it a versatile platform that businesses can align with their interests. These can be affiliated directly to Facebook like Instagram or not, for example, Survey Monkey. For Facebook affiliated programs, ad sharing is possible, which makes its use convenient. The integration can allow for smoother transition with applications already in use by businesses in various stages of their internal processes. It can save time for companies that have a presence across different social media platforms with their activities appearing on Facebook and other applications simultaneously.

Amazon's Artificial Intelligence Activities

The AI activities from Amazon are many with their focus being on continuous improvement of their systems that are giving them a competitive edge within the marketplace.

The actions have grown it into a behemoth of online trading with a wide variety of products that potential customers have access to through their accounts. Amazon AI activities can benefit businesses of different sizes as their platform is versatile, allowing both digital and physical products. The actions have their basis in deep learning and machine learning which helps Amazon consistently improve on their offerings to potential clients.

The developments are helping in breaking down barriers that were due to geographical limitations. For physical products, Amazon has an AI-backed tracking system that allows customers to have real-time information on the location of their packages. The transparency has built their reputation as trustworthy, which is giving them a presence worldwide in terms of trade. Businesses can tap into this brand trust to move their items through the platform of Amazon around the world. Their experience with shipping is unmatched, which can save smaller businesses from dealing with the challenges that come with logistics. Companies can outsource tasks that Amazon can handle to focus on their core competencies, leveraging on their AI activities in the marketplace while achieving scale operations quicker.

The AI activities by Amazon span the world of payment processing with transaction confirmation occurring via automated email processing. The perception in the market of their ability to handle payments without fraud is positive enabling businesses to reach clients that trust its business model. Plugging into their robust system may mean growth for organizations as it exposes companies to new customer segments at a low cost. The AI activities at Amazon are allowing for cost calculation in a customer's local currency, making the transactions relatable. Businesses can, therefore, forecast their earnings in a currency that fits their local contexts.

Using AI, Amazon is allowing for the creation of personalized stores both for customers and for businesses which creates a better customer experience. One can control their purchasing or store collection conveniently with buying done from the comfort of one's home.

Companies can lead potential customers to their storefronts within the Amazon platform at no extra costs to their business. Organizations can change the look and feel of their digital storefronts conveniently with the touch of a button, which they can use to attain a competitive edge within the marketplace. Amazon is using robots as part of their AI activity strategy. With the machines assisting the human workforce in varied business processes, they can achieve a quick turnaround time. Companies can leverage this advantage to reach customers faster while saving on costs.

One of the areas where Amazon is integrating robots is within its warehouses to reduce errors and increase the speed of service. Businesses can use this strength to improve their customer experience, which may convert to increased market share. This investment is allowing Amazon to compete effectively with brick and mortar stores.

Amazon's innovation within the field of AI is allowing it to compete within the digital marketplace with the company creating its digital bookshop known as Amazon Kindle. Here, clients can access millions of books worldwide at the touch of a button which improves customer experience. Businesses can, therefore, go around the limitations of geographical barriers, which may increase their market reach. Uploading digital products is also convenient with individuals globally able to benefit from the technology. Amazon's AI activities, in this way, levels the field for businesses of smaller size to compete with the larger establishments.

Apple's Artificial Intelligence Activities

Apple's AI activities in the technology space are revolutionary with the company having a segment of customers who portray brand loyalty through their purchases. They run on the foundation of exclusivity with offerings of products and services available to those who select to purchase their devices. Data and machine learnings are part and parcel of the innovations within the company's portfolio of products. Their segmentation of customers can be a market source for businesses looking to serve their exclusive club. Such companies will not have to bear the cost of segmentation as Apple takes on the same. Apple, as a company, achieves exclusivity through the process of encryption. It does not allow non-affiliated systems to work with their products. The result is improved sales as customers have to keep updating their devices to remain in the exclusive club and the improved quality of services for their customers. The latter is through the passing of quality standards set by the company to be on their platform. Their customers also trust them giving them the advantage of brand loyalty that businesses can tap into to sell their products.

Given the characteristics of their customer segments, organizations can tailor their product promotions to align with the interests of their clients. Apple AI activities inform their sales strategy with precise segmentation, for example, aligning with expected income levels of potential customers. Apple devices are undergoing continuous improvement, establishing a perpetual sales cycle. Customers, will over time, update their devices through purchasing as changes reach a point of not being in tune with a tool. Businesses can align themselves with their sales strategy to come up with new product offerings that can be of interest to the customer segment within Apple's platform.

The companies can improve their sales revenue while riding on the business model of the Apple company. Apple AI activities come with challenges arising from their business model. Some are the attraction of those looking to hack into their system of exclusivity. There are scenarios where there are calls for the exclusivity to align with the political interests of societies. Some customers may not be able to keep up with the device changes in terms of purchasing, which may lead to a loss of customers. Due to geographical limitations, some customers may not access the latest innovations presented by the company to their client base. There has been a criticism of the company's ability to maintain a lead in AI innovation, given its model of exclusivity, which is an expectation of customers. Apple, as a firm, operates the Apple store that holds different products, which may be of interest to their customer base. The products in the store must pass their standards to be part of the portfolio. Businesses can work to attain their requirements to sell their products and services to the customers, which may expand a company's market share. The exclusivity may work to the advantage of a company as customers may perceive a brand to be exclusive when associated with the Apple company. The Apple company creates devices that are compatible with one another, and that cannot work with other third-party applications. Companies, depending on their strategic goals, can aim to have their devices work with the exclusivity of the Apple brand as a foray to new markets. Companies can focus on adjustability beyond the Apple Company. The effect could be achieving an extensive array of clients. Customers are now demanding products that are not restrictive which may be an opportunity for businesses. Versatility to a broader arena can mean working with more third-party applications as they would assume the products of a company are of the level of the Apple Company regarding the quality levels.

Conclusion

In the book, *Artificial Intelligence for Business Applications,* the reader will find information describing what artificial intelligence entails. The promises and challenges of the software are covered. There are discussions on how businesses can take advantage of the hopes of AI.

They will learn how AI is changing business processes. The processes discussed include new customer acquisition. One will find details on customer services that are coming up as businesses are implementing AI. The book discusses the topic of virtual assistants in business settings. The author describes how companies are using AI in the context of focus and strategy where the reader will find details on how to plan one's AI strategy.

Business owners can learn how to predict the behaviors of their target customers by reading the book. The book contains discussions on chatbots and responders. One will find extensive descriptions of what they are in the context of AI.

The author shares information on marketing platforms that have AI capabilities. Businesses can find information on how to use AI to improve their email marketing processes with the benefits of the same discussed in detail. The book details why companies should take the idea of applying AI in email marketing seriously. The book contains ideas on how a business can exploit the AI of big companies. One will find specifics on big companies providing AI and how they can take advantage of the same. The book details the type of AI the companies are currently running on their platforms.

Python Programming

A Comprehensive Smart Approach for Total Beginners to Learn Python Language Using Best Practices and Advanced Features

By: Ethem Mining

Introduction

This book is designed to be a step-by-step guide for total beginners to learn to program with Python. This book covers all the basics of Python programming languages from the data object types to debugging methods for large programs. This book has eight chapters where each chapter discusses a specific topic with code examples provided. The present book is structured as follows. The first chapter of this book provides the big picture of Python programming language, its features as well as its strengths. It also presents the necessary tools in order to start using Python languages and be able to test the examples provided in the book. The second chapter provides a general idea of what is a variable in Python, how to declare a variable as well as the difference between global and local variables. Chapter three of this book presents the set of a built-in data object in Python. It also presents the necessary functions and methods to process these data object type. Chapter four presents first the basics of Python syntax. Although Python is designed as readable with an easy syntax, there are some basic rules to follow which are given in this chapter. This chapter presents the if test and loops syntax and Python exceptions that are used to process data objects that were presented in chapter three. Chapters five and six discuss how to make your code and scripts more general, reusable, and sharable with other programmers via the notion of functions and modules. Chapter five is dedicated to functions and chapter 6 is dedicated to modules. Chapter seven of this book is dedicated to debugging with Python. It is common among programmers to use debugging in order to fix any errors in their programs after they are developed. This chapter presents the Python debugger and its commands.

Finally, chapter eight covers processing files with Python. Files are important whether to read from or to write processed data. Writing and reading of the files will also be explained in this chapter. Plenty of books on this subject are available in the market and we thank you for choosing this one. This book was made with care to make it a useful Python basic book for total beginners that wish to learn to program with Python.

Chapter 1: What You Need to Know Before You Start

The aim of this chapter is to get you started with Python and explain the basics behind Python programming. In fact, this chapter provides you with basics that you need to know before you start learning the basic Python programming language. In this chapter, we discuss what is Python and the Python features that make it an attractive programming language for large domain applications. We also present how you can download and install Python according to your Operating System. We also expose ways on how to launch and execute Python code. Of course, like in any programming language, we will show you how to develop your first famous program 'Hello World'. We won't actually start coding until the next chapters. We expose here just some examples so you can get the general picture behind Python.

What is Python?

Python is a programming language that has several features that makes it very attractive to programmers and developers. First of all, Python is a free programming language which means it is available for anybody.

Python is also an open-source language which means you can contribute to the source code if you wish. In fact, Python is a language that is supported by a community that gathers its effort through the internet to improve this language. Python is a language that belongs to the category of high-level languages. This implies that Python does not require compiling like other languages such as C or C++, Fortran, and so on. It implies also that the syntax of Python is very easy to use and learn. These features make Python programs to be easily developed, interpreted, and maintained at low cost. Therefore, it allows sharing and collaborating to develop applications based on Python very efficient.

Being an easy syntax and high-level programming language does not mean that Python is a very slow programming language. In fact, Python is considered a very competitive and productive language. When compared to other programming languages that are low-level and known to be fast, a Python script can be 3rd or 5th size of a similar script developed with C++ or Java. In addition to requiring less typing and debugging, Python does not require compiling. Once a Python script is developed, it can be run directly without additional steps of compiling or linking to other tools or libraries.

Another feature that makes Python an interesting programming language is its portability. Python language is portable and can be run in any Operating environment or system without any changes.

The same Python code can be run on Windows, UNIX / LINUX, Mac, on large servers, Android, or iOs tablets. Even graphical user interface applications can be developed to be portable using options that are supported in Python. Different from other languages like Java or C, Python offers a dynamic typing environment. Variables in Python can be used without declaration or type specification prior to use. Any variable can be used without specifying its type which makes developing codes very straight forward.

A very attractive feature of Python is the libraries that come with it. These libraries, also called packages, are a set of code tools that allows performing basic and common tasks. Python comes with a default library called the standard library which includes a set of modules like the math module for mathematical and numerical programming. Moreover, Python supports using other libraries developed by third parties.

There is a wide range of third parties' packages that are available online and allows using advanced tools for a specific domain (e.g. Numpy library for Numerical programming with Python, Pandas, Matplotlib for developing figures and so on). Hence, when coding with Python language, you have access to a wide set of tools and pre-coded and built-in objects that can be easily used. You never start from scratch because there is a high chance that the function you want to use was already coded and made available for use by anybody.

Python can be considered as a hybrid language in the context that it allows integrating and to be integrated with other programming languages. For instance, you can use pre-coded or compiled libraries that are written in C or C++ within Python. You can also call Python codes from scripts that are written in C or C++.

Overall, If you opt for Python as a language to develop your applications, you get the following benefits: 1) easy syntax and less typing; 2)a program that is fast to execute; 3) a program that is portable and usable within any operating system; 4) a program that is easily maintained and well organized; 5) never start from scratch with access to a wide variety of packages and codes ready to be used; 6) integrated components that allow running codes in C, C++, or any other language to speed up execution of parts of the code. These are some characteristics and benefits of using Python as a language for programming.

What can you develop with Python?

Given the strong features of Python, this programming language can be used to develop a wide range of applications from stand-alone scripts, to graphical user interface applications or integrated programming. In fact, Python is considered as a scripting language to develop easy programs given its readability and easy syntax. However, because it evolved to be also an object-oriented programming language, Python has similar characteristics as the low-level object-oriented languages such as C++. This implies that you can develop modules and classes with Python that benefits from multiple inheritances, polymorphism, and operator overloading. A class is the main notion in object-oriented programming that allows defining an object with its attributes and methods to handle it.

So, Python offers the ability to define and develop modular applications. Python also supports shell script programming that allows developing system programs. Indeed, Python programs are usable on any platform without change, so it is very suitable for shell script programming.

These shell scripts are typically used to fetch files, directories, set/change paths, or execute and launch other programs. The POSIX bindings available among the Python standard library support all tools of the Operating system that includes the environment variables, files, filename expansions, command-line arguments, and much more. These tools can be easily handled within Python scripts for shell scripting programming. Graphical user interface (GUI) applications can be easily developed with Python using the package Tkinter. This library supports graphical user development that is compatible with any operating system, LINUX/UNIX, Mac, and Windows, with no change required.

Python also supports developing internet scripts. A standard Internet module is included in the standard library that comes with Python. This module allows developing scripts that perform networking jobs in the server and in the client. You can develop codes that get information from a server or transfer files via FTP. It allows also processing XML files, and emails (i.e. send, receive or parse). It allows developing scripts that sort and search internet pages via URL. In addition, you can perform Internet programming where you can develop scripts to generate HTML files and websites.

Python can be used as glue programming that launches or runs other programs. For instance, you can easily test libraries written in C or C++ using Python scripts for rapid execution and evaluation. Python supports numerical and engineering programming, data analysis, and image processing through its libraries Pandas, NumPy, and Matplotlib. Other libraries are available in particular for data analysis. Python also supports performing database programming. It offers tools to read, save, and perform all common tasks on the database.

Moreover, it supports an interface that allows using the traditional syntax of MySQL, Oracle, Sybase, ODBC, or Informix for those who prefer using them. Those were examples of what you can develop with Python programming language.

In general, you can develop anything you want given the panoply of tools and libraries that are available in Python. In addition, Python is a very popular and widely used language in a wide range of applications. Hence, it is always updated and new tools and third parties' libraries are always developed and made available for the public. In addition, Python has a very strong community to help resolve any issues with the language. Now that you are familiar with Python features and what can you do with Python, let's see how Python can be installed on any Operating System.

How to install Python in your Operating System?

Python is a free programming language that can be downloaded from Python's official website www.Python.org. Python is available as software that includes the standard libraries and the interpreter. The latter is a program in the form of an executable that works, as its name suggests, as an interpreter or translator to the hardware of the machine. Its purpose is to interpret Python codes into a binary form that the machine hardware is able to process. After downloading and installing Python on your machine, several components will be automatically generated that includes the interpreter as executable and the standard library of Python.

If you have Linux or Mac OS, Python might be already available on your operating system. To check if Python is already available, you can type in a prompt shell 'Python'. This should return a '>>>' if Python is available, otherwise, it will display an error message that Python is not recognized as a command line. Another way to check if Python is available in Linux is to search Python manually in the folders 'usr/local/bin'or '/usr/bin'. If it isn't already available on your LINUX environment, you can download Python for Linux from the Python official website. It comes in several rpm files that can be zipped easily. Python should then be compiled from the source code contained in the zipped directory using the make command and running the config. This should set automatically the configuration of Python in your system. Python generally comes with a README file that explains the instructions to follow in order to install Python.

On Mac OS, Python 2.0 is typically already installed, and basically, you don't have to install or configure anything. However, you can always install the latest version of Python, which is version 3, that is considered the most up to date. Before installing Python, you might need to install OSX-GCC which can be downloaded using Xcode. If you already have Xcode installed, then you don't need to install the GCC. Then you need to install Homebrew. To do so, you need to launch your OS prompt shell, then execute:

```
$ /usr/bin/ruby -e "$(curl -fsSL
https://raw.githubusercontent.com/Homebrew/install/master
/install)"
```

Once Homebrew is installed, you can add it to your path environment variable as follows:

```
export PATH = /usr/local/bin:/usr/local/sbin:$PATH
```

Now, you are ready to install Python using the following command:

```
$ brew install Python
```

If you are using a Windows Operating System, installing Python is very straightforward.

You can download from the Python official website the appropriate version for Windows. The downloaded folder is a zipped directory that comes as a self-installer. You unzip the folder and launch the executable. Then in the installer window, you can click Yes for every window to install Python with the default settings.

This should install Python with documentation, graphical user support, an IDLE development as well as the necessary settings you would need to run Python scripts appropriately. After the installation is finished, Python will figure in the start menu among the programs. Now that you know how to install Python on your machine, we are going to see how you can run Python scripts and, of course, how to make your first program that displays 'Hello World'.

You first 'Hello World' Program

Python can be started from a command line through the prompt of your Operating System. You simply type 'Python' in the prompt. In Windows, for example, this can be done in the WINDOWS DOS console. After running 'Python' command to launch Python interpreter in the prompt, it displays the following 2 Lines:

C:\Users***>Python

Python 3.7.1 (default, Dec 10 2018, 22:54:23) [MSC v.1915 64 bit (AMD64)] :: Anaconda, Inc. on win32

Type "help", "copyright", "credits" or "license" for more information.

>>>

Basically, it displays the information about the Python version installed and currently launched and commands to get more information. When the prompt displays '>>>', it means that it is ready to execute Python code. To exit Python from the prompt shell on Windows, you can type Ctrl-Z. On Linux or Unix environments, you can use Ctrl-D. Now, we are going to develop and execute your first 'Hello World' program.

After you have launched Python in your prompt shell, you can run the following command:

```
>>> print ('Hello World')
Hello World
```

The 'print' command is a function that tells Python to display anything between the parenthesis. We will go through built-in functions in the next chapters. Note here that we are working in an interactive session. Everything that we run is lost once the prompt shell is exited. The code that we type is executed instantly when we hit Enter but lost after ending the session. This is a good way to practice and test quickly some commands. However, it is best suited to save the code somewhere and run it every time you need it. This should save the time of re-writing a script whenever you need it. To do so, you can use a script Editor like Notepad++ to develop and write the script. Then the script should be saved in a file with '.py' extension. This would allow Python to recognize and read the scripts that are written in the file as Python script.

Now, you can write in a text editor the following commands:

```
print ('Hello World')
print ('\n Executing my first Python program')
```

You can save the file as Hello.py. Now, to run this code, you have to launch your operating system prompt shell, then call Python and pass as argument the name of the script we just developed. For instance, on Windows you would type in WINDOWS DOS console:

C:\Users***>Python Hello.py

Hello World

Executing my first Python program

Note that if in the prompt shell the directory where your Python file is saved is different from your working directory, you should pass as an argument to Python the entire path of your script file like follows:

C:\Users***> Python path_script/Hello.py.

In the second print of this example, we added '\n'; this tells Python to go into the following line.

Chapter 2: Variables in Python

This chapter discusses the Variables in Python. We will start with a definition of what a variable is in Python. Then, we will see how to declare and re-declare variables. We will also see the local and global variables and the difference between these two variables.

What is a variable?

A variable is typically a reserved memory to a saved value on your machine. According to the data type to be stored in a variable, a Python interpreter will allocate memory to save the variable. In Python, variables do not have to be explicitly declared before they are used. In other words, you don't need to define the type or size of any variable before it is used in Python. Basically, Python does not allocate any memory for variables prior to their use. Variables are defined and memory is allocated instantaneously when the variable is used. In Python, variables are objects that can be a number, string, list, dictionary, tuple, or a file. We will explain in detail each data object type in the next chapter. For the sake of simplicity and to explain variables and how to declare and manipulate them in this chapter, we will consider the basic data object number and strings. A number object type can be, for instance, an integer or a decimal.

Before going into how to declare and assign values to variables, there are some rules that should be followed to name a variable or a data object in Python. We cover more of this topic in chapter 4 of this book. First of all, only alpha-numeric characters and underscores can be used to name a Python variable. A variable name cannot start with a numeric. For instance, a variable name can be something like A_20. But 20_A cannot be used as a name for a variable. In Python, variables are case sensitive. For instance, PRICE, price, and Price are three different variables. We will cover more on variable names in Chapter 4 of this book.

How to declare, re-declare, and delete variables?

Remember that in Python, variables do not require any pre-allocation, type, or size specification prior to use. A variable is defined once a value is assigned to it. The equal operator '=' is the operator that assigns values to an object variable. The variable name is the left operand and the value to be stored in the variable is the right operand. For instance, we create the following variable:

```
>>> A = 200
>>> print (' The variable A is: ', A)
The variable A is: 200
```

Here we created a number variable. We can also declare or define several variables in a single statement as follows:

```
>>> A, B, C = 100, 200, 8
>>>print (' The variable A is:', A)
>>> ('\n The variable B is: ', B)
>>> ('\n The variable C is: ', C)
The variable A is: 100
The variable B is: 200
The variable C is: 8
```

In this example, we declared three number variables in a single statement. We can also declare in a single statement several variables of different types as follows:

```
>>> A, B = 12, 'Price'
>>> print (' The variable A is:', A)
>>> print ('\n The variable B is: ', B)
The variable A is: 12
The variable B is: Price
```

We can re-declare a variable by assigning a new value to the variable. For example:

```
>>> A = 2000
>>>print (' The variable A is: ', A)
The variable A is: 2000
>>> A = 400
>>>print (' The new value of the variable A is: ', A)
The new value of the variable A is: 400
```

We can also change the type of a declared variable by assigning a new type of data. For example, we can declare a variable as a number then we can change its value to a string.

```
>>> A = 100
>>>print (' The variable A is: ', A)
The variable A is: 100
>>> A = 'Date'
>>>print (' The new value of the variable A is: ', A)
The new value of the variable A is: Date
```

Variables in Python can be deleted using the function del. This function is used as followed:

```
>>> A = 100
>>> del A
```

Like assigning multiple variables, the function del can delete multiple variables as follows:

```
>>> A, B, C = 100, 200, 300
>>> del A, B, C
```

Now, if you want to access any variable, Python will throw an error message.

For example, if you try displaying variable B:

```
>>> B
Traceback (most recent call last):
File "<stdin>", line 1, in <module>
NameError: name 'B' is not defined
```

Now, you have learned how to declare and re-declare and delete variables in Python. In the next section, we will see what is a local and global variable in Python.

What are the local and global variables?

Remember that in Python, functions and modules can be defined. Variables that are defined inside of these functions are called local variables. Global variables are all variables that are declared in the main script outside of the functions. The global variables can be used inside or outside a function even if they are not defined inside a function. For instance, let's consider the following code:

```
>>> def my_fct():
...     print ('The value of the global variable is:', A)
```

In the code above, we defined a function that displays the value stored in the variable A which is not defined inside the function. So, the variable A is a global variable. Now, we can declare a variable A and print its value by calling the function my_fct() we defined as follows:

```
>>> A = 100
>>> my_fct()
The value of the global variable is: 100
```

242

Now, let's see how can we change any global variable within a function. For example, we define a function that multiplies the value of the global variable:

```
>>> def my_fct():
...     A = A * 2
...     print (' The value of the variable is: ', A)
```

Now, after we define a variable and call the function my_fct() we defined, we get the following output:

```
>>> A = 1
>>> my_fct()
UnboundLocalError: local variable 'A' referenced before
assignment
```

This code throws an error because Python is treating the variable 'A' as a local variable that is not defined inside the function. Therefore, Python cannot recognize it. To be able to change a global variable inside a function, we should use the global keyword. The global keyword is a keyword in Python that enables changing a global variable outside of the current script and makes the changes in a local environment (i.e. inside a function). The global keyword has some rules that should be followed when it is used. The global keyword is used only to read and write (i.e. make changes) to a global variable within a function. Using the global keyword outside of a routine or a function does not have any effect. A global variable defined outside a function is, by default, a global variable and a variable declared inside a function is, by default, a local variable. In the previous example, to change the global variable 'A' inside the function my_fct(), we should add the following command into the function script: global A. So, the function script should be like follows:

```
>>> def my_fct():
...     global A
...     A = A * 2
...     print (' The value of the variable is: ', A)
```

243

Now, if you define a variable 'A' outside of the function my_fct() and call the function, we get the following output:

```
>>> A = 1
>>> my_fct()
The value of the variable is: 2
```

Note that the variable is changed also in the script not only inside the function. If we display the variable 'A' outside the function, the value is

```
>>> print (' The value of the variable outside the function is: ',
A)
The value of the variable outside the function is: 2
```

If a local variable is declared in a function and then the same variable is declared as a global variable outside a function, calling the function does not change the value of the global variable. To make it more explicit, let's see an example:

```
>>> def f():
...      V = 'Charles'
...      print ('The local variable is:', V)
>>> V = 'John'
>>> f()
The local variable is: Charles
>>> print ('The global variable is:', V)
The local variable is: John
```

Local variables are only accessed within the function. In a script, a local variable cannot be accessed from outside the function where it is defined.

For instance, if we define a function as follows:

```
>>> def f1():
... var = 1
... print ('The local variable is:', var)
```

If we call the function we just defined, the output is as follows:

```
>>> f1()
The local variable is: 1
```

Python throws an error when we try to access the variable 'var' from outside the function as shown below:

```
>>> print(var)
Traceback (most recent call last):
File "<stdin>", line 1, in <module>
NameError: name 'var' is not defined
```

Chapter 3: Python data objects

In this chapter, we will cover the basic data objects in Python. We will also cover the operations that can be performed on these data objects and also how to manipulate them.

What are the Python data objects?

Python data objects are the variables in which save data that will be analyzed or processed. In Python, there are five major data objects types which are: number, strings, lists, dictionaries, and tuples. Numbers are the fundamental data type that also to store numeric variables. Strings in Python are a chain or a sequence of characters. Unlike other languages such as C, in Python, there is no character data object type to save a character singleton. Strings can be a single character or a sequence of characters. Lists are data structure in Python that allows saving items of different types. In fact, strings are a list that contains only characters. However, lists provide a flexible way to save multiple data of different types in a single data object. Dictionary is another flexible data object that allows in Python to save data of different types in the same data object or variable. The main difference between lists and dictionaries is how the data is stored and how it is fetched. In lists, items are saved from left to right position and are indexed. Items in lists can be accessed using index or position.

On the other hand, items in dictionaries are saved according to a key, meaning that items in dictionaries are not ordered and can be accessed using a key. Items in a dictionary are saved in a randomized way and the only way to access them is by key. In Python, the function type() allows verifying variables types. This function takes as input a variable and returns the type of the variable passed as input.

Let's some examples of applying this function.

```
>>> A = 200
>>> print ('Type of variable A is: ', type(A))
Type of variable A is: <class 'int'>
>>> A = 'chain of characters'
>>> print ('Type of variable A is: ', type(A))
Type of variable A is: <class 'str'>
>>> A = [1,'p', 300]
>>> print ('Type of variable A is: ', type(A))
Type of variable A is: <class 'list'>
```

In the first example, we defined the variable 'A' as an integer number, the type function returned as output class integer. In the second example, we declared the variable 'A' as a string, the type function returned a class string. Finally, in the third example, the variable 'A' is declared as a list and the function type returned a class list. Now that you know the different types of data objects in Python, in the next sections of this chapter, we will cover in detail each data type. Let's start with the most basic one, the number data type.

Number Data Object in Python

The number data object is the most basic data object that allows the processing of numeric variables in any programming language. This data object allows the processing quantity data. In Python, a number data object or variable can be an integer, a float number, or a complex number. Python also offers several functions that allow handling this data object. Python also supports normal integer, a long integer with unlimited precision. Basically, integers are a string of decimal digits that can be positive or negative. Float numbers can be a negative or positive number with a decimal point. Python supports the scientific representation of floating numbers with an exponent written with E or e indicating the power.

248

Even though a number with exponent is an integer, Python considers it as a floating number and uses float-point math functions when performing mathematical operations such as addition, subtraction, or multiplication.

Python offers all basic mathematical functions and operators to process number variables. The table below summarizes all comparison operators that can be used on number variables. Basically, these operators allow comparing between variables whether they are equal, or if the left operand is superior or inferior to the right operand.

Table 1: Comparison operators to be performed on number variables

Operator	Explanation
X > Y	X is strictly superior to Y
X >= Y	X superior or equal to Y
X < Y	X strictly inferior to Y
X <= Y	X inferior or equal to Y
X == Y	X is equal to Y
X != Y	X is different than Y

In the following table, we cover the logical operators that can be performed on number variables. These operators allow object comparison, whether two variables are true if a number variable belongs to other object data.

Table 2: Logical operators to be performed on number variables.

Operator	Explanation
X **and** Y	both X and Y should be true (i.e. Y is evaluated unless X is true)
X **or** Y	X or Y is true (i.e. Y is evaluated unless X is false)
not X	logical negation
X **is** Y	object comparison
X **is not** Y	object comparison
X **in**	X belonging to another object
X **not in**	X not belonging to another object
|	bitwise or
^	bitwise exclusive
&	bitwise and

The table below summarizes the mathematical operations that Python supports on number variables. These operations include addition, subtraction, multiplication, negation, and division.

Table 3: Mathematical operators to be performed on a number of variables.

Operator	Explanation
X + Y	X plus Y
X - Y	X minus Y
X // Y	X divided by Y
X % Y	The remainder of the division of X by Y
X * Y	X multiplied by Y
+ X	identity of X which equal to X
- X	negation of X
X ** Y	X power Y

Remember that when performing several mathematical operations in one single statement, the rules of mathematical operations applies. That being said, Python will always start by evaluating multiplication first, then it evaluates the other operations. For instance, if we consider the following statement $Z = A * X + Y$, Python will evaluate $A * X$ then add the result to Y.

If we want to specify a certain order of operations, let's say we want to evaluate first $X + Y$ then multiply the result by A, then we should add parenthesis around $X + Y$. To do so, the statement should be $Z = A * (X + Y)$. Therefore, the results returned by $Z = A * X + Y$ and $Z = A * (X + Y)$ are very different.

When adding parenthesis, Python evaluates first the expressions between parenthesis. Let's apply a real example of the two expressions given above.

>>> A = 4

>>> X = 5

>>> Y = 9

>>> Z = A * X + Y

>>> print ('Z = A * X + Y is:', Z)

Z = A * X + Y is: 29

>>> Z = A * (X + Y)

>>> print ('Z = A * (X + Y) is:', Z)

Z = A * (X + Y) is: 56

We can see from the example above that the first expression $Z = A * X + Y$ returns 29 for $A = 4$, $X = 5$ and $Y = 9$.

Python computes first A * X (i.e. 5 * 4) which is, in this case, 20 and adds Y (i.e. 9) to it which gives 29. For the second expression Z = A * (X + Y), Python evaluates first X + Y (i.e. 5 + 9) which is 14, then it multiplies it by A (i.e. 4) which gives 56.

Python supports evaluating multiple expressions in one single line and returns the results in a tuple. For instance, we can evaluate the two expressions A * X and Z +Y in one single line as follows:

>>> A = 4

>>> X = 5

>>> Y = 9

>>> Z = 56

>>> A * X, Z + Y

(20, 65)

As we have seen before, we can evaluate the two expressions and assign the results to two variables in one single line. The code below presents an example:

>>> A = 4

>>> X = 5

>>> Y = 9

>>> Z = 56

>>> B, C = A * X, Z + Y

>>> print (' A * X is:', B)

A * X is: 20

>>> print (' Z + Y is:', C)

Z + Y is: 65

In the following codes, we provide examples of applying some operators from the tables presented above.

```
>>> A = 4
>>> B = 20
```

Applying division:

```
>>> C= B // A
>>> print (' B divided by A is:', C)
B divided by A is: 5
```

Applying the modulus operator:

```
>>> C = B % A

>>> print (' The remainder of B divided by A is:', C)

The remainder of B divided by A is: 0
```

Operation on integers and float number:

```
>>> A, B = 2.4, 20

>>> C = B // 2.4

>>> print (' B divided by A is:', C)

B divided by A is: 8.0

>>> print (' The type of the results from an operation applied
to an integer and float is:', type(C))

The type of the results from an operation applied to an integer
and float is: <class 'float'>
```

As we can see from the example above, any operation applied to an integer and a float number always returns a float number type.

Python has several built-in mathematical functions available in the math module and comes within the standard library. These functions allow evaluating the trigonometric functions (i.e. cons, sin, tang...), the absolute value of a number, evaluating the integer part of a number, the power function, as well as rounding float number among others. The module math has also the number pi defined. In order to use these functions, the math module needs to be imported first. In the following codes, we present examples of applying these functions. First, we import the math module:

>>> import math

Remember, in order to use a function within a module, we need to type module.function_name. For example, for the math module, all functions are called math.function_name. The examples below illustrate how math functions are called.

Using the pi number of the math module:

>>> print (' The number pi is:', math.pi)

The number pi is: 3.141592653589793

Calling the trigonometric functions from the math module:

```
>>> alpha = math.cos (math.pi)
>>> print (' The cos of pi is:', alpha)
The cos of pi is: -1.0
>>> alpha = math.sin (1)
>>> print (' The sin of 1 is:', alpha)
The sin of 1 is: 0.8414709848078965
>>> alpha = math.tan (1)
>>> print (' The tan of 1 is:', alpha)
The tan of 1 is: 1.5574077246549023
```

Applying the power function is the same as using the operator **:

```
>>> print (' 3 ** 2 is:', C)
3 ** 2 is: 9
>>> C = math.pow (3, 2)
>>> print (' 3 power 2 with pow function is:', C)
3 power 2 with pow function is: 9.0
```

Note that the operator ** returns an integer when the two numbers are integers whereas the math.pow() function always returns a float number.

Functions presented in the following examples are from the standard library of Python and not included in the math module.

Evaluating the absolute value of a number:

>>> A, B = abs (-4), abs (6)

>>> print (' The absolute value of -4 and 6 are:', A, 'and', B)

The absolute value of -4 and 6 are: 4 and 6

Evaluating the integer part of a float number:

>>> A = int (6.7)

>>> print ('The integer part of 6.7 is:', A)

The integer part of 6.7 is: 6

Rounding the value of a float number:

>>> A = round (4.5)

>>> print (' The value of rounding 4.5 is:', A)

The value of rounding 4.5 is: 4

String Data Object in Python

Strings in Python are a sequence of characters stored in a list. Unlike other languages like C, for instance, Python does not support a char data object which a character singleton. In Python, a character singleton is basically a string of a single character. Strings in Python are immutable. In other words, once you define a string variable its size is fixed and cannot be changed after. As we mentioned before, a string is a sequence of characters stored in a list which means that string characters are saved in an orderly fashion from left to right. Each character in a string can be accessed by position because it is stored in a list. To declare a variable a string, both single and double quotes can be used. Triple quotes are used when a variable is defined as a block of strings that extends over a few lines. The codes below illustrate examples of declaring variables using single, double and triple quotes.

>>> Ex1 = ' This is a string defined in a single quote'

>>> print (Ex1)

This is a string defined in a single quote

>>> Ex2 = " This is a string defined in a double quote"

>>> print (Ex2)

This is a string defined in a double quote

>>> Ex3 = """ This is an example of a string

... that extends on

... three lines """

>>> print (Ex3)

 This is an example of a string

that extends on

three lines

In fact, using a single or a double quote does not make any difference. Strings defined using a single or double quote are the same. For instance, we create the same string using both methods, Python will return the same exact result as in the example below:

>>> ' My string ', " My string "

(' My string ', ' My string ')

Python supports several built-in functions that handle strings, unlike other languages. These functions allow concatenation of two strings, repeating the same string, find a sequence of characters in a string, replace a sequence of characters of a string, and splitting a string.

The following codes present these functions and illustrate with examples of how they can be used. To concatenate two strings the operator ' + ' can be used. This operator concatenate strings of any length. For instance, we will concatenate the following strings:

>>> A = ' This is the first element of the concatenation example'

>>> B = ' This is the second element of the concatenation example'

>>> C = ' and this is the third element'

>>> X = A + B + C

>>> print (' The result of concatenation with the operator + is: \n', X)

The result of concatenation with the operator + is:

This is the first element of the concatenation example This is the second element of the concatenation example and this is the third element

A sequence of a string can be repeated n times using the operator ' * '.

For instance:

>>> A = 'This is an example of repeating a sequence of string'

>>> B = A * 2

>>> print (' The string A repeated 2 times is: \n ', B)

The string A repeated 2 times is:

This is an example of repeating a sequence of string This is an example of repeating a sequence of string

To find a character or a sequence of characters within a string, Python has the function find(). This function is a method of the String class object that takes as input a character or a sequence of characters and returns the index of the first character of the sequence in the string. This method is used as in the example below:

>>> A = 'This is an example of the find function'

>>> A.find ('example ')

11

Remember that a string is a list and items of a string or its characters can be accessed by position. So, for the above example, the position returned by the find function is the position of the first character that was passed as an argument which is in this case ' e '. Therefore, if we try to get the 11th element of the string ' A ' we defined, we get the following output:

>>> A [11]

'e'

A sequence of characters in a string can be replaced using the function replace(). This function is also a method of the String class in Python like the find function and is called in the same manner. The replace function takes two arguments where the first argument is the sequence of characters to be replaced and the second argument is the sequence of characters to be replaced with.

Let's see an example:

>>> A = ' This is an example of using the replace method'

>>> A.replace ('method', 'function')

' This is an example of using the replace function'

In the example above, we replaced ' method ' by ' function ' in the string variable ' A '.

To split a string into several strings, the split function is used. Like the previous methods, the split function is a method of the String class and is used in the same manner. The split function basically split a string according to the spaces in the string.

The output is a list of strings where each item is a sequence of characters that forms the strings according to the spaces. The example below illustrates how this function works:

>>> A = 'This is an example of the split function'

>>> C = A. split()

>>> print (' The output of the split function is:\n', C)

The output of the split function is:

['This', 'is', 'an', 'example', 'of', 'the', 'split', 'function']

To evaluate the length of a string, the function len is used. This function takes as an argument a variable and it returns its length. In the code below, we illustrate how this function is applied:

>>> A = 'This is an example of the len function'

>>> L = len (A)

>>> print ('The length of the string variable A is:', L)

The length of the string variable A is: 38

List data object in Python

List data objects are a flexible heterogeneous data object that can contain items of different types. In addition, lists can expand, shrink, and change upon request. A list can be formed by any other data object including lists. Data is typically saved in lists in an orderly manner from left to right. Because items in lists are ordered, they can be accessed by indexing or position. We can perform slicing and indexing and concatenation. Lists in Python are mutable which means their size can be modified after they are defined.

This means that we can delete items from a list or add new items to the list by index assignment. Python offers all basic functions to manipulate lists that include concatenation, sorting items in a list, deleting an element from a list, evaluating the length of a list, extending a list, reversing elements of a list, adding an element to a list, or repeating a list n times. The following examples illustrate how to apply these functions and to handle lists in Python.

Lists are defined in Python using brackets. This means that in order to define a list, items to be saved in the list should be written between brackets. For instance:

>>> A = [100, 40, 50]

>>> print (' My first list in Python is:', A)

My first list in Python is: [100, 40, 50]

Sometimes, it is useful to create an empty list in which we save items as we process information within a loop. We can create an empty list like in the example below:

>>> A = []

>>> print (' My first empty list in Python:', A)

My first empty list in Python: []

Items of a list can be extracted or accessed by their positions. In Python, indexing starts by 0 meaning that the position of the first element is 0. For example:

>>> A = [100, 40, 50]

>>> print (' The first item in my first list is:', A [0])

The first item in my first list is: 100

Python supports slicing to extract or modify items in a list. Note that an item can also be modified by its position. Slicing is typically used when we want to extract multiple elements at the same time. The examples below illustrate, in more detail, slicing.

>>> A = [100, 90, 600, 40, 500]

>>> print (' The first two elements of the list A are:', A [0:2])

The first two elements of the list A are: [100, 90]

>>> print (' The prior to the last element of the list A is:', A [-2])

The prior to the last two elements of the list A is: 40

>>> print (' The last two elements of the list A are:', A [-2:])

The last two elements of the list A are: [40, 500]

>>> print (' The three first elements of the list A are:', A [:3])

The three first elements of the list A are: [100, 90, 600]

As you can notice from the examples above, the last index of the slicing is not returned. It only indicates to Python where it should stop the slicing and the actual item corresponding to that index is not returned. The following example is an illustration of the changing values of a list using slicing.

>>> A = [100, 90, 600, 40, 500]

>>> A [2:3] = [0,0]

>>> print (' The list after slicing assignment is:', A)

The list after slicing assignment is: [100, 90, 0, 0, 0, 40, 500]

263

When using slicing assignment, the number of new items should be the same as the number of items being replaced. Like in the example above, although we are assigning the same value (i.e. 0), we should assign a list of two items to change the value of the two items. If we try to assign a single value in this case, Python will throw an error like follows:

>>> A [2:3] = 0

Traceback (most recent call last):

 File "<stdin>", line 1, in <module>

TypeError: can only assign an iterable

To concatenate two lists, the operator ' + ' is used like for string data object. Concatenation conserves the same order in the lists passed as argument. For example:

>>> A = [100, 90, 600, 40, 500]

>>> B = [900, 34, 89, 789, 57]

>>> C = A + B

>>> print (' The concatenated lists is:', C)

The concatenated list is: [100, 90, 600, 40, 500, 900, 34, 89, 789, 57]

Like strings, a list can be repeated n times using the operator ' * '. For example:

```
>>> A = [100, 90, 600, 40, 500]

>>> C = A * 2

>>> print (' My list repeated 2 times is:', C)
```

My list repeated 2 times is: [100, 90, 600, 40, 500, 100, 90, 600, 40, 500]

The length of a list can be evaluated by the basic function of Python the len function. This function returns the number of elements saved in a list.

```
>>> A = [100, 90, 600, 40, 500]

>>> print (' The length of the list A is:', len (A))
```

The length of the list A is: 5

To sort elements of a list, the sort function is used. This function is a method specific to the list class object.

In the example below, we present how this method is used.

```
>>> A = [100, 90, 600, 40, 500]

>>> A.sort()

>>> print (' This is an example of sorting a list and the result
is: \n', A)
```

This is an example of sorting a list and the result is:

[40, 90, 100, 500, 600]

The sort function sort items of a list in ascending order. To reverse the items of the list, the method reverse is used. This method is specific to the list class object and is as the sort function. Now, we can get the list sorted in a descending manner by applying both sorts and reverse like follows:

>>> A = [100, 90, 600, 40, 500]

>>> A.sort()

>>> A.reverse()

>>> print (' The reserved or sorted list A in descending order is: \n', A)

The reserved or sorted list A in descending order is:

[600, 500, 100, 90, 40]

To add an item to a list, the append function is used. The append function is different than concatenation in the sense that appends is a method specific to list class object and take as input value while concatenation process two lists. They yield the same results in different ways. The append function is useful when you are processing data in a script and updating a list by adding each new item when available. The append function is called like the sort and reverse methods as follows:

>>> A = [100, 90, 600, 40, 500]

>>> A.append(10000)

>>> print (' This is an example of the append function and the result is: \n', A)

This is an example of the append function and the result is:

[100, 90, 600, 40, 500, 10000]

266

Another function specific to the list class object is extended. This function allows also to add new items to a list. Unlike the append method, extend takes as in input argument a list. The following example illustrates how to add new items with the extend method.

>>> A = [100, 90, 600, 40, 500]

>>> A.extend([400, 900, 60])

>>> print ('This is an example of adding items with extend function: \n', A)

This is an example of adding items with extend function:

[100, 90, 600, 40, 500, 400, 900, 60]

In Python two functions allow deleting items from a list which are pop and del functions. The first one, the pop function, deletes and returns the last item of a list. This function is a specific method for the list class object. The second function, the del function, is more general and allows deleting any item or any number of items from a list by position. In the next examples, we illustrate how to use these two functions.

>>> A = [100, 90, 600, 40, 500, 400, 900, 60]

>>> A.pop()

60

>>> print (' This is an example of deleting with pop function: \n', A)

This is an example of deleting with pop function:

[100, 90, 600, 40, 500, 400, 900]

>>> del A [2:]

>>> print (' This is an example of deleting items with del function: \n', A)

This is an example of deleting items with del function:

[100, 90]

In the example, we deleted all elements from the second item of the list using slicing.

Dictionary data object in Python

The dictionary data object is another flexible data object supported in Python. Dictionaries are heterogeneous data object that enables saving data of different types including another dictionary. Dictionaries and lists both have some similarities in the context that they are both flexible and can shrink and extend upon request. The main difference between lists and dictionaries is that the way items are saved in these data objects and how they can be fetched. If items in lists are ordered and can be accessed by position, in dictionaries, items are not ordered and are accessed by key.

Because dictionaries are a built-in object of Python, they support many data structures that you perhaps can need in developing an application and would have to define manually when working with low-level programming languages.

In the same context, they also support several searching algorithms that would need to develop in low-level languages like C for instance. Indeed, using the indexing for dictionaries allows a fast search task. Dictionaries can be used as records or symbols for tables for other languages, or a representation of data structures that are sparse. The main characteristics of dictionaries are as follows. Items of a dictionary are accessed by keys. In fact, items in a dictionary are associated with a key. In other words, a key is assigned for each set of values. When fetching a dataset, keys are used to extract the data that are saved in a particular key. Indexing operations can also be used to extract items out of a dictionary, however, the index is in the form of a key not a relative position within the dictionary. Items are unordered in a dictionary. Unlike lists, items in a dictionary do not follow a particular order. Python saves items in a dictionary in a random way which allows a fast lookup. The keys that are assigned for each set of data does not provide a physical position but a symbolic position of an item within a dictionary. The length of a dictionary is variable meaning that it can expand or shrink without creating a new copy of the dictionary in question. They are heterogeneous in the sense that they can save in other types of data including lists or another dictionary. Items of a dictionary can be modified in place using index assignment. However, they do not allow the operations in sequences like strings or lists. Items in dictionaries do not follow any order. Therefore, all operations that are based on a fixed order such as slicing or concatenation are not permitted and do not make any sense when working with dictionaries.

However, dictionaries are the single data structure within Python that supports a representation of the category of mapping type meaning that objects can be mapped with keys to values. Finally, dictionaries can be considered as unordered tables.

In fact, Python implements dictionaries as hash tables that can start with a small size, then expand if needed. Python uses algorithms that are optimized in order to find keys that make extracting items very fast. Dictionaries in Python are defined by a set of keys for which a set of values are assigned and separated by a comma and enclosed between curly braces. Like lists, Python has several built-in functions that allow handling dictionaries that we are going to cover in the following code examples. The following table summarizes the operations that can be performed on dictionaries.

Table 4: List of operations to be performed on the dictionary data object.

Operator	Explanation
Dic = {}	Declaring an empty dictionary
Dic = {'age':10, 'name': 'john'}	Declaring a dictionary of two items
Dic ['age']	Indexing a dictionary by key
Dic.has_key ('age')	Test of membership
age' in Dic	Test of membership
Dic.keys ()	Get a list of keys
Dic.values ()	Get list of values
Dic.copy ()	Copies items of dictionary
Dic.get (key, default)	Get items
Len (Dic)	Get length of the dictionary
Dic [key] = value	Modifying or adding a value
Del Dic [key]	Deleting items

In the table above, we have an example of defining an empty dictionary and a dictionary of two items. We can also create a dictionary from other dictionaries. To get a sense of how to do so and how to use the functions in the table above, let's practice with some examples in the interactive session of Python. To create an empty dictionary, we pass empty curly braces:

>>> Dic = {}

>>> print (' This is an example of an empty dictionary:', Dic)

This is an example of an empty dictionary: {}

270

To define a dictionary of items, values are assigned to keys. The following codes present an example:

>>> Dic = {'Name': 'John', 'Age': 100}

>>> print (' This is an example of an empty dictionary:', Dic)

This is an example of an empty dictionary: {'Name': 'John', 'Age': 100}

In the following example, we will see how we can define a dictionary that contains a dictionary.

>>> Dic = {' Pers': {' Name': 'John', 'Age': 10}}

>>> print (' This is an example of nested dictionary:', Dic)

This is an example of nested dictionary: {'Pers': {'Name': 'John', 'Age': 10}}

A dictionary can be also defined from lists. In the previous examples, each key is associated with single values. In the following examples, we illustrate how we can define a dictionary where each key is associated with a list of values.

>>> LL = ['John', 'Mike', 'Dave']

>>> Ag = [20, 30, 40]

>>> Dic = {'Name': LL, 'Age': Ag}

>>> print (' This is an example of a dictionary defined from lists:', dic)

271

This is an example of a dictionary defined from lists: {'Name': ['John', 'Mike', 'Dave'], 'Age': [20, 30, 40]}

To extract items from a dictionary, we use the same syntax of position indexing used for lists. The difference is we use keys instead of position. Let's see some real examples of how to extract items from a dictionary.

>>> LL = ['John', 'Mike', 'Dave']

>>> Ag = [20, 30, 40]

>>> dic = {'Name': LL, 'Age': Ag}

>>> print (' This is an example of extracting an item from a dictionary: \n', dic ['Name'])

This is an example of extracting an item from a dictionary:

['John', 'Mike', 'Dave']

To extract keys of a dictionary, the keys method is used as follows:

>>> LL = ['John', 'Mike', 'Dave']

>>> Ag = [20, 30, 40]

>>> dic = {'Name': LL, 'Age': Ag}

>>> print (' This is an example of extracting keys of dictionary, keys are: \n', dic.keys())

This is an example of extracting keys of dictionary, keys are:

dict_keys (['Name', 'Age'])

We can verify if a key is part of a dictionary by using the logical in. The following presents an illustration of verifying the existence of a key in a dictionary.

```
>>> LL = ['John', 'Mike', 'Dave']

>>> Ag = [20, 30, 40]

>>> dic = {'Name': LL, 'Age': Ag}

>>> print ('This is an example of verifying if a key (here Age)
is in dictionary:', 'Age' in dic)
```

This is an example of verifying if a key (here Age) is in dictionary: True

The len function is a general function in Python that returns the length of a data object. It is applied to the dictionary the same as it is applied to lists and strings.

```
>>> LL = ['John', 'Mike', 'Dave']

>>> Ag = [20, 30, 40]

>>> dic = {'Name': LL, 'Age': Ag}

>>> print (' The length of the dictionary is:', len (dic ))
```

The length of the dictionary is: 2

Values stored in a dictionary are extracted using the method values.

This function is used as follows:

```
>>> LL = ['John', 'Mike', 'Dave']
>>> Ag = [20, 30, 40]
>>> dic = {'Name': LL, 'Age': Ag}
>>> print (' This is an example of extracting values of a
dictionary:\n', dic.values ())
This is an example of extracting values of a dictionary:
 dict_values ([['John', 'Mike', 'Dave'], [20, 30, 40]])
```

Values stored in a dictionary can be replaced in place without creating a new dictionary. To do so, position indexing by key is used. The following code presents an example of changing values by key.

```
>>> LL = ['John', 'Mike', 'Dave']
>>> Ag = [20, 30, 40]
>>> dic = {'Name': LL, 'Age': Ag}
>>> print (' Dictionary before replacement:', dic)
Dictionary before replacement: {'Name': ['John', 'Mike', 'Dave'],
'Age': [20, 30, 40]}
>>> dic ['Name'] = ['Markus', 'David', 'Peter']
>>> print (' Dictionary after replacement:', dic)
Dictionary after replacement: {'Name': ['Markus', 'David',
'Peter'], 'Age': [20, 30, 40]}
```

Items from a dictionary can be deleted using position indexing and the del function. For instance

>>> LL = ['John', 'Mike', 'Dave']

>>> Ag = [20, 30, 40]

>>> dic = {'Name': LL, 'Age': Ag}

>>> print (' Dictionary before deletion is:', dic)

Dictionary before deletion is: {'Name': ['Markus', 'David', 'Peter'], 'Age': [20, 30, 40]}

>>> del dic ['Age']

>>> print (' Dictionary after deletion is:', dic)

Dictionary after deletion is: {'Name': ['Markus', 'David', 'Peter']}

Items can be added to a dictionary using position indexing like in the following example:

>>> LL = ['John', 'Mike', 'Dave']

>>> dic = {'Name': LL}

>>> print (' Dictionary before adding new item is:', dic)

Dictionary before adding new item is: {'Name': ['Markus', 'David', 'Peter']}

>>> dic ['Age'] = [90, 30, 50]

>>> print (' Dictionary after adding new item is:', dic)

Dictionary after adding new item is: {'Name': ['Markus', 'David', 'Peter'], 'Age': [90, 30, 50]}

275

So far, we covered in this chapter all basic and flexible data objects supported by Python. In the next section, we will cover the last data object which is tuples. This data object is relatively simple to handle, and as you can see, you already learned basics functions that might be used on tuples too from reading these sections about the other data objects.

Tuples data object in Python

Tuples like dictionaries and lists are a collection of data of different types. Tuples are very similar to lists. However, tuples cannot be changed. Indeed, tuples are less flexible than lists and are immutable. Items of tuples are typically written between parenthesis instead of brackets like lists. Tuples have similar characteristics as lists. Items in tuples are ordered according to their positions. Items in a tuple can be accessed by their positions.

Therefore, tuples support indexing, slicing, concatenation, repetition, and globally all operations performed on strings and lists. Tuples are similar to string in the context that both do not allow changing in size or items in place. Tuples cannot expand or shrink and their size is fixed once it is defined. The heterogeneous data object supports storing data of different types. In the following code examples, we illustrate how to perform some operations like indexing, concatenation, slicing, and others on tuples.

First, we illustrate some examples of defining a tuple.

```
>>> A = ()
>>> print (' This is an example of an empty tuple: ', A)
```

This is an example of an empty tuple: ()

```
>>> A = (1,)
>>> print (' This is an example of a one item tuple: ', A)
```

This is an example of a one item tuple: (1,)

```
>>> A = (1, 'John', 6.7, 90)
>>> print (' This is an example of a 4 items tuple: ', A)
```

This is an example of a 4 items tuple: (1, 'John', 6.7, 90)

```
>>> A = 1, 'John', 6.7, 90
>>> print (' This is another example of a 4 items tuple same as
the one before: \n', A)
```

This is another example of a 4 items tuple same as the one before:

(1, 'John', 6.7, 90)

```
>>> A = 1, 'John', (6.7, 90)
>>> print (' This is an example of a nested tuple: ', A)
```

This is an example of a nested tuple: (1, 'John', (6.7, 90))

Note from the examples above that if values assigned to a variable without brackets or parenthesis, Python will automatically consider the variable as a tuple. Although in the case of tuples, parenthesis is optional. In order to declare a variable as a tuple, it is a best practice to use parenthesis. This also helps code readability. Note also that parenthesis in Python encloses an expression. So, if a tuple from a single item is to be declared, use the syntax presented in the examples above. If a single value is written between parenthesis, it will not consider it as tuple but rather just a value.

Tuples have no specific methods like lists. However, the basic Python operations performed on lists and strings apply to tuples as well.

To concatenate two tuples, the operator ' +' is used. For example:

>>> A = (1, 4, 60)
>>> B = (90, 50, 40)
>>> print (' This is an example of tuple concatenation: ', A + B)
This is an example of tuple concatenation: (1, 4, 60, 90, 50, 40)

To repeat a tuple n times, the operator ' *' is used as in the example below:

>>> A = (1, 4, 60)
>>> print (' This is an example of tuple repeated 2 times: ', A * 2)
This is an example of tuple repeated 2 times: (1, 4, 60, 1, 4, 60)

To extract an item from a tuple, we can use either indexing or slicing as illustrated in the examples below:

>>> A = (1, 4, 60)
>>> print (' This is an example of extracting an item from a tuple by indexing: ', A [1])
This is an example of extracting an item from a tuple by indexing: 4
>>> print ('This is an example of extracting an item from a tuple by slicing: ', A [:1])
This is an example of extracting an item from a tuple by slicing: (1,)

Note that when extracting items from a tuple, it returns a tuple even though it is a single value. To sort items stored in a tuple, it should be converted to a list then sorted. Like mentioned before, tuples do not have specific methods like lists. The following example illustrates how to order a tuple:

```
>>> A = (100, 4, 60)
>>> print (' This is a tuple before sorting: ', A)
This is a tuple before sorting: (100, 4, 60)
>>> T = list (A)
>>> print (' This is a tuple converted to a list: ', list(A))
This is a tuple converted to a list: [100, 4, 60]
>>> T.sort ()
>>> print (' This is the list sorted', T)
This is the list sorted [4, 60, 100]
>>> A = tuple (T)
>>> print (' This is the tuple sorted: ', A)
This is the tuple sorted: (4, 60, 100)
```

Note that the function list() allows converting an item to a list and the tuple() function convert an object to a tuple. In fact, both functions list() and tuple() create new objects. Here, we just have overwritten the existing ones which makes it like a conversion of data types. The immutability characteristics apply only to the tuple data object and not to items that it contains.

For instance, if a tuple contains a list, the size of the list can be changed but not the tuple itself. Let's see an example to make it more comprehensible.

```
>>> A = (' Name', [20, 40, 50], 0)
>>> print (' This is an example of a tuple containing a list:', A)
This is an example of a tuple containing a list: ('Name', [20, 40,
50], 0)
>>> A [1][2] = 9000
>>> print ('This is an example of changing an item in a list
within a tuple:', A)
This is an example of changing an item in a list within a tuple:
('Name', [20, 40, 9000], 0)
```

If we try to change an item from the tuple like follows, Python throws an error.

```
>>> A [1] = 'Age'
Traceback (most recent call last):
 File "<stdin>", line 1, in <module>
TypeError: 'tuple' object does not support item assignment
```

In this chapter, we covered all built-in data objects in Python which are number, strings, lists, dictionaries, and tuples. The last data object, tuples, are heterogeneous data object that allows storing data of different type like lists and dictionaries but is less flexible. You are probably wondering why to use tuples. If they are not flexible, using lists instead would make more sense. Indeed, lists are more flexible, but they can be changed through your script. On the contrary, tuples cannot be changed or altered after they are defined. In addition, tuples may be of interest where lists cannot, for instance, as keys for dictionaries. Also, some functions in Python require variable in the form of tuples, not lists. As a general rule, lists are the go-to when the data need to be in ordered data structure and may be changed throughout the script. Otherwise, tuples are the best choice.

Chapter 4: Python Operators

I n this chapter, we will cover the different statements in Python as well as the Boolean expressions and conditional statement which are the if tests and loops. Overall, we will cover the statements that allow processing data that are stored in the data object that we presented in the previous chapter. At the end of this chapter, you will acquire basic skills to develop and run some logic Python scripts.

Python Statements Syntax

Before diving into logic if test and loops and logic conditions, we are going to run over the basic syntax of Python. Statements are basically the expression you write that instruct what the Python interpreter should do. In other words, statements are instructions into your program. In the following table, we present a global statement that can be used in Python.

Table 5: List of Statements supported in Python.

Statement	Explanation	Illustration
Assignment	Create a variable	A, B = 90, 'Age'
print	Display objects	print (' This is an example')
call	Launching a function	stdout.write('Example\n')
while else	Global loop	while T: print ('Example')
for else	Iteration in a sequence	for i in list: print(i)
		if A in text: print ('Example if
if/elif/else	Selection of tasks	test')
break and	To jump into a specific	
continue	task in loops	while T: if not A: break

try, except and finally	Exceptions catching	try: tasks / except: print ('Example Error')
raise	To trigger an exception	raise Endlocation
import	Module importing	import math
import from	Import from a module	from sys import stdout
def, return and yield	Defining functions	def fct(a): return a * 3
class	To build objects	class subclass: newData=[]
global	Defining a global variable	def fct(): global a, return a * 3
del	To delete items	del data
assert	To check to debug	assert A == B

Statements that are related to larger programming subjects like developing functions, modules, and debugging will be covered separately in the upcoming chapters of this book. Chapters are dedicated to each programming subject. In this chapter, we will cover the assignment syntax, expression statements, the if test, and the loops. Let's start with the basic statement which is the assignment.

So far, in this chapter, we have been already using the assignment statement. The assignment statement allows assigning a data object to a variable name. Basically, you write an assignment statement using the operator '=' where on the left, you have the target, and the on the right is that the data to be assigned. The target can be either a variable name or component of an object. On the right can be a single value or an expression that evaluates an object. Overall, the assignment is very simple, but you should consider some properties. Assignment in Python saves objects references in names or data structure. When an assignment is used, it does not copy the object, but it creates a reference to the object.

Unlike C language, for example, variables in Python are similar to pointers and not just data storage. This means when you use or modify a variable inside a function, it is modified through the entire script not just locally.

282

On the contrary, if a variable in C is modified in a function, it is modified only locally and not in the whole script. When first assigned, names are created. In Python, a variable name is created on the first time you assign a value to it. Python does not require a pre-declaration of variable names beforehand. When assigned, the variable name is replaced by the value that references in each expression they belong to. Before being referenced, the variable name must be assigned.

If a variable name is used before it is assigned to a reference data object, Python throws an error. Python uses some other implicit assignments when importing modules, defining functions or classes, in function arguments that we will see later in this book. Assignment works the same in any context and whether it is implicit or explicit, the assignment always binds an object reference to a variable name. Assignment has a few forms that are presented in the table below.

Table 6: Forms of Assignment Statements

Statement	Explanation
A = 5	Basic assignment form
A, B = 5, 6	Multiple assignment
A = 5, 6	Assignment of tuple
A = (5, 6)	Assignment of tuple
A = [4, 5]	Assignment of list
A = B = 'true'	Multiple target assignment

The first two forms of the assignment are the most basic forms. The three following forms of assignment (list and tuple assignment) are called list / tuple unpacking assignment. In these forms of assignment, Python creates first a tuple / list of the elements on the right. Then it pairs from left to right to the variable name. The last form assignment, multiple target assignment, Python assigns the same data reference to multiple target variables. This assignment is the same as writing two lines of codes to assign A = 'true' and B = 'true'.

283

In the following code examples, we will cover some illustration of assignment forms and tricks coding in Python. Here we present some basic unpacking assignments.

```
>>> Age = 30
>>> Name = 'John'
>>> A, B = Age, Name
>>> print (' This is an example of tuple unpacking assignment:
')
>>> A, B
(30, 'John')
>>> [X, Y] = [Age, Name]
>>> print (' This is an example of list unpacking assignment: ',
X, Y)
This is an example of list unpacking assignment: [30, 'John']
```

The reference values found on the right is stored in a temporary tuple. Since the temporary tuple is defined by Python, tuple unpacking assignment may be used to replace 2 variables while not having to define a temporary variable. The following example illustrates how to swap two variables with unpacking assignment.

```
>>> Age = 30
>>> Name = 'John'
>>> Age, Name
(30, 'John')
```

```
>>> Name, Age = Age, Name

>>> print ('This is an example of swapping variables with
unpacking assignment: ')
```

This is an example of swapping variables with unpacking
assignment:

```
>>> Age, Name

('John', 30)
```

In Python, any sequence of values or data can be assigned to a tuple or list on
the condition that the sequence has the same length. A list of values can be
assigned to a tuple and vice-versa. A string can also be assigned to a tuple. In
general, Python would assign the right items to the left items in sequence from
left to right by position. Let's see some illustrations.

```
>>> [X, Y, Z] = (30, 400, 50)

>>> print (' This is an example of assigning a tuple to a list:')
```

This is an example of assigning a tuple to a list:

```
>>> X, Y, Z

(30, 400, 50)

>>> (X, Y, Z) = 'ade'

>>> print (' This is an example of assigning a string to a tuple:')
```

This is an example of assigning a string to a tuple:

```
>>> X, Y, Z

('a', 'd', 'e')
```

An unpacking assignment allows assigning a sequence of integer to multiple variables. In fact, Python has a built-in function which is a range that returns a sequence of integers. This function is very useful when working with for loops that we are going to see later in this chapter.

In the next example, we provide an illustration of assigning a series of integers to a tuple.

>>> A, B, C = range (3)

>>> print (' This is an example assigning a sequence of integers:', A, B, C)

This is an example assigning a sequence of integers: 0 1 2

Now that we have covered the assignment statement, it is worth mentioning that rules should be respected when choosing a variable name. We have already seen in Chapter 2 of this book that variable names should always start by an underscore or a letter and only alpha-numeric characters are permitted. In general, a name of a variable should respect the following syntax: letter or underscore + letter, underscore or digit. A named variable like 1_var, var# or $%var is not permitted variable names. In Python, the case is important and variables names are case sensitive. For instance, Var, var, and VAR are three different variable names. Python has reversed words that are permitted to be variable names. Basically, these reversed words are lowercase and are used by the Python system. For instance, if you try assigning a value to 'and' Python will throw a syntax error:

>>> and = 4

File "<stdin>", line 1

and = 4

^

SyntaxError: invalid syntax

The same variable name can be used if it is uppercase:

```
>>> AND = 4
>>> AND
4
```

Overall, the reversed words cannot be redefined. This applies also to module and function names. You might be able to define a module as ' and.py' or a function as ' and() ', but Python will generate an error when you try to call the function or import the module. The following table presents all reversed words that are not permitted as variable names.

Table 7: Reverse word in Python not permitted as variable names.

and	elif	global	or	yield
assert	else	if	pass	def
break	except	import	print	continue
class	exec	del	from	for
finally	in	is	return	try
lambda	while	not	raise	

In addition to the rules mentioned above to name a variable, there are some conventions that should be considered. They are a requirement but considered the common practice. The names of the variables that end and start with 2 underscores, for example, __X__, are typically considered by the interpreter of Python as system variable names. Naming variables in that manner should be avoided. The statement ' from module import ' cannot import names with a single underscore like _name. If a variable name starts with two underscores and does not end with another two, it is located to enclosing classes.

287

A name that is only in the form of a single underscore (i.e. _) save the last expression result in the interactive session of Python. These were the major naming rules and conventions that you should consider when choosing a name to a variable. In the following examples, we are going to cover some useful assignment statement that is commonly used within the if test and loops that we are going to cover later in this chapter. These assignment statements are inspired by the C programming language and mainly a shorthand. They typically combine an assignment with a binary expression. The following table summarizes these statements known as augmented assignment statements.

Table 8: List of Python augmented assignment.

Assignment	Equivalent	Assignment	Equivalent
A += B	A = A + B	A -= B	A = A - B
A &= B	A = A & B	A ** = Y	A = A ** B
A // = B	A = A // B	A /= B	A = A / B
A %= B	A = A % B	A | = B	A = A | B

Let's go back to the Python interactive session and see some examples of these assignments. We start first by the operator '+='.

>>> A = 10
>>> A = A + 1
>>> print (' A incremented by traditional assignment:', A)
A incremented by traditional assignment: 11
>>> A = 10
>>> A += 1
>>> print (' A incremented by augmented assignment:',

A)

A incremented by augmented assignment: 11

Note that both yield to the very same results. However, the augmented assignment ' A += 1 ' is faster because Python needs to evaluate the variable 'A' one time. On the contrary with the basic form ' A = A + 1', the variable needs to be evaluated twice because it appears in the expression twice. This augmented assignment '+=' works as concatenation when applied to strings and, as mentioned, works faster than the basic concatenation formulation.

>>> A = 'Example'

>>> A += ' number 1'

>>> print (' This is an example of augmented assignment on strings type:', A)

This is an example of augmented assignment on strings type: Example number 1

The same augmented assignment can be applied to a list.

For instance,

>>> List = [30, 40, 50]

>>> List += [2, 5, 8]

>>> print (' This is an example of augmented assignment on List type:', List)

This is an example of augmented assignment on List type: [30, 40, 50, 2, 5, 8]

In short, augmented assignment perform faster because variables on the left need to be evaluated once and require less typing. In addition, they allow the interpreter to choose automatically the best technique to evaluate the expression. If an object supports in-place modification like lists, the augmented assignment would perform the in-place modification instead of creating a copy.

Syntax rules in Python

Before diving into if test and loops, in this section, we are going to address the syntax rules that should be followed when coding with Python. Python syntax is generally simple. However, there are some rules to respect. Globally, there are no braces or parentheses around the statements block in Python. Instead, Python relies on indentation to delimit or group blocks of code nested under a header. Unlike other programming languages, Python does not use a semicolon to indicate the end of the statement. The line end is the statement end on that particular line. When launched, program statements are executed by Python from first to last until there is an indication to jump a block of statements. Python would jump a block of statements if it meets an if a test or a loop as we are going to see later in this chapter. These statements are called the control flow because they control which statements to run or to jump. Blank lines are generally ignored by the interpreter as well as lines starting by a ' # ' character. In fact, any line that starts with the ' # ' character is considered a comment. Hence, it is ignored by the Python interpreter.

There is another type of comments supported by Python that is known as the documentation strings. They are also known as docstrings in short. This form of comment is retained by the Python interpreter. They show up at the header of a program file. They are associated with objects and can also be printed alongside the documentation. Although Python interpreter retains the docstrings, they are ignored.

Remember that indentation is very important in Python and indicates the level of a block. If the indentation is not used appropriately and consistently, Python throws an error. The if statements and loops generally have a header line as we are going to see in the following chapters.

290

Block of codes to run each header whether it is a loop or an if test. Globally, when developing a Python program, the form or syntax of the program should look like:

Code block level 0

Header statement:

Code block level 1

Header statement:

Code block level 2

....

Code block level 1

Code block level 0

Note that in the example syntax presented above, each code block line up to the right in the same distance as considered from the same block. Codes that are deeply nested are just more intended to the right compared to the upper enclosing code.

If a statement doesn't fit in a single line because it is too long, there are few rules to respect to make them continue on a few lines. Python support continuing a statement in more than one line if it is enclosed between brackets, parenthesis, or curly braces. All statements that are between parenthesis, assigning lists, dictionaries, and tuples can be performed on more than one line. These statements end at the line where the closing part appears. Only the first line where the statement begins should be intended correctly and the continuous lines can be at any level.

For instance, we declare in the following example a list on several lines:

```
>>> A = [ 9,
... 8,
... 10,
... 100]
>>> print (' That was a list declaration on multiple lines:', A)
That was a list declaration on multiple lines: [9, 8, 10, 100].
```

This type of statements continuing on several lines can be used for anything between () like expressions, or function headers or arguments.

For example:

```
>>> A = 2
>>> B = 3
>>> if (A == 1
... and B == 3):
... print ('YES')
... else:
... print('NO')
...
NO
```

Note that in this example, only the statement under the header of the if and else statements should be intended. The continuing line of the if the header does not have to be intended.

Python support writing more than one statement in one line separated by a semicolon. For instance:

>>> A = 3; B = 90; C = 900

>>> print (' That was an example of multiple statements in a single line:', A, B, C)

That was an example of multiple statements in a single line: 3 90 900

Python If Test and Its Variations

This chapter section will cover the if test which is a statement that allows choosing from a series of possible operations according to the result of a test. In this, we will cover also the Boolean expressions and truth tests. We will also see in detail the embedded statement syntax.

The if statement is typically a formal procedure in programming languages. This statement is in the form of if test then a set of options of operations to perform or another elif (i.e. else if) and ends with a block of else. The block of else is optional. After every test (if and elif) and else, there is an embedded block of operations that is indented under the test header. When running Python on if test, it performs the block of operations that are assigned to the first test which is satisfied (i.e. returns true) otherwise, it performs the else block if all tests are not true.

293

Basically, the if statement takes the general form presented below:

```
if < condition or test >:
        < block of statements >
elif < condition or test >:
        < block of statements >
else:
        < block of statements >
```

Only the if statement and the associated block are required. The other elif and else blocks are optional. Let's practice some examples in the interactive session and see how the if statement how works under Python. In the very basic case, an if statement can be run alone when you need to run an operation when a condition is met. The following code example provides an illustration.

```
>>> X = 9
>>> if (X == 9):
... print ('YES')
...
YES
```

Notice here that the prompt changed to ' ... ' which means the continuation of lines in the basic Operating system. If working in IDLE, you have to intend the block after the If header. Here in the interactive session, a blank line ends the statement and runs the if block.

In the following code, we illustrate the most common form used of the if test:

```
>>> X = 0
>>> if (X == 9):
... print (' YES ')
... else:
... print (' NO ')
...
NO
```

In the next code example, we provide an illustration of the complete form of the if statement with all blocks. This is typically used when you have multiple conditions to evaluate in order to choose to right operations to perform within your code.

```
>>> A = ' TIGER '
>>> if (A == 'John '):
... print ('HOW are you, John?')
... elif (A == 'Dog'):
... print (' What is the name of the dog? ')
... else:
... print (' WARNING: DANGER ')
...
WARNING: DANGER
```

Note that, in this example, Python runs through all blocks because they all return false statement. Now, you might be wondering how to select an action based on the value of a variable. In fact, Python does not have a switch or case statements like C programming language or Pascal. If you are not familiar with these programming languages, the switch and case are statements that allow performing an action according to its value. In Python, the if/elif/else statement is used in series instead. In the following example, we provide an illustration of performing an operation based on the value of the variable ' A '.

```
>>> A = 3

>>> if (A == 1):

... print ('The month is January')

... elif (A == 2):

... print ('The month is February')

... elif (A == 3):

... print ('The month is March')

... else:

... print ('This is another month')

...

The month is March
```

Another way to implement this example and requires less typing is by using a dictionary. In fact, a dictionary associates with each key value.

To use a dictionary in the previous example, we should do something like:

```
>>> B = {'1': ' The month is January ', ' 2 ': ' The month is February ',

...      '3': ' The month is March '}

>>> print (B.get (' 1 '))

This month is January

>>> print (B.get (5))

None
```

Note here that when a key is not found in the dictionary, it returns None by default which would be like the else statement in an if test. In short, dictionaries can be a very good alternative to implement a simple procedure that selects an option according to variable possible values where these possible values are the keys of the dictionary. In the rest of this section, we are going to discuss the truth test that is usually used within an if test. In the previous chapters, we have introduced comparisons operator used on strings and numbers and so on.

Basically, these are Boolean operators that return True or False, 0 or 1 depending on the operation or the comparison used. Overall, true is returned when an object is a non-zero number or not empty. False is returned if an object is zero number or empty or is None. The equality test and comparisons are applied to data objects and return 1 or 0. The logic operators 'and' and 'or' returns true or false.

Let's see some examples in the Python interactive session.

```
>>> A = 3
>>> B = 5
>>> A == 3 and B == 4
False
>>> A == 3 or B == 4
True
>>> [] or 5
5
```

Note here that in the last line, Python evaluates both the left and the right side and returns the right value or because the left is false. Basically, when used in an if test or a while loop, Python uses a Boolean which is a logical true or false.

Loops in Python (while and for loop)

In this section, we discuss the main two loops in Python that repeats a block of code over and over. The first loop format is the while loop which supports a general looping statement and the second loop format is the for loop that goes through elements of a sequence data structure and runs a specific code. Other forms of loops are supported in Python that includes 'break' and 'continue' which we will cover in the next section. A while loop is a broad form of iteration construct.

The while loop typically runs the same code over and over as long as a condition is true. When this is evaluated to false, Python interpreter skips the code intended under the while header and runs the following code statements. In the simplest form of the while loop, the syntax is as follows:

while < test or condition >:

Block of code

Python will run, in this case, the block of code until the test is evaluated to false.

The other form of Python is more complex looks like:

while < test or condition >:
Block of code
else:
Block of code 2

In this form, Python will run the block of code 2 if it does not exit the while loop with a break. Now, let's go back to the interactive session of Python and see some examples of a while loop.

```
>>> A = ' NAME '
>>> while A:
... print (' This is an example of while loop:', A)
... A = A [1:]
...
This is an example of while loop: NAME
```

This is an example of while loop: AME

This is an example of while loop: ME

This is an example of while loop: E

In this example, the while loop runs the code as long as the variable 'A ' is not empty. The code consists of printing the value of the variable 'A' and removing one character. Note that one major problem that you should pay attention to when using the while loop is that this loop may run forever if the test is always evaluated as true. Hence, checking and making sure that the test is evaluated to false at some point to exit the loop. The for loop consist of iterating through elements of a sequence object that can be string, list, dictionary, tuple or any other class object. Basically, the number of iterations is known beforehand unlike the while loop that runs according to a test value. The for loop syntax is very easy and takes the form of a header line and block of statements to run over and over and optionally an else statement like the while loop.

The header of the for loop indicates a target and the data object that it iterates trough. The general syntax is as follows:

for < i > in < data object >:

      block of code

else:

      block of code 2

When running a for loop, Python attribute elements of the data object to the 'i' variable. Then it evaluates the block of the code for each item of the data object stored in 'i'. This variable 'i' is assigned in the header of the loop and can be changed inside the loop and is updated automatically to the next element in the sequence whenever the control is evaluating the header of the loop.

Typically, this variable takes the value of the last item evaluated in the sequence when the loop is over. If the loop did not exit with a break statement and was run accurately, the variable 'i' would refer to the very last item in the sequence. The optional else block works similarly as for the while loop. If the for loop did not exit with a break, it will run the code block assigned to the else statement. Now, let's see examples in the interactive session of Python. The first example presents an illustration of applying a for loop on a list of strings. This example goes through string items of a list and prints each element.

```
>>> List = ['John', 'Brian', 'Mike', 'James']
>>> for i in List:
... print ('Name is:', i)
...
Name is: John
Name is: Brian
Name is: Mike
Name is: James
```

Note here that in the loop, each string element is assigned to the variable 'i'. We can also use the position indexing to loop over items of a list. For the previous example, we would do:

```
>>> List = ['John', 'Brian', 'Mike', 'James']
>>> for i in range (len (List)):
... print ('Name is:', List [i])
...
Name is: John
Name is: Brian
Name is: Mike
Name is: James
```

The second application of the for loop is useful when you are assigning elements from the sequence to another sequence by position. We will see in the next example an application of the for loop on a list of numbers.

In this example, we compute the sum of elements of a list.

```
>>> A = [10, 200, 4, -100]
>>> X = 0
>>> for i in A:
... X+= i
... print (' A loop example on list of numbers, the sum is:', X)
...
A loop example on list of numbers, the sum is: 10
A loop example on list of numbers, the sum is: 210
A loop example on list of numbers, the sum is: 214
A loop example on list of numbers, the sum is: 114
```

If a single statement is to be evaluated within the loop body, the for loop header and the statement can be written in the same line. For instance, the previous example becomes without the print statement as:

```
>>> A = [10, 200, 4, -100]
>>> X = 0
>>> for i in A: X+=i
...
>>> print (' This is an example of for loop in a single statement, the sum is:', X)
```

This is an example of for loop in a single statement, the sum is: 114

The for loop works the same on a sequence of tuples where the target value will be assigned a tuple. The following two examples illustrate how the for loop work on a tuple sequence.

>>> T = ('John', 'Mike', ' Samuel')

>>> for i in T:

... print ('Name in the tuple is:', i)

...

Name in the tuple is: John
Name in the tuple is: Mike
Name in the tuple is: Samuel

If a list of tuples is provided the loop for works the same. For instance:

>>> T = [('John', 30), ('Mike', 40), ('Samuel', 40)]

>>> for i in T:

... print ('Name and age in list of tuples is:', i)

...

Name and age in list of tuples is: ('John', 30)
Name and age in list of tuples is: ('Mike', 40)
Name and age in list of tuples is: ('Samuel', 40)

In the above example, at each iteration, the target variable ' i ' is assigned a tuple that is in the list sequence. Another way to use the loop for, in this case, is to iterate through two-variable targets where each variable is assigned an element of the tuple in the list.

We can apply this to the previous example as follows:

```
>>> T = [ ('John', 30), ('Mike', 40), ('Samuel', 40)]
>>> for (i, j) in T:
... print (' Name in the list tuple is', i, 'Age in the list tuple is', j)
...

Name in the list tuple is John Age in the list tuple is 30
Name in the list tuple is Mike Age in the list tuple is 40
Name in the list tuple is Samuel Age in the list tuple is 40
```

A function that is useful when working with loops, in particular, the for loop is the range function. This function basically takes as an input of one or two arguments. Then it generates a sequence of order values according to the value of the input arguments. If only one argument is supplied as input, then it generates values in the range 0 to the input value. If it is supplied with two input arguments, then it generates values from the first input value to the second input value. The following code presents an illustration of the range function supplied with one and two arguments.

```
>>> for i in range (4):
... print ('Example of range with one input argument here 4, values are:', i)
...

Example of range with one input argument here 4, values are: 0

Example of range with one input argument here 4, values are: 1

Example of range with one input argument here 4, values are: 2

Example of range with one input argument here 4, values are: 3
```

```
>>> for i in range (3, 6):

... print ('Example of range with 2 input arguments here 3 & 6,
values are:', i)

...

Example of range with 2 input arguments here 3 & 6, values are: 3

Example of range with 2 input arguments here 3 & 6, values are: 4

Example of range with 2 input arguments here 3 & 6, values are: 5
```

We can pass optionally the third argument to the range function. When supplied, this argument is used as a step to generate values from the first to the second input argument values. The next example provides an illustration of the range function supplied with three input arguments.

```
>>> for i in range (3, 10, 2):

... print ('Example of range with 3 input arguments here 3 & 10
& 2, values are:', i)

...

Example of range with 3 input arguments here 3 & 10 & 2, values
are: 3

Example of range with 3 input arguments here 3 & 10 & 2, values
are: 5

Example of range with 3 input arguments here 3 & 10 & 2, values
are: 7

Example of range with 3 input arguments here 3 & 10 & 2, values
are: 9
```

Notice that whether it is supplied by one or two input arguments, the range function does not include this input value in the returned range values. As you can see from these examples, the range function is very useful with loops to repeat a sequence of operations over and over for a specific number of times. The while loop and the for loop can have a much-complicated syntax that allows jumping or exiting the loop when a specific condition is met or a test that evaluates to true. In general, loops can be associated with the statement's break and continue. In the next section, we cover the usage of break and continue within loops of Python.

Continue, Break and Pass Statements with Python Loops

Now that you have seen Python loops, while and for, we will cover the two statements continue and break. These statements only work within a loop. We will also see in more detail the else statement which is related to the break statement. The break statement allows jumping all the codes enclosed in the closest loop. In other words, it exits the enclosing loop. The continue statement, on the other hand, jumps to the closest enclosing loop header. The pass statement is equivalent to not doing anything which is basically a placeholder of an empty statement.

The pass statement is typically used when there is no required action to take and works as an empty body for a statement that is compounded.

Given these definitions, the general complex format of the while loop is as follows:

```
while < test or condition >:

        Block of code

        if <test 1 or condition 1>: break

        if <test or condition 2>: continue


else:

        Block of code 2
```

Note that the break and continue can be placed anywhere within the body loop. However, they are typically placed within an if test to operate as a response to the returned value of a test or a condition as presented above. Now, let's go back to an interactive session to see some examples. In this first example, we will see how the continue statement allows jumping nested statements. The illustration presented displays all odd numbers inferior to 10 and jumps even numbers.

```
>>> A = 10
>>> while A:
... A = A - 1
... if ((A % 2) == 0): continue
... print(A)
...
9
7
5
3
1
```

In this example, there is no need to enclose the print statement within an if test because the continue statement will skip it if the test ' (A % 2) == 0 ' is evaluated to true. Hence, the print statement is run only if the continue statement is not run. The continue statement used here is similar to a 'goto' in other programming languages. If you are just starting with Python, it is best to use continue sparingly. The above example can be written in a more readable way with the print statement assigned to an if test as follows:

```
>>> A = 10
>>> while A:
... A = A - 1
... if (A % 2 != 0) :
... print(A)
...
9
7
5
3
1
```

The next example provides an illustration of the while loop with a break statement. In this example, we read input data from the user until he writes an end.

```
>>> name= []

>>> while name != 'end':

...        name = input ('Enter a name, to stop enter end: ')

...

Enter a name, to stop enter end: 'John'
Enter a name, to stop enter end: 'Mike'
Enter a name, to stop enter end: 'Liam'
Enter a name, to stop enter end: 4
Enter a name, to stop enter end: end
>>>
```

The function input() here is a function of Python version 3 that reads input from the keyboard. Note that when the loop keeps reading from the standard input until the end is entered. Then Python returned >>> into the prompt which means it is ready to take other statements.

In the following example, we illustrate how to combine the break and the else statements in a while loop. In this example, we determine if a given number is prime or not by looking for the numbers factors which are superior to 1.

```
>>> A = 7
>>> B = A / 2
>>> while B > 1:
... if (B % A == 0):
... print (A, ' is factor of', B)
... break
... B = B - 1
... else:
... print (' The number', B, 'is prime')
...
The number 0.5 is prime
```

The break here is very useful that works as a flag when exiting the while loop. In this example, instead of adding an if test to evaluate the value after the while loop is over, a break is inserted to exit when a factor is found.

Otherwise, if the break is not met, the loop assumes that a number is a prime number. Note that even if the loop does not run at all in case the header is false, to begin with, it will return or run the statement assigned to the else because it did not exit with a break in this case. If we try that on the previous example (i.e. B == 0), we still get the message 'The number is prime'.

```
>>> B = 0
>>> while B > 1:
... if (B % A == 0):
... print (A, ' is factor of', B)
... break
... B = B - 1
... else:
... print (' The number', B, 'is prime')
...
The number 0 is prime
```

The else might seem a bit confusing because it is specific to Python's programming. You can think of the else as a way of coding some flags that catch the exit of a loop without explicitly hard coding test to check those flags. Let's say that you are coding a loop that search for an item in a sequence of values and you want to know, after the loop is over, whether it was found or not.

You might think of coding something that looks like the following code:

```
>>>A = [20, 200, 2, 90]
>>>inList = 'NO'
>>>i = 0
>>> while (i < len (A) and inList == 'NO'):
...      if (A [i] == 0):
...              inList = 'YES'
...      else:
...              i = i+1
>>>if (inList == 'NO'):
...      print ('Is not in list ')
... else:
...      print ('Is in list')
Is not in list
```

Here, we have set a flag 'inlist' initialized as 'NO' that we check after the loop is executed to know if the item is in a list or not. This structure of code is what the break and the else statement are designed for. By implementing these two statements, the above code is optimized. First, the loop is stopped once the item is found in the list by inserting the break statement. Second, the else code will be displayed if the loop is run over all items and not found the item. In addition, we have fewer intermediate variables to handle.

The optimized code with break and else statement is as follows:

```
>>> A = [20, 200, 2, 90]
>>> i = 0
>>> while (i < len (A)):
...      if (A [i] == 0): break
...      i = i+1
... else:
...      print ('Is not in the list')
Is not in the list
```

In the same manner, the for loop uses the else and break statements to exit the for loop when a condition is satisfied. The complex form of the for loop is as follows:

```
for < i > in < data object >:
        block of code
        if < condition 1 or test 1 >:
                block of code 2
                break
        if < condition 2 or test 2 >:
                block of code 2
                continue
else:
        block of code 3
```

Like the while loop, when test 1 is evaluated to true, the for loop is exited and the else block is not run. When test 2 is evaluated to true, every statement that appears after is ignored and the loop goes to the header (i.e. evaluate the next item). Now that you understand the sophisticated format of the for loop, let's see some examples in an interactive session.

The following example is similar to the last example of the while loop. We search for an item in a list. This example illustrates also how to use nested loops. We use the break and else statement to exit and return if the item is on the list.

```
>>> A = [20, 40, 90, 50, 60]
>>> B = [9, 90, 'no', 90, 20, 100]
>>>for j in B:
...     for i in A:
...             if j == i:
...                 print ('Element', j, 'is in list')
...                 break
...     else:
...             print ('Element', j, 'is not in list')
Element 20 is in list Element
100 is not in list Element
90 is in list Element
100 is not in list Element
100 is not in list
```

In this example, the first loop goes through the first list 'B's that stores the items being searched for and the second loop goes through the list that is being searched. Both loops are running together. When an item is found in list 'A', the second loop is exited. The else here is assigned to the second loop to return that the item is not the list. The code presented here is just to present an illustration of using a break and else. This code can be optimized by using the 'in' operator that looks for any match in a sequence. The optimized code is as follows:

```
>>> A = [20, 40, 90, 50, 60]
>>> B = [9, 90, 'no', 90, 20, 100]
>>> for j in B:
...     if j in A:
...         print ('Element', j, 'is in list')
...     else:
...         print ('Element', j, 'is not in list')
Element 9 is not in list
Element 90 is in list
Element no is not in list
Element 90 is in list
Element 20 is in list
Element 100 is not in list
```

This code only works for the lists defined here. It would be helpful to be able to run the same code on other lists, too. This is when the function comes very handy. We will cover this topic in the next chapter. The loops we have covered in this section will also be used in chapter 8 of this book that covers files. Indeed, loops are very handy to repeat the same task as long as it is necessary. Files come in the form of several lines that contains several characters. They are the typical use of the for loops. In chapter 8, we will cover how to use loops to read and write files.

Python Exceptions

Python exceptions are events that can have an impact or change the control flow of a script. Exceptions in Python are raised on errors. They can be raised and intercepted by the script. In Python, exceptions are handled using three statements that we will cover in this section. The first statement try has two variations which are ' try/ finally ' and ' try/ except'. The first variation, 'try/ except', catches the exceptions and recovers from it by Python or by the user. The second variation, ' try/finally ', performs a clean-up whether the exception is raised or not. The second statement is ' raise ' and it triggers an exception in the code manually. The third statement is ' assert'. This statement raises an exception conditionally in the script. Now you must be wondering why to use exceptions in a script.

Exceptions are very handy in large programs to keep track if the code is running as expected. In other words, exceptions allow jumping pieces of code when something goes wrong.

Depending on what is expected from the program, when an exception is raised, the code might execute some tasks to recover from the exception that was raised or exit the code completely. In Python, exceptions are used for a wide range of purposes. Exceptions can be used to handle errors. Python is able to automatically trigger errors when it is running. These errors can be caught and assigned a code/task as a response or can be ignored. If the error is being ignored, Python would use the default handling of the error. The program will stop running and an error message will be displayed. Otherwise, if you develop a try statement as a response when the error is being raised, Python would ignore the default handling and would jump to your coded try statement. Hence, your script will continue running after the try.

Exceptions can also be used as a notification for events. In this context, exceptions are used as a validation condition signal without handling and coding flags that are processed in the program. For example, a routine that searches for a particular element might trigger an exception when failed instead of returning a Boolean or integer, as a result, to be tested after. Exceptions can serve to handle a special case. A special case is a condition that can occur rarely. Instead of convoluting the code to take action, an exception can be inserted to take action when unusual cases occur.

Exceptions can be used to stop actions. As mentioned before, the ' try/finally ' statement guarantees that code final closing tasks are executed whether an exception is raised or not during run time. Finally, the exceptions can be used as flow control similar to a ' goto ' statement available in other programming languages. Now that you got the general idea behind exceptions, let's try some examples in the interactive session.

Try/except statement

The syntax for this exception statement is in the following form:

```
try:
    statement or task to run
except < name >:
    statement
```

In order to illustrate the ' try/except ' statement, let's consider a function that we will run as a task in the try block. We define a function that takes as input two arguments where the first is a list and the second is an index. This function returns the element of the index passed as a second argument. Don't worry about functions at this step. We will cover them in more detail in the next chapter.

```
>>>def fct (myList, ind):
...      return (myList[ind])
```

Now, if we try to call this function with the list and the index defined below, we get something like:

```
>>> myList = [20, 40, 50, 70]

>>> ind = 3

>>> A = fct (myList, ind)

>>> print (' element is: ', A)

element is: 70
```

Now, if we try to pass an index equal to superior to 3, Python will throw an error as follows:

```
>>> ind = 8
>>> A = fct (myList, ind)
Traceback (most recent call last):
File "<stdin>", line 1, in <module>
File "<stdin>", line 2, in fct
IndexError: list index out of range
```

Python detects automatically that the index passed is out of the range of the list indices. Then, it raises an error handled by the default IndexError exception which prints a message error along with the number of the lines where the error occurred.

Here we are working in an interactive session, so the lines are not meaningful. If real applications where the program is not run in the interactive session, the program will be stopped from execution by the default top handler. Python throws this error because it is not being raised by the defined function. You can also try to catch the exception when running the function and not trigger the default Python hander using the ' try/except ' statement.

317

The code will be, in this case, to run the function as follows:

```
>>> try:
...         fct (myList, 9)
... except IndexError:
...         print (' This is an exception')
...
This is an exception
>>>
```

In this case, Python ignores the default handler and jumps to the defined handler. The try has stopped the function from running. Then Python displays >>> in the prompt which means it is ready to run statement. In more complex programs and real applications, to recover and catch from the exceptions, you can use the try statement. Then, we would define something like:

```
>>> def catcher():
...         try:
...                 fct (myList, 9)
...         except IndexError:
...         print (' This is an exceptions')
... print (' Will continue running')
...
>>> catcher()
This is an exception
Will continue running
```

Now, the exception is being raised by try, and the program continued running after the exception by printing the message ' Will continue running'. The program resumes normally and runs the following statements.

Try /finally statement

In this sub-section, we illustrate how the ' try/finally ' works. The ' try/finally ' syntax is similar to the ' try/exception ' syntax and is in the form presented below:

```
try:
 statement or task to run
finally:
 statement or task to run
```

This exception statement runs the code assigned to finally, whether try raised an exception or not.

```
>>> Mylist = [20, 300, 900, 90]

>>> ind = 2

>>> try:
...     fct (Mylist, ind)
... finally:
...     print (' This is the finally block')
...

900

This is the finally block
```

Here the finally block is launched with the try block that runs normally without any exception being raised and the script continued running after the try block. This code is similar to displaying the message in the finally block after running the function. So, the code is similar to the following statements:

```
>>> ind = 2
>>> myList = [20, 300, 900, 90]
>>> fct(myList, ind)
900
>>> print ('This is the finally block')
This is the finally block
```

However, in a real application where the code is run outside of the interactive session if the function triggers an exception every code statement after it is not executed. So, we might try a code that resumes after the try statement if something went wrong. For example,

```
>>> def after():
...     try:
...         fct (myList, 9)
...     finally:
...         print ('This is the finally block')
...     print ('This the block after try and finally')
...
>>> after()
This is the finally block
Traceback (most recent call last):
  File "<stdin>", line 1, in <module>
  File "<stdin>", line 3, in after
  File "<stdin>", line 2, in fct
IndexError: list index out of range
```

Now, you can notice the code did not display the message 'This the block after try and finally'. The reason is that the control flow does not continue when an exception is triggered in the try/finally statement. Python executes the code assigned to finally. Then it propagates the error raised in the try section through the code to the default handler in this case. If the function call is changed for a case where it does not raise an error, the code after the try/finally would run.

The code below shows an example:

```
>>> def after():
...     try:
...         fct(myList,0)
...     finally:
...         print ('This the finally block')
...         print ('This the block after try and finally')
...
>>> after()
This the finally block
This the block after try and finally
```

Chapter 5: Functions in Python

This chapter of the book covers functions that are a piece of code that can be executed repeatedly with different variables to generate a different outcome. We have been already using this notion in the previous chapters whether it is using Python's built-in function like print() to display a message in standard output of Python or the function that we defined in the section illustrating exceptions. This chapter makes the emphasis on how to develop functions that compute and return values and how to code a script to be reused easily.

Function Utilities in Programming

Functions are a fundamental concept in any programming language. They are also known as procedures or routines in other programming languages. Functions are very handy when you need to run the same code with different variable values. For instance, you want to compute the factorial of different numbers. Instead of coding the same code for each number, you would define a function that takes as input the number of interests, computes its factorial, and returns the result. This way you just have to call the same function for each number inside a loop for instance. In this context, functions serve for two main purposes. The first is to make the code reusable. They provide a way to package your code such that it is used more than once or in multiple places in the same or different program.

So far, illustrations and code examples presented in this book are run immediately in the interactive session. With functions, the code can be wrapped and generalized to be used several times after. The second purpose of functions is to decompose a program into several pieces where each piece is assigned a role. This is very useful when coding a large program or a framework that replicates the functioning of a complex system. Functions allow us to break down the system into pieces where each piece is coded by a function.

Each function would serve to perform a task in a large system. This way of coding makes it easy to implement complex systems than just implementing a whole system in one chunk of code. You can think of functions as a procedure that allows replicating how to do something. Coding functions does not imply different syntax. In the following sections, we will cover the keywords and the basics to develop functions with Python.

Function Concept, Declaration and Calling in Python

We have been using and calling functions that are built-in Python in the earlier chapters of this book. For example, to compute the length of an object, we call the function len. In this section, we are going to learn how to define new functions. Every new function you define in Python works exactly the same as the built-in functions of Python. Functions are called through statements or expressions and can take input arguments and return a result. Developing new functions requires using additional statements that were presented in table 5 shown in Chapter 4.

In Python, functions act differently compared to complied programming languages (e.g. C or C++).

'def', a new statement, defines the Python functions. This is also an executable code. When you develop a new function, it is not recognized by the Python until it hits a 'def' statement and runs through it. Sometimes, the 'def' statement is inserted in if test or a loop or maybe inside other 'def' statement. In a real application, the 'def' statements are defined within modules. When the module is imported in the Python environment workspace, the functions are generated automatically. We will cover modules in more detail in the next chapter. The 'def' statement makes a new object (i.e. a function) and assigns a name to it. A function object is created and given a name every time a 'def' statement is found by Python. This name is the reference of the function which can be saved in a list or given another name. Functions can send back an object result after they are called. When Python goes through a statement that calls a function, it runs through the function code until it finishes. Then it resumes to the following statements.

If a function returns a value, it communicates it back to the control flow as a return statement. This result is then the outcome of calling this function. Functions can take optionally input arguments that passed as a reference.

Unlike other programming languages such as C or C++, references (i.e. variables) are shared across the function and Python called. This means that a variable that is modified within a function is also modified automatically within the entire code. In other words, if you define a variable name outside a function. Then, later in the code, you call a function that shares the same variable name (i.e. reference) that changes its values.

When the function is finished running and the control is given back to the controller, the variable has the same value that was assigned inside the function and not the value that was assigned before the function call. As we have mentioned in Chapter 2, variables that are assigned inside a function are, by default, local variables. They are defined only inside the function. Once the function finishes running, these variables don't exist anymore. Like any other object data, the function does not need any declaration of any kind prior to use. Inputs arguments, as well as output arguments, can be of any type of data object. Hence, the functions can be called with different data types.

To create a new function, we use the 'def' statement with the following syntax:

def < function name> (argument 1, ..., argument n):

statements or tasks to perform

Like any compound statement in Python, indentation is very imported. All statements that constitute the function body should be intended unless it is one single statement that can appear after the header (i.e. after the colon). The function body is executed every time the function is called. After 'def' is the name of the function which attributed to reference to the function object, followed by the arguments.

The name of arguments is attributed to the data object that is passed to the function when called. If no argument is to be passed to the function, then the syntax is as follows:

def < function name> ():

statements or tasks to perform

Usually, a function returns an output argument or statement. In this case, the syntax of the function includes a return statement as follow:

def < function name> (argument 1, ..., argument n):

statements or tasks to perform

return < output value>

In Python, the 'def ' can appear anywhere in the code, even inside other statement. For example, we can define a function according to a test like follows:

If < condition >:

def my_function():

statement 1

else:

def my_function(argument):

statement 2

326

In the syntax example given above, the function my_function is defined with or without input argument depending on whether the condition is satisfied or not. The 'def' statement works as any Python assignment statement and the function is not defined until the code goes through the 'def' statement. The function name can also be changed anytime by assigning it to another name. For instance, we can do:

Name2= my_function

To call a function we just type in the name of the function with arguments if it takes any.

function_name (argument 1, argument 2, …, argument 3)

Or   function_name ()

In the following sections of this chapter, we are going to present explicitly how functions use arguments and return values with some examples.

Function Expressions, Arguments, and Returned outputs

As we have seen in the previous section, arguments of a function, also called parameters, are passed between parenthesis. When the function is called, Python uses these arguments to reference the date object passed as input.

There is no requirement to declare the type of the data object that the function is expecting as input. Usually, functions are defined within modules and run outside of the interactive session. For the sake of simplicity and the fact we are using simple basic examples, the interactive prompt would be sufficient to run the examples of this book.

The following code is an example of a function that takes as an argument a number, computes and displays a factorial of a number.

```
>>> def Xfactorial (X):
...     P = 1
...     for i in range (1, X + 1):
...         P *= i
...     print ('Factorial of', X, 'is:', P)
```

Now, to call this function, we simply type the name of the function with the number for which we want to compute the factorial. For example:

```
>>> Xfactorial (3)
Factorial of 3 is: 6
```

If we want to save the output of this function in a later use in the code, we use the return statement when defining the function as follows:

```
>>> def Xfactorial (X):
...        P = 1
...        for i in range (1, X + 1):
...                P *= i
...        return P
```

Then when calling the function, we assign the function to a variable as follows:

```
>>> A = Xfactorial (3)
>>> print ('Factorial 3 is:', A)
Factorial 3 is: 6
```

Now, let's consider a simple function that returns the value of X times Y with X and Y two input arguments.

```
>>> def Prod (A, B):
...        return A * B
```

Now, let's call this function with input arguments of different types.

```
>>> A = Prod (2, 3)
>>> print ('This is an example of calling the Prod function
with two integers:', A)
```

This is an example of calling the Prod function with two integers: 6

>>> A = Prod (1.5, 3)

>>> print ('This is an example of calling the Prod function with a float and integer:', A)

This is an example of calling the Prod function with a float and integer: 4.5

>>> A = Prod ('name', 3)

>>> print ('This is an example of calling the Prod function with a string and integer\n:', A)

This is an example of calling the Prod function with a string and integer:

namenamename

>>> A = Prod ('name', 'name')

Traceback (most recent call last):

 File "<stdin>", line 1, in <module>

 File "<stdin>", line 2, in Prod

 TypeError: can't multiply sequence by non-int of type 'str'

In the examples above, we called the function and passed two integers, a float and integer, and a string and an integer. In the first case, it returned an integer. In the second, it returned a float, and in the third, it returned a string. In the final example, we passed two strings input arguments and Python raised an error because multiplication between strings does not exit. Overall, there is no declaration or restriction on the data type that can be passed to a function as long as the operations in the function body are defined. Overall, Python functions allow defining code scripts that are reusable as many times as it is needed.

There are no restrictions on the data object type passed as arguments.

The code becomes general and used in any context as long as the operations inside the function are defined. Moreover, you can define your own operations inside these functions or include exception statements that can handle issues in this case. By coding a script within a function, it makes it easy to make a modification if needed and to be made in one single place. You can also insert a function code within a module file. This way, the function can be imported by importing the module and used within any program or shared with other programs for wide broad use. In fact, this is exactly how packages are developed and used in Python. In the next chapter, we are going to cover this specific topic on how to develop modules with Python.

Chapter 6: Modules in Python

Modules, also known as packages, are a set of names. This is usually a library of functions and/or object classes that are made available to be used within different programs. We used the notion of modules earlier in this chapter to use some function from the math library. In this chapter, we are going to cover in-depth on how to develop and define modules. In order to use modules in a Python program, the following statements are used: import, from, reload. The first one imports the whole module. The second allows import only a specific name or element from the module. The third one, reload, allows reloading a code of a module while Python is running and without stopping in it. Before digging into their definition and development, let's start first by the utility of modules or packages within Python.

Modules Concept and Utility Within Python

Modules are a very simple way to make a system component organized. Basically, modules allow reusing the same code over and over. So far, we were working in a Python interactive session. Every code we have written and tested is lost once we exit the interactive session. Modules are saved in files that make them persistent, reusable, and sharable. You can consider modules as a set of files where you can define functions, names, data objects, attributes, and so on. Modules are a tool to group several components of a system in a single place. In Python programming, modules are among the highest-level unit.

They point to the name of packages and tools. In addition, they allow the sharing of the implemented data. You only need one copy of the module to be able to use across a large program. If an object is to be used in different functions and programs, coding it as a module allows share it with other programmers. To have a sense of the architecture of Python coding, we go through some general structure explanation. We have been using so far in this book very simple code examples that do not really have high-level structure.

In large applications, a program is a set of several Python files. By Python files, we mean files that contain Python code and have a .py extension. There is one main high-level program and the other files are the modules. The high-level file consists of the main code that dictates the control flow and executes the application. Module files define the tools that are needed to process elements and components of the main program and maybe elsewhere. The main program makes use of the tools that are specified in the modules.

In their turn, modules make use of tools that are specified in other modules. When you import a module in Python, you have access to every tool that is declared or defined in that specific module. Attributes are the variables or the functions associated with the tools within a module. Hence, when a module is imported, we have access to the attributes of the tools as well to process them. For instance, let's consider we have two Python files named file1.py and file2.py where the file1.py is the main program and file2.py is the module. In the file2.py, we have a code that defines the following function that we have used in the previous chapter:

```
def Xfactorial (X):

    P = 1

    for i in range (1, X + 1):

        P *= i

    return P
```

In order to use this function in the main program, we should define code statements in the file1.py as follows:

```
Import file2

A = file2.Xfactorial (3)
```

334

The first line imports the module file2.py. This statement means to load the file file2.py. This gives access to the file1.py to all tools and functions defined in file2.py by the name file2. The function Xfactorial is called by the second line. The module file2.py is where this function is defined using the attributes' syntax. The line file2.Xfactorial() means fetch any name value of Xfactorial and lies within the code body of file2. In this example, it is a function that is callable. So, we have provided an input argument and assigned the output result to the variable A.

If we add a third statement to print the variable A and run the file file1.py, it would display 6 which is the factorial of 3. Along Python, you will see the attribute syntax as object.attribute. This basically allows calling the attributes that might be a function or data object that provides properties of the object.

Note that some modules that you might import when programming with Python are available in Python itself. As we have mentioned at the beginning of this book, Python comes with a standard large library that has built-in modules. These modules support all common tasks that might be needed in programming from operating system interfaces to graphical user interface. They are not part of the language. However, they can be imported and comes with a software installation package. You can check the complete list of available modules in a manual that comes with the installation or goes to the official Python website: www.Python.org. This manual is kept updated every time a new version of Python is released.

How to Import a Module

We have talked about importing a module without really explaining what happens behind in Python. Imports are a very fundamental concept in Python programming structure. In this section, we are going to cover in-depth how really Python imports modules within a program. In fact, Python follows three steps to import a file or a module within the work environment of a program. The first step consists of finding the file that contains the module. The second step consists of compiling the module to a byte-code if required.

Finally, the third step runs the code within the module file in order to build the objects that are defined. These three steps are run only when the module is imported for the first time during the execution of a program. This module and all its objects are loaded in the memory. When the module is imported further in the program, it skips all three steps and just fetch the objects defined by the module and are saved in memory. At the very first step of importing a module, Python has to find the module file location. Note that, so far in the examples we presented, we used import without providing the complete path of the module or extension .py. We just used import math, or import file2.py (an example of the previous section). Python import statement omits the extension and the path. We just simply import a module by its name. The reason for this is that Python has a module that looks for paths called 'search path module'. This module is used specifically to find the path of module files that are imported by the import statements. In some cases, you might need to configure the path search of modules in order to be able to use new modules that are not part of the standard library. You need to customize it in order to include these new modules. The search path is simply the concatenation of the home directory, directories of PYTHONPATH, directories of the standard library, and optionally if the content of files with extension .pth when they exist. The home directory is set automatically by the system to a directory of Python executable when launched from the interactive session, or it can be modified to the working directory where your program is saved. This directory is the first to be searched when import a module is run without a path. Hence, if your home directory points to a directory that includes your program along with the modules, importing these modules does not require any path specification.

The directory of the standard library is also searched automatically. This directory contains all default libraries that come with Python. The directories of PYTHONPATH can be set in order to point toward the directory of new modules that are developed.

In fact, PTYHONPATH is an environment variable that contains a list of directories that contains Python files. When PTYHONPATH is set, all these paths are included in the Python environment and the search path directory would search these directories too when importing modules. Python also allows defining a file with .pth extension that contains directories, one in each line. This file serves the same as PTYHONPATH when included appropriately in a directory.

336

You can check the directories' paths included when you run Python using sys.path. You simply print sys.path to get the list of the directories that Python will be searching for.

Remember, when importing a module, we just use the name of the module without its extension. When Python is searching for a module in its environment paths, it selects the first name that matches the module name regardless of the extension. Because Python allows using packages that are coded in other languages, it does not simply select a module with .py extension but a file name or even a zip file name that matches the module name being imported. Therefore, you should name your modules distinctly and configure the search path in a manner that makes it obvious to choose a module. When Python finds the source code of the module file with a name that corresponds to the name in the import statement, it will compile it into byte code in case it is required. This step is skipped if Python finds an already byte code file with no source code.

If the source code has been modified, another byte code file is automatically regenerated by Python while the program runs in other further executions. Byte code files have typically .pyc extension. When Python is searching and finds the module file name, it will load the byte code file that corresponds to the latest version of the source code with .py extension. If the source code is newer than the byte code file, it will generate a new one by compiling the source code file. Note that only imported files have corresponding files with .pyc extension. These files, the byte code files, are stored on your machine to make the imports faster in future use.

The third step of the import statement is running the module's byte code. Each statement and each assignment in the file are executed. This allows generating any function, data objects, and so on defined in the module. The functions and all attributes are accessed within the program via importers. During this step, you will see print statements if they exist. The 'def' statement will create a function object to be used in the main program.

To summarize the import statement, involve searching for the file, compiling it, and running the byte code file. All other imports statement uses the module stored in memory and ignore all the three steps. When first imported, Python will look in the search path module to select the module.

337

Hence, it is important to configure correctly the path environment variable to point to the directory that contains new defined modules. Now that you have the big picture and the concept of modules, let's explore how we can define and develop new modules.

How to write and use a module in Python?

Modules in Python can be created very easily and do not require any specific syntax. Modules are simply files with a .py extension that contains Python code. You can use a text editor like Notepad++ to develop and write modules then save them in files with the .py extension. Then, you just import these files like we have seen in the previous section to make use of the contained code. When you create a module, all the data object including functions that are defined becomes the module attributes. These attributes are accessed and used via the attribute syntax like follows: module.attribute. For instance, if we define a module named ' MyModule.py ' that has the following function:

```
def Myfct (A):

    print (' A by 2 is: ', A * 2)

    return A * 2
```

The function ' Myfct ' becomes the attribute of the module ' MyModule.py '. Basically, you can call a module any Python code that you develop and save in a file with a .py extension if you are importing them in later use. Module names are referenced variables. Hence, when naming a module, you should follow the same rules as for variable naming. You might be able to name your module anything you want. But if the rules are not respected, Python throws an error.

For instance, if you name your module $2P.py, you will not be able to import it and Python would trigger a syntax error.

338

Directory names that contain the module and Python packages should follow the same rules. In addition, their names cannot contain any space. In the rest of this section, we are going to provide some code examples of defining and using modules. There are two statements that can be employed to make use of a module. The first one is the import statement we have covered in the previous section. Let's consider again the previous example to illustrate a module 'MyModule.py' that contains ' Myfct' function:

```
def Myfct(A):

    print (A, 'by 2 is: ', A * 2)
```

Now, to use this module, we import it using the following statements:

```
>>> import MyModule
>>> MyModule.Myfct(2)
2 by 2 is: 4
```

Now, the MyModule name is being used by Python to load the file and as a variable in the program. The module name should be used to access all its attributes. Another way to import and use a module attribute is by using the 'from import' statement.

This statement works in the same manner as the import statement we have been using. Instead of using the module name to fetch for its attributes, we can access the attributes by their names directly.

For example:

```
>>> from MyModule import Myfct
>>> Myfct (2)
2 by 2 is: 4
```

Basically, this statement makes a copy of the function name without using the module name. There is another form of 'from import' statement that uses an *. This statement allows copying all names that are assigned to objects in the module. For example:

```
>>> from MyModule import *
>>> Myfct (2)
2 by 2 is: 4
```

Because modules names become variables (i.e. references to objects), Python supports importing a module with an alias. Then we can access its attributes using the alias instead of its name. For instance, we can attribute an alias to our module like follows:

```
>>> import Mymodule as md
>>> md.Myfct(2)
2 by 2 is: 4
```

Data objects other than functions are accessed the same way with attribute syntax. For instance, we can define and initialize data objects in modules than used them later in the program. Let's consider the following code to create a module named ExModule.py.

```
A = 9

Name = 'John'
```

In this example, we initialize both variables A and Name. Now, after importing the module, we can get both variables as follows:

```
>>> import ExModule

>>> print ('A is: ', ExModule.A)

A is: 9

>>> print ('Name is: ', Exmodule.Name)

Name is: John
```

Or we can assign the attributes to other variables. For instance:

```
>>> import ExModule

>>> B = ExModule.A

>>> print ('B is: ', B)

B is: 9
```

If we use the 'from import' statement to import the attributes, the names of the attributes become variables in the script. For example:

>>> from Exmodule import A, Name

>>> print ('A is: ', A, 'and Name is: ', Name)

A is 9 and Name is John

Note that from the import statement supports importing multiple attributes in one single line. Python allows changing objects that are sharable. For instance, let's consider the following code to define the module named ExModul1.py:

A = 9

MyList = [90, 40, 80]

Now, let's import this module and try to change the values of the attributes to see how Python behaves.

>>> from ExModule1 import A, MyList

>>> A = 20

>>> myList [0] = 100

Now, let's re-import the module and print those two attributes and see what changes Python has made.

> >>> import ExModule1
>
> >>> print (' A is: ', ExModule1.A)
>
> A is: 9
>
> >>> print ('My list is: ', ExModule.myList)
>
> My list is: [100, 40, 80]

You can notice that Python has changed the value of the first element of the list but did not change the value of the variable 'A' to the value we assigned before. The reason is that when a mutable object like lists is changed locally, the changes apply also in the module from which they were imported. Reassigning a fetched variable name does not reassign the reference in the module from which it was imported. In fact, there is no link between the reference variable name copied and the file it was copied from. In order to make a valid modification in the script and the module it is imported from, we should use the import statement like follows:

> >>> import ExModule1
>
> >>> ExModule1.A = 200

The difference between changing the attributes 'A' and 'myList' is the fact that 'A' is a variable name and 'myList' is an object data. That is why modification to the variable 'A' should use import to be applied in the module file, too.

We have mentioned that importing a module for the first time in a script implies going through three steps that are searching for the module, compiling the module, and running the module. All other imports of the module later in the script skip all these three steps and access to module loaded in the memory. Now, let's try an example to see how this really works. Consider we have a module with the following code and named ExModule2.py:

```python
print (' Hello World\n')

print (' This is my first module in Python')

A = 9
```

Now, let's import this module and see how Python behaves when importing this module:

```
>>> import ExModule2

Hello World

This is my first module in Python

>>>
```

You can notice that when importing this module, it displays both messages. Now, let's try to reassign a value to the attribute ' A', then re-import the module with the import statement.

```
>>> ExModule.A = 100

>>> import Exmodule2

>>>
```

As you can note from the example, Python did not display the messages, 'Hello World' and 'This is my first module in Python' because it did not re-run the module. It just used the module that is already loaded in the memory. In order to make Python really goes through all steps of importing a module for the second time in a script, we should use the reload statement. When using this statement, we force Python to import the module as it would for the first time. In addition, it helps make modifications in the program while it is running without interrupting it. It also helps see instantly the modifications that are made. The reload is actually a function and not a statement in Python that takes as argument a module that is already loaded in memory.

Because reload is a function and expects an argument, this argument should be already assigned an object which is a module object. If for some reason the import statement failed to import a module, you will not be able to reload it. You have to repeat the import statement until it imports the module successfully.

Like any other function, the reload takes the module name reference between parenthesis. The general form of using reload with import is as follows:

import module_name

list of statements that use module attributes

reload(module_name)

list of statements that use module attributes

The module object is changed by the reload function. Hence, any reference to that module in your scripts is impacted by the reload function. Those statements that use the module attributes will be using the values of the new attributes if they are modified. The reload function overwrites the module source code and re-runs it instead of deleting the file and creating a new one.

In the following code example, we will see a concrete illustration of the reload functioning. We consider the following code to create a module named ExModule3.py:

```
my_message = ' This is my module first version'

def display ():

    print (my_message)
```

This module simply assigns a string to the variable 'my_message' and print it. Now, let's import this module in Python and call the attribute function:

```
>>> import ExModule3

>>> Exmodule3.display()

This is my module first version

>>>
```

Now, go to your text editor and edit the module source code without stopping the Python prompt shell.

You can make a change as follows:

```
my_message = ' This is my module second version edited in the text editor'

def display ():

    print (my_message)
```

Now, back to the interactive session of Python in the prompt shell, you can try to import the module and call the function:

>>> import ExModule3

>>> Exmodule3.display()

This is my module first version

>>>

As you can notice that the message did not change although the source code file was modified. As said before, all imports after the first import use the already loaded module in memory. To get the new message and access the modification made in the module, we use the reload function:

>>> reload (ExModule3)

<module 'ExModule3)>

>>> Exmodule3.display()

This is my module second version edited in the text editor

Note that the reload function re-runs module and returns the module object. Because it was executed in the interactive session, it displays < module name> by default.

Chapter 7: Python Debugging

In some cases, a program is developed, but when running, it does not provide the desired outcome or it gets stuck somewhere in the workflow. This implies that the program should be scrutinized while it is running on a test in order to get a sense of where the program should be corrected or where things go wrong. This action is what is named by programmers debugging. This task is actively used in order to make sure that a program is running as it is supposed to be. In this chapter, we will cover this topic and present the commands that are available to debug Python programs. First, let's talk in-depth about what is debugging.

What is debugging?

Debugging is simply the process of finding and fixing errors in a program. Debugging verifies the functioning of a program to fix statements of operations that make the program stack and not running appropriately. The simplest and most obvious way to debug a program is using the print function in order to spot the output of functions or variables. In general, the print allows getting information to have a look inside of the functioning of the program. However, this method has several drawbacks. The major is that you need to add changes to the code several times in order to add the print in places where you need to extract information. These places are commonly known as breakpoints. Then you have to run the program every time. There are some advanced debugger tools that can be used.

These tools mostly are very efficient and allow saving a great amount of time when used compared to debugging with print. Python has a debugger that comes by default with the software when installed. This debugger is simply a tool that gives ways to get a look at the code while it is running. When using this tool, you can make changes instantly in the code and alter the values of the variables all while you run the code in chunks. The debugger that comes with Python is named pdb. This tool is in the form of a command-line interface.

This debugger, as any package, is imported with the import statement in order to be able to use it.

import pdb, pdb.set_trace.

In order to be used, the debugger should be imported into the program you wish to debug. When Python interpreter runs this line, you will be redirected to a prompt command on your terminal in which the program is launched. Typically, this is the prompt of Python with commands that allows you to evaluate your code. We cover the list of these commands in the following section.

Python Debugger Commands

Python default debugger has several debugging commands which are presented in the table below. Here we cover the most basic one. The first command, list, allows you to list the line where the control workflow is on.

You can check specific parts of your code by passing their first and last lines as arguments to the list command. You can also check the code around a specific line bypassing only the number of this line to the list command. The up and down commands allow navigating around the code of your program. By using these commands, you are able to know which statement is calling the function that is currently running or understand reasons why the interpreter is behaving or running certain code parts. The next and step are commands that allow resuming execution of the code line by line. The next command will jump to the following line of the function that is currently running even if it calls another function. On the contrary, the step function allows you to go deeper in the code chain rather than just executing the following line. Finally, the break is a command that enables adding new breakpoints with no requirements to make any modifications in the source code.

Table 9: List Python debugger commands

Debug command	Explanation
Alias or a	allows creating an alias to the command
args or rgs	allows showing the list of arguments
break or b	allows setting breakpoints.
disable	allows disabling breakpoints supplied as a list separated by a space
ignore	allows setting a count for a number of breakpoints
commands	allows specifying a command list for a number of breakpoints
continue or c or cont	continue running the code until it reaches a breakpoint
exit	quit the debugger
interact	launch an interpreter that is interactive
list or l	allows showing the code for specific lines
next or n	resumes execution until the following line of the function currently running
restart	allows restarting the program
step or s	run expression in the current line
unalias	removes alias
where or w	displays a trace of the recent last frame
down or d	goes to the next line down
up or u	goes to the above line
clear or cl	allows clearing all breakpoints
enable	allows enabling breakpoints

condition	allows setting conditions for breakpoints as a test that should be evaluated to true in order to set the breakpoint
p	allows evaluating the expression in the current line
help or h	If no argument is supplied, displays list of commands, otherwise, displays information about the command passed as an argument
jump or j	allows setting the number of the line to run next; it allows jumping code parts or running the code from the start
longlist or ll	allows showing the whole code for the function currently running
quit or q	exit the debugger and abort the program
return or r	continue running the code until hits a function return
tbreak	allows making a temporary breakpoint
until or ill	if no argument is passed, it continues running the code until a line which has a number superior to the current is reached
whatis	displays the expression type

Now that you know the concept behind debugging and its basic commands, let's see a real example. We consider the following code saved in a file named test.py.

```
def Myfct1 (A):

    print ('A by 2 is:', A * 2)

return A * 2


def Myfct2 (B, A):

    C = B * A

A = 4

B = 'name'

Myfct2 (B, A)
```

You can notice that this code does not import Python debugger, the pdb module. Instead, we are going to launch the function in the prompt with Python in a debugger mode with the following command:

```
C:\Users\***\Desktop>Python -m pdb test.py

> c:\users\***\desktop\test.py(1)<module>()

-> def Myfct (A):

(Pdb)
```

As you can see, Python did not return the usual >>> in the prompt but it returned instead (Pdb). This means that the debugger is waiting for debugger commands. Now, let's test some of the commands listed in Table 9 above to get a sense of how the debugger works. We start by the list command.

```
(Pdb) list
1 -> def Myfct1(A):
2 print ('A by 2 is:', A * 2)
3 return A * 2
4
5 def Myfct2(B, A):
6 C = B * A
7
8 A = 4
9 B = 'name'
10 Myfct2(B, A)
[EOF]
```

In this example, we applied the list command with no argument. It returned the content of the file with line numbers. If we pass arguments (i.e. line numbers) to the list command, it will return only the code that shows between these lines. For instance:

```
(Pdb) list 2, 3
 2 print ('A by 2 is:', A * 2)
 3 return A * 2
(Pdb)
```

If we use now the next command it will return, the next line after where the current curser is:

(Pdb) next

> c:\users***\desktop\test.py(5)<module>()

-> def Myfct2(B, A):

(Pdb)

We skip lines in the debugger using the jump command as follows:

(Pdb) jump 8

> c:\users*****\desktop\test.py(8)<module>()

-> A = 4

(Pdb)

If we try to print the variable 'A', Python will display a name error because this statement is not yet executed. The curser is just pointing to this line:

(Pdb) A

*** NameError: name 'A' is not defined

(Pdb)

Now, in order to print variable names, we should actually run the program with commands that actually run the program not just show its content. Among these commands is the continue command. So, let's run now the continue command:

(Pdb) continue

Traceback (most recent call last):

File "C:\Users****\Anaconda3\lib\pdb.py", line 1697, in main

pdb._runscript(mainpyfile)

File "C:\Users****\Anaconda3\lib\pdb.py", line 1566, in _runscript

self.run(statement)

File "C:\Users****\Anaconda3\lib\bdb.py", line 585, in run

exec (cmd, globals, locals)

File "<string>", line 1, in <module>

File "c:\users****\desktop\test.py", line 8, in <module>

A = 4

NameError: name 'Myfct2' is not defined

Uncaught exception. Entering post mortem debugging

Running 'cont' or 'step' will restart the program

> c:\users*****\desktop\test.py(8)<module>()

-> A = 4

Now, here that the continue launched different built-in functions of the debugger. It finally displayed an Error name for the 'Myfct2' because the 'def' statement of this function was not executed. Now, if we try to print the value of the variable ' A ', we get:

```
(Pdb) A
4
(Pdb)
```

If we reach the bottom of the file and run, for instance, the next command, Python debugger returns:

```
(Pdb) next
Post mortem debugger finished. The test.py will be restarted
> c:\users\***\desktop\test.py(1)<module>()
-> def Myfct1(A):
```

The longlist command allows showing the entire code. For instance:

```
(Pdb) longlist
1 -> def Myfct1 (A):
2 print ('A by 2 is:', A*2)
3 return A * 2
4
5 def Myfct2 (B, A):
6 C = B * A
7
8 A = 4
9 B = 'name'
10 Myfct2(B, A)
(Pdb)
```

357

Now, to run a code, we use the command step. For instance, let's quit the debugger with the command q() and restarted it again to test the command step.

(Pdb) q()

C:\Users****\Desktop>Python -m pdb test.py

> c:\users****\desktop\test.py(1)<module>()

-> def Myfct1 (A):

(Pdb) step

> c:\users****\desktop\test.py(5)<module>()

-> def Myfct2 (B, A):

(Pdb)

As you can notice, when a step command is run, the current line is def Myfct2 (B, A). This means that it is executed the 'def' statement of the first function. We can test that by calling this function:

(Pdb) Myfct1 (3)

A by 2 is: 6

6

(Pdb)

We can also pass an argument to step function to specify which line to run. For instance, we pass as argument Line 8. The debugger will run everything before line 8. As we can see from the example below, we can both print the variable A and call the function Myfct2 because these statements were both executed.

(Pdb) step 8

> c:\users****\desktop\test.py(8)<module>()

-> B = 'name'

(Pdb) A

4

 (Pdb) Myfct2 (5, 3)

(Pdb)

Because we have reached the end of the file, let's use continue to go back to the beginning of the file and test other commands.

(Pdb) cont

The program finished and will be restarted

> c:\users****\desktop\test.py(1)<module>()

-> def Myfct1 (A):

As you can see when running continue command at the end file, the debugger shows a message that lets you know that the program has finished and it is restarting. Now, we are going to test the whatis command:

(Pdb) whatis 2

<class 'int'>

(Pdb)

This command returns the type of the data object of the expression that appears in the Line passed as an argument. Now, let's set some breakpoints using the command break.

(Pdb) break 3

Breakpoint 1 at c:\users*****\desktop\test.py:3

(Pdb)

This command displays a message regarding where the breakpoint was added along with the Python file. We can clear breakpoints with the clear command. After running this command, the debugger will display a message that asks whether you want to clear all breaks or not.

Then it prints a message to confirm that the breakpoint was deleted along with the path of the Python file.

(Pdb) clear

Clear all breaks? Y

Deleted breakpoint 1 at c:\users****\desktop\test.py:3

(Pdb)

If you run a longlist after adding a breakpoint in your Python script, it will show you where the breakpoint was added. So, you don't have to go check in your Text Editor.

For instance, we add a break in line number 2:

(Pdb) break 2

Breakpoint 2 at c:\users****\desktop\test.py:2

(Pdb) longlist

1 def Myfct1 (A):

2 B print ('A by 2 is:', A * 2)

3 return A * 2

4

5 def Myfct2 (B, A):

6 C = B * A

7 A = 4

8 B = 'name'

9 -> Myfct2 (B,A)

(Pdb)

To resume this chapter, using debugger tools are very efficient to get a look inside of the program while it is running. It let you know what's going on when the program is running without having to make any changes in its source code. In addition, you can see all the changes you make and breakpoints you add while you are debugging with the Python module pdb. Moreover, this Python default debugger has numerous commands listed in Table 9 that allows an efficient scrutinization of your code.

Chapter 8: Files in Python

Files are a wide notion that is used to call any storage of your computer and handled by the operating system. Files are used to store data and information. When programming, you need tools that extract this information from the files or tools to save processed information in a file. In this chapter, we are going to cover how to handle files in Python.

Reading and writing files in Python

In Python, files are considered as a data object. In fact, Python has a built-in data object type assigned specifically for files. Unlike other data types we have seen in chapter 3, the file data object is associated only with common methods used to process files. The built-in method open is a function that allows creating a file data object to be processed. In short, this method links the file data object to the file stored in the hardware of your machine. Once you call open function, you have access to the file in order to read it or write it using the read and write attributes of the file data object. Table 10 presented below lists all common methods used to process files. In order to read a file, the function open is called with file name along with the mode to process the file which is 'r' in this case. To write a file, the process mode is 'w'. This mode creates a new file. If a file exists with the same name used to open a file in a writing mode, it will be overwritten. In order to write or add content into the existing file, the file should be open with mode append (i.e. 'a').

The file name can include or not the file path of the directory that contains or will contain the file. If the path is not specified, then Python would assume that the file is in the working directory which is the directory where the current program is running.

Table 10: List methods to process files.

Method	Explanation
File2Read = open (file_path/file_name, 'r')	Defines a file data object to write
File2write = open (file_path/file_name, 'w')	Defines a file data object to read
content = File2read.read()	Reads the whole file and assign the content to a single string
content = File2read.read(X)	Reads only X bytes
Line = File2read.readLine()	Reads following line
Lines = File2read.readLins()	Reads the whole file and stores the content in a line strings list
File2write(data)	Writes data in the file
File2write.writeLine(List_line)	Writes in the file the strings line of the list List_line
File2write.close()	Closes the file manually

After you open a file, you have a file data object. Then, its methods can be used in reading and writing with the methods presented in the table above. In either case, the file data object methods take and return only strings in Python. In other words, the read method returns as a data object type as a string. The write method takes as data object type as string, too. Both methods have different varieties.

The role of the close method is closing the connection between Python and the external file residing in the hardware of your machine. Python also liberates the space in memory that was occupied by an object after it is no longer referenced in the script. Python would also close automatically the close if required. Hence, in Python, it is not necessary to call the close method in order to delete the file object reference manually. However, it is good practice to call the close method after you finish reading or writing a file.

Example File Processing in Python

In this section, we are going to present some examples of processing files in Python using the methods presented in Table 10. The first example illustrates how to write the 'Hello World' in a file. So, let's go back to prompt shell and launch Python for practice.

```
>>> File = open (' MyFile.txt', 'w')
>>> File.write(' Hello World! \n')
>>> File.close()
```

In the first statement, we called the method open in write mode (i.e. 'w') to create the file. The second statement writes the line 'Hello World!' with a newline marker. The third statement closes the file object.

In the following code example, we are going to open the file in reading mode (i.e. 'r') and get the line written in the file:

```
>>> File = open (' MyFile.txt', 'r')

>>> A = File.readline()

>>> print (' This is an example of reading a file with readline: \n', A)
```

This is an example of reading a file with readline:

Hello World!

```
>>> File.close()
```

Now, we are going to add a second line in our file. To do so, we are going to open the file in mode append (i.e. 'a') and write the line 'My first file in Python':

```
>>> File = open (' MyFile.txt', 'a')
>>> File.write(' This is my first file in Python')
>>> File.close()
```

If we open the file again and check its content with the read method, we get the following output:

```
>>> File = open (' MyFile.txt', 'r')
>>> A = File.read()
>>> print (' This is an example of reading a file with read: \n',
A)
This is an example of reading a file with read:
Hello World!
This is my first file in Python
>>> File.close()
```

As you can notice when opening a file with append mode, it adds whatever you write in the file at the end. We can also change what is already in the file by opening the file in mode 'r+'. When you open the file in this mode and write in it, it will overwrite everything in it.

For instance:

>>> File = open (' MyFile.txt', 'r+')

>>> File.write(' This is my first file Python opened in mode r+')

>>> File.close()

>>> File = open (' MyFile.txt', 'r')

>>> A = File.read()

>>> print (' Checking file after opening in mode r+: \n', A)

Checking file after opening in mode r+:

This is my first file Python opened in mode r+

>>>File.close()

Remember, loops are very handy when it comes to repeating the same tasks for a specific number of times. In particular, loops are very useful in processing the file data object. We have seen through the above examples that we can read the content of the whole file in one single step using the read method. In some cases, we need to read the file line by line.

In this case, we would use the readLine method. We might also need to write the file line by line in the case of formatted files, in which case, the writelines is handy. Let's practice some examples. First, we are going to write using writelines method. Then we are going to read the same file line by line.

For both tasks, we will use a while loop.

>>> List_string = [' This is an example of \n',

... 'writing a file \n',

... ' on multiple lines\n',

... ' using write Lines \n',

... ' inside a while loop']

>>>print (' List of strings is:\n ', List_string)

List of strings is:

[' This is an example of \n', 'writing a file \n', ' on multiple lines\n', ' using write Lines', ' inside a while loop']

>>> File = open ('Test', 'w')

>>> File.writelines (List_string)

>>> File.close ()

Remember that all file object methods process only strings. Therefore, we created a list of strings where each element end with /n for newline maker.

Now, we open the file for reading:

```
>>> File = open ('Test', 'r')
>>> while 1:
...     Line = File.readline ()
...     if not Line: break
...     print (Line)
...
This is an example of
writing a file
on multiple lines
using write Lines inside a while loop
>>> File.close ()
```

As you can notice, we have a break statement in the while loop. This ensures that the while loop stops when there is no line to read. In other words, it ensures that the loop exit when it reaches the end of the file. Because 1 is always evaluated to true, the loop will continue running until it runs to the break. Hence, this loop reads the file line by line until it reaches the end of the file. If we open the file and use the read method, we get exactly the same results:

```
>>> File = open ('Test', 'r')
>>> A = File.read ()
>>> print ('This is the output from reading the file with
reading method: \n', A)
This is the output from reading the file with reading method:
This is an example of
writing a file
on multiple lines
using write Lines inside a while loop
>>> File.close ()
```

Note in this last example, we did not specify the file extension. In fact, Python allows handling and processing any type of files that the extension does not matter. These methods work the same on any file.

Conclusion

Thank you for making it through to the end of *Python Programming: A Comprehensive Smart Approach for Total Beginners to Learn Python Language Using Best Practices And Advanced Features*. Let's hope it was informative and able to provide you with all of the tools you need to achieve your goals whatever they may be.

This book provides the basics of Python language programming. It also covers some advanced topics such as developing modules, debugging, and handling files. This book does not require any programming prerequisites. On the contrary, this book is designed to provide total beginners with the right tools to start programming using the Python language.

In the very first chapters, chapter 1 to chapter 3, we cover the most basics of any programming language which are how to install the language and how to run scripts. We also cover the data object type and how to process them. In chapter 4, we start diving into more details about Python syntax, operators, and if test and loops specifics to process data objects. In the rest of the book, we cover more advanced topics such as developing functions and modules to make any script reusable and widely sharable with others. We also cover debugging which allows finding and fixing code errors, and finally, how to process files. All chapters of this book provide code examples that allow practicing while you are learning the language. After finishing this book, you will not only be able to develop scripts to accomplish simple tasks, but you will be also able to develop your own modules. You will also be able to use these modules within any program. In short, you will be able to master basic programming with Python with some advanced features. You will also be able to debug and scrutinize your programs while they are running. Once you master these skills, you will be able to pick up more advanced skills easily.

Finally, if you found this book useful in any way, a review on Amazon is always appreciated!

371

Python Machine Learning

Understand Python Libraries (Keras, NumPy, Scikit-lear, TensorFlow) for Implementing Machine Learning Models in Order to Build Intelligent Systems

By: Ethem Mining

Introduction

For decades, artificial intelligence has been more promise than delivery. With the advent of increasing computing power and the arrival of big data, however, things have started to change. Over the past 15 years or so, a new and relatively quiet revolution began in the area of artificial intelligence. Finally, the hype began to meet with the substance. It should be made clear that the old visions of human-like robots running around and eventually displacing humans still remain quite far-fetched. What we are seeing instead is that computers are doing what they've always done, helping aid humans working in areas where humans aren't really that suitable. Nonetheless, the impact on business over the past decade has been enormous, and more big changes are ahead.

In this book, we hope to get the reader interested in and informed about a branch of artificial intelligence called machine learning. The aim of this guide is to get you acquainted with some of the tools used in machine learning that make it accessible and practical. Those who become familiar with the python libraries and tools that can be used in machine learning are going to find it surprisingly easy to use.

We will begin the book with some background material, to make sure that all readers are on the same page. First, we will introduce the concept of machine learning and explain what it's all about, and how it can be applied in the real world.

Then we will discuss the two main types of machine learning, supervised and unsupervised machine learning. From there, we will describe the tools available in python that can be used to do machine learning.

Python is very accessible and easy language to learn. If you are not familiar with python, there are many fine books on the topic, and you can find many websites that will teach you how to use the language. Those who already have experience with computer programming will find that using python is comparatively easy as compared to most programming languages.

There are plenty of books on this subject on the market, thanks again for choosing this one! Every effort was made to ensure it is full of as much useful information as possible, please enjoy it!

Chapter 1: An Introduction to Machine Learning

Artificial intelligence is a branch of computer science that seeks to develop computer systems that are capable of humanlike intelligence. This is something that can be viewed from many different directions. The first thing that might come to mind when you think of human intelligence is that it is general in nature. You can learn to do many different things, from mathematics to learning a new language, or visual recognition.

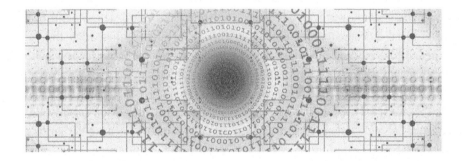

The second aspect of human intelligence that is important is that humans learn from experience. As we will see, this is going to be a critical aspect of machine learning. The experience that you learn from might come in different forms. You can learn by doing, or you can be guided through learning by an instructor. One way you learn is by memorizing, which is a form of experience. The key point here is that the human brain adjusts itself, basically restructuring itself, when it is exposed to new information.

In the end, whether or not you are learning how to play tennis or do calculus, everything is basically information of some kind.

Of course, human intelligence can be broken down into specialties, so you can have artificial intelligence that replicates the human mind implemented this way rather than just having a computer system that mimics and the entire human brain. In fact, the latter is probably something very far off, if it is ever achieved. However, artificially intelligent computer systems are quite good at performing specialized tasks. Computer vision, for example, is one area that has taken off and continues to get better and better. Artificially intelligent systems also run independently. Think of it as educating a child in school. The child is taught in school, and when they become an adult, they become an independent operator. Most adult humans don't need to consult their teachers or parents all the time in order to make decisions. Computer systems based on artificial intelligence need to be trained, but once trained they can operate on their own without human intervention.

Another aspect of human intelligence can be captured by the phrase "practice makes perfect". Or put another way, the more data you are exposed to the better you get at solving problems related to that data. Computer systems based on artificial intelligence get better at what they do the more data they are exposed to. They self-adjust to make themselves perform better. This is quite a contrast with conventional computer systems, which can do a lot of powerful things, but are essentially dumb. They only do what you tell them to do, and without humans rewriting the programs that run them, they don't get any better at what they do. This is an important point to focus on, because the kinds of systems that we are going to talk about in this book will adjust themselves and get better, without any human intervention whatsoever.

Once they are deployed, the human operators might not even understand why the artificially intelligent computer system makes the decisions it does, or how it is making those decisions. The worth of the systems can only be judged on results alone.

What is Machine Learning and How Has it Developed?

Machine learning is actually an old technology, as far as computer technology is concerned. The first machine learning system was constructed in the mid-to-late 1950s. It was developed at IBM, and described in a paper published in the peer reviewed literature. This system was able to learn how to play checkers. The system has some key components that make us recognize it as machine learning.

The first item to note is that the system was not designed to play checkers. Instead, the system was designed to learn, and to self-adapt. It learned to play checkers by being exposed to playing checkers. The second item to consider is that the more the system played checkers, the better it got. This is an illustration of the ability of these types of computer systems to benefit from the experience. Just like a human being, the more experience they have at doing something, the better they get. There is one key aspect that you should be aware of when considering a program like this. A human being can learn to play checkers, and they can also learn to play monopoly and guitar. Although years ago researchers in the field hoped to build computers that were like this too, the machine learning systems in use today are not like that.

In short, they are one trick ponies. So, our system that we are describing here was really good at playing checkers. It could not do anything else. Once you have a system that does something, that is what it does, period. With the first system built some 60 odd years ago, you might be wondering why it is only recently that this type of computer system has become relevant to the real world. There are two reasons. One is the messy way that research develops in any human enterprise. A few years after this development, computer scientists got extremely hot on the idea of general artificial intelligence. Huge promises were made, and lots of hype developed around the field. This was when the idea of fully functioning "android" robots caught fire. These would be human-like computer systems packaged in a human-like form, often indistinguishable from humans. The movie Alien captured this idea quite well with the ship scientist named Ash; the other crew members didn't even know he was an android. The idea of artificial intelligence was also portrayed in the famous science fiction movie 2001: A Space Odyssey.

This was a more realistic portrayal, the computer was not human-like in form, but it clearly had a mind. One of the key themes in the film is the fact that the system has faults, and can make bad decisions as a result. This is probably a warning we should take to heart, but we probably won't. The system in the movie brags that it never makes mistakes, but it clearly does. Unfortunately, people today place too much faith in computers. Machine learning is great, but don't worship it. Another aspect of the HAL 9000 computer portrayed in the film was actually realistic in the sense of what artificially intelligent computer systems can actually do in the real world, and what they might actually be used for. The system in the movie detects a coming fault in a communications device.

In the movie it turns out to be in error, but the point is many machine learning systems are being developed that will hopefully detect faults in electronics and machines before humans become aware of them. We don't want to get too carried away with science fiction stories, but the analogies and interpretations of what is possible are interesting to consider. It turns out that hype won the day, and after a few decades of pursuing the holy grail of artificial intelligence, in effect creating a computer system that worked like a human brain, computer scientists began to change direction. They turned more attention to machine learning, which is something that can be thought of as using humanlike intelligence but applied to a very narrowly tailored task. Something that was missing, however, was data.

Big Data and Machine Learning

In order to learn something, a system that is capable of machine learning needs to be exposed to a lot of data. Going back several decades, computers didn't have access to all that much data, in comparison to what they can access today. Computers were slow and quite awkward. Most data at that time was stored on paper, and so it was not readily accessed by computer systems. There was also far less of it. Of course, companies and large businesses, along with governments have always collected as much data as they could, but when you don't have that much data and it's mostly in the form of paper records, then you don't have much data that is useful to a machine learning computer system.

The first databases were invented in the late 1960s. A database is not really what we think of when considering the relationship between data and machine learning, although it could be in some circumstances. Databases collect very organized information. To understand the difference, think about a collection of Facebook posts, versus a record of someone registering to enroll at a university. The collection of Facebook posts is going to be disorganized and messy. It is going to have data of different types, such as photos, videos, links, and text. It's going to be pretty well unclassified, maybe only marked by who posted it and the date. In contrast, when you say database you should think completely organized and restricted data. A database is composed of individual records, each record containing the same data fields. At a university, students when enrolled might enter their name, social security or ID number, address, and so on.

All of these records are stored in the same format, together in one big file. The file can then be "queried" to return records that we ask for. For example, we could have it return records for everyone in the Freshman class. Relational databases allow you to cross reference information and bring it together in a query. Following our example, you could have a separate database that had the courses each student was taking. This could be stored in a separate database from the basic information of each student, but it could be cross referenced using a field as a student ID. Tools were developed to help bring data together from different databases. IBM, a company that always seems to figure large in many developments in computer science, developed the first structured query language or SQL, that could be used to do tasks like this. Once data could be pulled together, it could be analyzed or used to do things like print out reports for human operators.

As computers became more ubiquitous, companies and government agencies began collecting more and more data. But it wasn't until the late 1990s that the amount of data and types of data began to explode. There were two developments that led to these changes. The first was the invention of the internet. The second was the development of ever improving and lower cost computer storage capacity. The development and commercialization of the internet meant that over a very short time period, nearly everyone was getting "online". Businesses moved fast to get online with websites. Those that didn't fall behind, and many ended up going out of business. But that isn't what's important for our purposes.

The key here is that once people got online, they were leaving data trails all over the place. This kind of data collection was increasing in the offline world as well, as computing power started to grow. For example, grocery stores started offering supposed discount and membership cards, that really functioned to track what people were buying, so that the companies could make customized offers to customers, and so they could adjust their marketing plans and so forth.

The internet also brought the concept of cloud computing to the forefront. Rather than having a single computer, or a network of computers in one office, the internet offered the possibility of harnessing the power of multiple computers linked together both for information processing and doing calculations and also for simple data storage. A third development, the continual decline in the costs of storage components of computer systems along with increased capacity had a large impact in this area. Soon, more and more data was being collected. Large companies like Google, and eventually Facebook, also started collecting large amounts of data on people's behavior.

This is where machine learning hits the road. For the first time, the amounts of data that machine learning systems needed to be able to perform real world tasks, not just do things like playing checkers, became possible. Machine learning systems are trained on data sets, and now businesses (and governments) had data of all kinds to train machine learning systems to do many different tasks.

Goals and Applications of Machine Learning

Machine learning is something that can be applied whenever there is a useful pattern in any large data set. In many cases, it is not known what patterns exist before the data has been fed to a machine learning system. This is because human beings are not able to see the underlying pattern in large data sets, but computers are well suited to finding them. The types of patterns are not limited in any way. For example, a machine learning system can be used to detect hacking attempts on a computer network. It can be trained for network security by feeding the system past data that includes previous hacking attempts.

In another case, a machine learning system can be used to develop facial recognition technology. The system can be presented with large numbers of photographs that contain faces, so that it can learn to spot faces, and to associate a given face with a particular individual. Now let's consider another application of machine learning, which is completely different from the other two we've looked at so far. Machine learning can be used to approve or disapprove a loan application. During the training phase, the system will be exposed to a large number of previous loan applications and the ultimate results. In other words, did the borrower pay the loan off early or default on the loan? During the exposure to all the data, the system will learn what characteristics or combinations of characteristics best predict whether or not a given applicant is going to default on a loan.

This is all done without human input, and so the machine may find patterns in the data that human observers missed and never suspected were there. The fact is that human minds are not very good at being able to analyze large data sets, and some would probably argue that we can't do it at all. One of the earliest applications of machine learning was in the detection of email spam. This is a good example to look at, because it illustrates a particular type of problem that machine learning systems are good at solving. Determining whether or not an email is spam or not is something that can be framed as a classification problem. In other words, you take each email, examine it, and classify it as spam or not spam. This is not something that can be taken to be absolute, and detecting all spam messages can be tricky.

Fraud detection with credit and debit cards is yet another application of machine learning. By studying past data, the system can learn to detect patterns in usage that indicate that the card is being used in a fraudulent manner.

In many cases, the patterns that are detected are going to be things that human observers are completely unaware of, or wouldn't associate with fraud detection even if they knew the patterns existed. So, we see that machine learning can be applied in virtually any situation where there is a large amount of data available, and there are patterns in the data that can be used for the purposes of detection or prediction. Machine learning is quite general, able to learn anything from playing chess to spotting fuel waste for an airline like Southwest. This is not the artificial intelligence that was once imagined by science fiction writers in the 1960s or 1970s, but it does have many characteristics of human learning. The first is that it's quite general. The second is that it will perform better, the more data that it is exposed to.

Now let's consider the goals of machine learning. The central goal of machine learning is to develop general purpose algorithms that can solve problems using intelligence and learning. Obviously one important goal of machine learning is to increase productivity. This is true whether or not the user of the system is a business, a military branch, or a government agency. The second goal is to replace human labor with better machine labor. Of course, this has been a goal of technology ever since the industrial revolution started, and it continues to be an important goal today. However, the way that this is being done in the case of machine learning is a little bit different. The first thing is using machine learning to perform tasks that require a level of attention and focus that human beings are not able to provide. Even when humans are excellent workers who will provide maximum focus, a human suffers from many flaws, like fatigue, and the ability to be distracted. Also, the amount of information that a human observer can pay attention to at any given time is very limited.

Consider a machine learning system instead—focus is never an issue. A computer system is able to generate laser-like focus in a way that a human being never could. Second, it is able to analyze and sample a far larger data set, and of course it will never be subject to fatigue and it's not going to need restroom breaks or lunch. One application—in a general sense—that is being used in many businesses today is using machine learning to spot waste. Several large corporations have already had great success with this.

384

We've already mentioned one, Southwest Airlines famously used machine learning to analyze the activity of airlines on the tarmac, and they found a great deal of waste in terms of time and fuel was spent by planes idling on the tarmac. UPS has also used machine learning to spot wasteful driving routes that cost the company time and money, at the expense of having thousands of trucks waste gallons of fuel. Machine learning can also be applied to find out what employees are doing and how they can better use their time.

Benefits of Machine Learning

There are a large number of benefits for businesses that use machine learning. We can summarize a few of them here:

- Machine learning can easily find patterns in any underlying data set.

- Systems based on machine learning get better with experience. The more data they see, the better they are going to get.

- Machine learning is quite general, and can be applied to nearly any application, from detecting hacking attempts on a computer network to picking winning stocks.

- Machine learning systems can handle multidimensional problems that would overwhelm human observers.

- Once a system has gone through the learning phase, further human intervention is not required. This is a true system that uses automation.

- Machine learning can be applied across a broad spectrum, and it can be used to solve nearly any problem that a business may encounter.

How Machine Learning Works

Machine learning begins with a human guide in the form of a data scientist. A problem has to be identified that a machine learning algorithm can be used to solve it. In order for the process to work, there must be a significant amount of data that can be used to train the system before it is deployed in the real world. There are two basic ways that machine learning can proceed, and we will discuss these in detail in the next chapter. They are called supervised and unsupervised learning. In the training phase, the data scientist will select appropriate training data, and expose the system to the data. As the system is exposed to data, it will modify itself in order to become more accurate.

This phase is a crucial part of a development with the system, and the data scientist must choose the right data set for the problem at hand. In other words, the impression that human beings are not involved at all is completely false. Human beings are involved in choosing and framing the problem, and in choosing the right training data. The human being is also involved in the process of evaluating the performance of the system. As we will see, there are tradeoffs that must be made that have large implications for the viability of the system. If the data scientists that are working on the problem are not careful and correct, to the best of their abilities, in interpreting the results produced by the system, a dysfunctional system can be deployed that will err when attempting to do its job. The training phase may have several iterations, depending on how the results turn out. Once the system is deployed, it will more or less operate in an autonomous fashion, but data scientists that are involved in this work should be continually evaluating the performance of the system. At some point, the system may need to be replaced or it may need to be subjected to more training, if it is not producing the kinds of results that are accepted.

Steps in Machine Learning

The data scientist must follow a certain procedure in order to implement machine learning. In the following chapters we will learn the two different approaches that are used in "training" the system.

Machine learning involves artificial intelligence, and so any system that has artificial intelligence is just like a human being, in that the system needs to learn it's skill before it goes out into the real world. It is up to the data scientist to provide the training that the system needs. In this section we are going to outline the general steps that are needed, in the following two chapters we will discuss the specific methods used.

Define the Problem

Each step in the machine learning paradigm is critical. If you make a mistake early on, this is going to make the entire enterprise fall flat. When you say artificial intelligence, while you get the impression that there is an all-powerful computer, like the HAL 9000 system from 2001, the reality is a little more down to earth.

It is true that there is not a specific, line by line set of instructions written in code by human engineers that tell the computer what to do, and once a machine learning system is deployed people might not really understand how it's working. Nonetheless, there is a lot of direct human involvement in the process. And given our propensity to make mistakes, it's important to be careful at each step along the way. Think of yourself as a teacher guiding a child so that they learn a new skill.

The first step is having a clear definition of the problem that you are facing. The end goal must be in mind, so you must know what you expect the machine learning system to do when it is up and running.

Gather and Prepare Data

The second step is to gather the data that is necessary to use in order to train the system. If you define the problem but there is little or no data that can be used to train it, then this procedure is not going to work. Machine learning must have enough data so that the system can determine patterns and relationships in the data that will allow it to make predictions and classifications in the real world. The assumption is going to be that enough data of the right type has been collected. But simply having the data is not enough. As we will see, if you simply feed the system raw data, this can create problems for a number of reasons. So you will have to take a look at the data and apply some human judgment to it. Think of data as consisting of a large number of fields or properties. Are all of the properties relevant to the problem at hand?

In many cases, a machine learning system is going to find relationships among different properties that do have a predictive value that humans will miss–so there is a balancing act between cutting down the data versus removing something that might be very important, even though it doesn't seem relevant to the human operator. Nonetheless, you don't want to have too much information in the data set that can make it impossible to learn. So, you might have to discard some data to reduce the complexity of the problem, if this is possible. We will discuss more details about this in later chapters.

Choose the Style of Learning

We will see in the next few chapters that there are different methods of learning. These are going to be based on the nature of the problem and the type of data that you have. This is an easy step in the process, since that will dictate the style of learning used. The main types of learning are supervised learning, unsupervised learning, semi-supervised learning, and representational learning. We will learn what types of problems each type of learning is suitable for and how the structure of the input data differs in the next couple of chapters.

Select the Most Appropriate Algorithm

Once you have settled on whether or not the data and the problem you are solving is best suited for supervised or unsupervised learning, then you need to decide which algorithm to use. Certain situations might dictate whether one algorithm is better than another algorithm. Choosing the right algorithm might have an influence on the types of errors that you see in the results. This means that as someone who is using machine learning, understanding the main types of algorithms is going to be important.

Train and Test

Now at this point, everything is ready to go. The first step is to expose the system to the training data so that it can learn. Then you will test the system and evaluate.

Improve

When you evaluate the performance of the system with training and test data, the error will need to be quantified. If the error is not acceptable, adjustments may have to be made. As you would with regular coding, you can go through a cycle of more training and making adjustments to reduce errors. In some cases, you might have to scrap the system and start over, but one of the benefits of machine learning is that the system is adaptive. The more data it sees the better it learns. So, improvement may be possible by simply exposing the system to more training data.

Deploy

Once the system is working to the degree that has an acceptable level of error, then it is ready to be deployed.

Chapter 2: How Machine Learning is Applied in the Real World

It's one thing to talk about machine learning in the abstract. To get a better handle on machine learning, we also want to understand how it's being used in businesses and other large organizations today in order to perform useful functions. First, let's understand where machine learning fits into the overall framework of computer science and artificial intelligence.

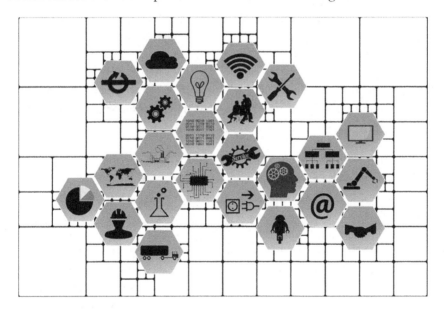

When Does Machine Learning Work?

When faced with a problem that is suitable for the deployment of a computer system, the first thing that you should ask about the problem is whether or not it is rigid and unchanging, or is this something that requires an adaptive system?

At first glance this seems like a simple question. For example, suppose that you were considering a ballistics program for the military. Ballistics follow the laws of physics.

These are precisely known, and so it should be a simple matter to do calculations to get the accurate results that are desired. Hard coded computer programs can be used to predict how things will work in real situations. Indeed, as soon as Newton's laws were known in the 17th and 18th centuries, armies were using people to do the calculations by hand, and this helped to revolutionize warfare and military efficiency. Today it's done even better and faster using powerful computer technology. But a recent example shows that there is often more to any situation than meets the eye. Consider an EKG, which can give a doctor a picture of the performance of the heart. An EKG is used to diagnose a heart attack, arrythmias, and many other problems. It's very narrowly focused, and patterns on the EKG are associated with specific conditions. Health professionals are trained to recognize those patterns, and they can study an EKG chart and determine which patients need medical intervention and which don't. This is as straightforward as the ballistics problem.

However, when artificially intelligent systems were developed using machine learning to study EKGs, it was found that they outperformed doctors by a significant margin.

The machine learning systems that have been developed are able to predict which patients will die within a year with 85% accuracy. For comparison, doctors are able to make the same prediction with 65% to at most 80% accuracy.

The key here is the difference. When there are EKGs that look completely normal to the human eye—the machine learning system is able to determine that in fact, they are not normal. The engineers that designed the system can't explain it. They don't know why or how the machine learning system makes its predictions. But the way it works, generally speaking, is that the machine learning system is able to detect patterns in the data that human minds cannot detect. This example serves to illustrate that adaptive learning can be used in nearly every situation. Even in ballistics, there may be many different factors that human engineers have not properly accounted for. Who knows what they are, it could be the humidity, wind, or other factors. The bet is that although line-by-line coded software works very well in deterministic situations, adaptive software that is not programmed and only trained with data will do better.

Complex and Adaptive

When there is any situation where experience—that is exposure to more data— can improve performance, machine learning is definitely called for. If the data is complex, this is another situation where machine learning can shine. Think about how the human mind can handle mathematical problems. Even two-dimensional problems in calculus and differential equations are difficult for most people, and even the smartest people struggle while learning it for the first time.

It gets even more difficult when you move to three dimensions, and the more complexity that is added, the harder it is for people to digest. If you are looking at a data set, you are going to be facing the same situation. If we have a small data set of 20 items, each with 3 fields and an output, a human operator might be able to extract a relationship between the inputs and outputs. They could even do linear regression by hand or plug it into a simple program like Microsoft Excel. Even simply eyeballing the data can reveal the relationships. But the more data you add to the problem, the less able a human operator is able to determine what the relationships are. The same problem with output but 20 inputs might make it very difficult. If there are no outputs, and you ask human operators to see if there are any patterns in the data, it might become virtually impossible. One way that we get around complexity in the real world is to program computers in the standard way. This helps humans get around many large data problems and solving problems that would involve tedious work. Consider weather prediction, early efforts at predicting the weather or modeling the climate were based on standard line-by-line coding, using the laws of physics and inputs believed to be important by the operator. However, when there is a large amount of complexity in a problem, such as predicting the weather, this is a signal that machine learning is probably going to outperform any method by a wide margin. Think about climate modeling. Using conventional techniques, the scientists and programmers are going to make estimates of what factors (such as carbon dioxide level) are important. But using machine learning, simply training the system on raw data, the system would probably detect patterns in the data that human observers don't even know are there, and it would probably build an even more accurate system that would be better at making future predictions.

393

To summarize, when you have a problem that is adaptive and complex then it is well suited for machine learning. But there is a third component, and this is big data.

The Role of Big Data

Over the past two or three decades, there has been a quiet revolution in computing power that went unnoticed at first. Developments in technology made it possible to develop more storage capacity, and the costs of this storage capacity have continually dropped. This phenomenon combined with the internet to make it easy for organizations that are large and small to collect enormous amounts of information and store it. The concept of big data was born.

Big data is of course large amounts of data. However, experts characterize big data in four ways.

Simply having a static set of large amounts of data is not useful unless you can quickly access it. Big data is characterized by the "four V's".

- *Volume*: Huge amounts of data are being created and stored by computer systems throughout the world.

- *Velocity*: The speed of data movement continues to increase. Speed of data means that computer systems can gather and analyze larger amounts of data more quickly.

- *Variety*: Big data is also characterized by collection methods from different sources. For example, a consumer profile can include data from a person's behavior while online, but it will also include mobile data from their smart phone, and data from wearable technology like smart watches.

- *Veracity*: The truthfulness of the data is important. Do business leaders trust the data they are using? If the data is erroneous, it's not going to be useful.

The key to focus on here is that big data plays a central role in machine learning. In fact, without adequate amounts of accurate (truthful) data that can be accessed quickly, machine learning wouldn't work. The basic fundamentals of machine learning were developed decades ago, but it really wasn't until we moved into the 21st century that the ability to collect and move data around caught up to what was known about machine learning. The arrival of big data is what turned machine learning from an academic curiosity into something real that could be deployed in the real world to get real results.

Where Does Machine Learning Fit In?

Now that we understand the relationship of machine learning to big data, let's see where machine learning fits in with other concepts in computer science. We begin with artificial intelligence.

Artificial intelligence is the overarching concept that entails computer systems that can learn and get better with experience. Artificial intelligence can be characterized by the following general characteristics:

- The ability to learn from data.

395

- The ability to get better from experience.
- The ability to reason.
- It is completely general, as the human brain. So, it can learn anything and can learn multiple tasks.

Machine learning is a subset of artificial intelligence. Rather than being completely general and engaging in humanlike reasoning, machine learning is focused on a specific task. There are four major areas of machine learning, and within each of these there are specialties:

- *Supervised learning*–good for predictions of future outputs.
- *Unsupervised learning*–good for classifying objects.
- *Reinforcement learning*–a type of learning that encourages ideal behavior by giving rewards.
- *Deep learning*–A computer system that attempts to mimic the human brain using a neural network. It can be trained to perform a specific task.

Some Applications of Machine Learning

We have touched on a few ways that machine learning is used in the real world. To get a better feel for machine learning and how it's applied, let's go through some of the most impactful ways that it is being used.

Crimes and Criminal Activity

When you think about machine learning, think patterns. One very practical use of machine learning is exposing a system to past data from criminal activity.

This data can contain many different fields or features. They could include:

- Type of crime committed.
- Location of the crime.
- Time of day.
- Information about the perpetrator or perpetrators.
- Information about the victim.
- Weapons used.
- Day of the week and day of the month.
- Year when the crime occurred.

By studying the data and looking for hidden patterns, a machine learning system can be built to predict the incidents of future crimes. This doesn't mean that it is going to be able to predict a specific crime "there will be a robbery at 615 main street at 6 PM", but rather it will predict overall patterns of criminal activity.

This activity might vary in ways that even experienced law enforcement officers are unable to predict–reflect back on the EKG example.

How can this help in the real world? It can help law enforcement agencies deploy resources in a more efficient manner. Even if they don't understand why a given system is making the predictions it's making, they can benefit by moving more law enforcement resources into areas that the system is telling them are going to experience more criminal activity, on the days and at the times when those resources are needed the most. This can help police and emergency personnel respond to crimes more rapidly, and it can also help deter crime with a greater police presence.

Hospital Staffing

Hospital staffing suffers from a similar problem. Human managers attempt to guess when most doctors and nurses are needed and where they should be deployed. While these estimates are reasonably accurate, improvements can be made by deploying a system that uses machine learning. Again, think back to the EKG example–a doctor is pretty good, giving results with 65-80% accuracy. But the machine learning system is even better with 85%, picking out situations the doctors miss. That kind of difference can be a large matter of life or death when it comes to efficiently allocate staff in a large hospital. To put together systems of this type, large medical organizations tracked the locations and movements of nurses. This allowed them to provide input data to the system, which was able to identify areas of waste. As a simple example, it might have discovered that a large number of nurses were idle on the 7th floor, while there were not enough nurses in a different ward of the hospital, and so patients there were not getting needed attention, and some may have died as a result.

The Lost Customer Problem

For a business, a loyal customer is worth their weight in gold–or far more. A loyal customer is one that is going to return to make repeated purchases. Or even better, they will subscribe.

What do you think is more valuable to companies like Verizon and T-Mobile, selling you the phone, or the fact that you sign up for possibly years of regular monthly payments?

Since loyal customers keep business profitable, learning why customers leave is very important. Even just a decade ago, this had to be done using guesswork. But now, vast sums of data have been collected on customers by large corporations. Preventing their customers from switching to a different company is something they are heavily focused on, and machine learning is enabling them to look for patterns in the data that can help them identify why a customer leaves, and even predict when a customer is about to leave. This data can include basic demographics, usage patterns, attempts to contact customer support, and so on. The first step where machine learning can be used is that customers that have switched to another company can be identified, and then the system can learn what underlying patterns there are that would enable it to predict what customers are going to leave in the future. Another way that this data can be used, is to study retention efforts. Once a customer is identified that is likely to leave, perhaps they can be offered a special deal. For example, a cell phone company could offer a large discount on a new phone, if they sign up for another two year contract. Or they could offer them free minutes or unlimited data. Over time, more data is going to be collected. Machine learning can be applied again, this time to determine which methods work the best and what patterns exist—in other words what method works best for what customers. Maybe you will find that customers of different ages, genders, or living in different locations, or working at different types of jobs, will respond in different ways to inducements offered to retain the customer. This type of analysis will allow the company to tailor it's responses to each additional customer, improving the odds that they can keep the customer. The customers themselves will be happier, feeling that the company is responsible for their personal needs.

The data will also help the company anticipate future market changes and help them adapt using predictive analytics.

Robotics

Using machine learning to develop better and more capable robotics is a huge area of inquiry. Robotics started out simple, performing rote tasks that don't require a huge amount of thought. For example, in the 1980s robotics were introduced on assembly lines to put in a screw or do some other task. The problem then was simple, the robot would perform a small number of exact, rote tasks that could be pre-programmed. Now robotics are becoming more sophisticated, using cognitive systems to perform many tasks that are tedious but were once thought to be something that only human beings could do. For example, recently robots have been developed that can work as fast food cooks. This is going to have major implications for unskilled labor, because there are two factors at play in the current environment. Activism is pushing up wages for hourly employees doing unskilled labor, while the costs of robotics that can perform the same tasks are dropping. Moreover, the abilities of the robots to perform these tasks continually improves. A breakeven point is going to be reached. That is the cost of buying and operating a robot will be less than the costs of hiring a human employee. The robot will never waver in efficiency, it won't require the payment of employment taxes, and it's never going to file a lawsuit or allege discrimination. From the employer's perspective, automation is going to be preferable and this trend probably can't be stopped.

Over the past year, many sophisticated robots have been revealed to the public. Boston Dynamics, for example, has built robots that can work in warehouses. They are able to identify packages that need to be moved, pick them up, and then place them where they need to be. At the present time, the only thing preventing widespread adaptation of this type of technology is cost. A working robot like this has to be able to interact with the environment that it is in, in addition to performing the required task. This means that a sophisticated computer system has to be in place in the robot that includes many machine learning systems. The machine learning systems will include movements required to perform the task, and the ability to avoid running into someone or another robot. Another form of artificial intelligence, computer vision, plays a significant role in the development of robotics, helping it to identify objects (and people) that are in the robot's environment. Since modern robotics is using machine learning, the ability of the robots to do their jobs and navigate the environments they are in will improve with time.

Virtual Assistants

One way that machine learning is having a direct impact on people right now is via personal assistants. Not only are these systems able to "think" in simple ways, look things up and follow instructions, but they are also able to understand language and engage in conversation. Think about the computer systems portrayed in Star Trek back in the 1960s—the users of the system would engage it using speech. Perhaps they were prescient or maybe the show actually directed where computer science research went, but today we have Alexa and Siri that basically work in the same way. Of course, these systems are far from perfect, but they are improving with time, and the number of tasks and the complexity of the tasks they are assigned to do will increase.

Robo Advisors

One of the breakthroughs in machine learning is using machine learning systems to determine what stock trades to enter into in order to earn an investor profit. This amazing technology is called a robo-advisor, with a robot taking over the role of a financial advisor. Robo-advisors started out as tools used by traders looking to make lightning fast trades, but over time their use has expanded. If there is one place where there is big data, the stock market certainly qualifies. Using the data of past trends in stock prices under different conditions, machine learning systems can learn how to invest and trade stocks and other financial securities like options in order to make profits, no matter what your goals are. The systems allow users to specify what their investment or trading goals are, and then the robo-advisor will make the trades that it determines will help the investor reach those goals. Robo-advisors are also becoming popular on the Forex market, where traders are engaged in making fast, short-term trades in order to make profits. As time goes on, there is no question that robo-advisors are going to see an increasingly prominent role in the financial markets, and declining costs will help to make these tools available to more people.

Underwriting

One of the biggest components of financial work is underwriting for insurance and loans. Increasingly, large companies that use underwriting are relying on systems built around machine learning, rather than using human beings. One thing that is driving this trend is the fact that over the decades, companies have gathered enormous amounts of data on applicants that can be used by machine learning systems to predict the outcome of giving someone a loan or life insurance. The data will include information like age, gender, occupation, income, and so forth. Again, while it might seem "obvious" what factors will determine who is a good risk and who isn't, the EKG example showed us that significant improvements could be made using machine learning, which will detect patterns in the data that human observers are not aware of. By using these types of systems to approve loans and engage in other financial decisions, companies can reduce the risk of default and other problems.

Customer Service

Many large companies are increasingly using machine learning as the basis of their frontline customer service. Admittedly, this is working with mixed results, and it is obvious there is more work to be done. One way that these types of systems are being used is through the use of chatbots. While these systems have not been brought anywhere near perfection, they are saving companies money by having an automated system in place to solve the most basic problems that arise in customer and technical support.

With these systems in place, a great deal of low-skilled human labor can be eliminated, and human workers can be reserved to deal with more extensive problems and consumer inquiries. Chat bots can be used for bill paying and other rote activities as well. With time, the performance of these systems is sure to improve.

Real Time Pricing

One of the biggest problems anyone in business faces is setting the right price for their product or service. Large amounts of data have to be analyzed in order to make the right decision, and by the time a human manager could make the decision, market conditions may have changed. Machine learning gives companies an edge they didn't have before, by giving them the ability to use dynamic pricing models. A machine learning system can look at real data collected over long time periods, and determine optimal prices that will help companies deal with the tradeoffs of quantity sold versus profit earned, and then incorporate that into dealing with any issues related to competition and shifting market conditions. Machine learning can then respond in real time, lowering prices when demand drops to stimulate sales, or responding to a price cut by a competitor.

Product Recommendations

Machine learning systems on the internet are constantly tracking our behavior, and they attempt to learn from our behavior to predict what we are going to want to buy.

These systems are another example of a system that is not perfect, they cannot tell if you are genuinely interested in something or looking something up for a friend, or looking at something you would never buy out of curiosity. Many people find them annoying and consider this an invasion of privacy, but one thing that we can be assured of is that over time the systems will improve dramatically as they continually learn from gathering huge amounts of data. We can expect that in the coming years these types of systems will be able to avoid the false positives that many people find annoying. The privacy issue is probably the big unknown here, if the kind of tracking that is necessary for these systems ever gets banned or regulated, they might not be in use at all in the future. The rub here is that data sharing between the big tech companies is necessary for these systems to work. Google collects data on people searching the internet, and companies like Amazon are also tracking searches on their sites, while Facebook is tracking what you look at and like.

Then all these data are shared between the companies so that advertisers can target specific and appropriate customers.

Self-Driving Cars

Multiple machine learning systems are being integrated into self-driving cars, creating one of the most sophisticated technologies ever devised. Although driving can be thought of as a relatively trivial skill for a human being to learn, it involves the integration of many different cognitive skills, including vision, interpretation, signs recognition, object recognition, following the road, avoiding collisions and so forth.

While driving split-second decisions are often essential for safety, and the hope is that self-driving cars will be able to make those decisions better than a human being can. Using machine learning, and gathering data by having test cars out on the road, remarkable progress has been made in a few short years. How far this technology is going to go is uncertain. Due to many thorny issues that are involved including liability questions and personal preferences, the self-driving capability may be limited to a role as an optional or supportive feature. Some people have visions of self-driving technology completely revolutionizing transportation, including the use of self-driving trucks for long-haul transport, but it is hard to imagine the freeways packed with self-driving semi-trucks. However, you can at least see the possibilities of a self-driving transport system and robots that would load and unload the trucks, completely automating logistics in the transportation industry.

Video Recommendations

Sites like YouTube and streaming services such as Netflix are using machine learning to help users navigate the world of online video. Every time you use one of these sites, your behaviors are collected, stored, and analyzed. This data includes everything from the type of videos you watch, to whether or not you pause or rewind, or whether you leave the video early. This information is then used to offer you a set of recommended videos or programs.

The recommendations are dynamic, so if your behavior changes, you will see your recommendations change as well. Of course, this is another area where the systems are not perfect. The human mind is as mysterious if not more so than machine learning, and someone who has a long history of watching World War 2 documentaries might suddenly feel an urge to watch a comedy, and no machine learning system in existence today is going to be able to detect that. Of course, if you start showing patterns, say wanting to watch a comedy after having watched a certain number of war documentaries, then the system will be able to learn from that and show you comedies you might want to watch at the appropriate times. But what these systems cannot do in most cases, is predict the unexpected when it comes to these specific applications.

Fraud Detection

We've talked about machine learning for fraud detection involving credit card theft, but it can be applied and is being used in other applications as well. For example, identity theft is something that can be rooted out using machine learning. Another area where machine learning is proving useful is with rooting out fraud in loan applications and even on tax returns. Recall that in the case of credit or debit card theft, certain anomalous behavior is going to be observed by the system. In the same way, the system can use clustering methods to spot anomalies when it comes to loan applications, filing of insurance claims, or the filing of a tax return. Of course, an anomaly is not a guarantee that fraud has occurred. But what can be done at that point, is when the system detects an anomaly it can be passed on to human operators who can investigate the situation.

This saves a lot of labor at a company, since human resources can be deployed for more in-depth investigation and critical decision making, rather than having to deploy people to do the tedious task of trying to identify the anomalies in the first place, and more than likely missing anomalies that the computer systems will detect. Spotting anomalies is something that is particularly susceptible to human flaws such as fatigue and inability to maintain the required level of focus for long time periods.

The large amounts of data that are collected by large companies and organizations like the IRS also make this problematic for human operators. Conventional computing is also not very good at this, because conventional computer systems would not be able to anticipate situations that are invisible to human operators. Another factor to consider is that bad actors are always changing their approach, and so learning the new ways of committing fraud is something that a system must be capable of doing. Of course machine learning systems are ideal in those circumstances.

Drug Discovery

The development of new drugs can be massively increased and improved with all the data that is being collected in the medical and pharmaceutical fields. Data on genetics, illness patterns, and so forth can be fed to machine learning systems, which can then evaluate large numbers of possible pathways to save pharmaceutical companies a great deal of time and help them to avoid blind alleys. One of the biggest problems that come about when designing new drugs is many of them are going to prove ineffective.

Machine learning systems are able to reduce the probability that a drug is not going to work. Another major advantage is that machine learning systems can combine data on DNA with other information to help design medications that can be laser targeted to individuals. Because of the particular genetic makeup of different individuals, some drugs are going to work better for one person, but not for another.

By using machine learning, companies can develop new drugs that can be targeted for specific genetic markers. Another way that machine learning is being used in the pharmaceutical industry is to find multi-drug combinations that will work better for specific individuals based on their genetic makeup when they have come down with a serious disease. Safety is also an issue, people with certain genetic markers may be more susceptible to serious side effects, and machine learning can help to identify the proper treatments for this subset of patients.

Facial Recognition

One longtime area of research in the world of artificial intelligence that has been going on for decades is computer vision. At first, computer vision systems were quite simple and one of the things that plague computer vision is the enormous amount of data that is required for learning. But now in today's world, yesterday's liability is now an asset. The ability to quickly process large amounts of data has made it possible to take computer vision to a new level. By exposing a machine learning system large numbers of images of faces, the systems have learned to take certain points on faces and use them to be able to identify individuals.

We already see many applications of this machine learning technology. For example, Facebook uses facial recognition technology to identify individuals in any image that a user uploads, and people can be automatically "tagged" if they appear in an image. The error rate for this is surprisingly low.

The second application of this technology will be familiar to many readers. Apple introduced facial recognition technology with the iPhone X, and used it as a way to unlock the phones. It is probably going to be the case that facial recognition technology will find wider applications when it comes to security. For example, you could deny access to unauthorized users when they try and enter a building that is secured, whether it is an office or at home. Facial recognition is also being used in public by authorities as well. The systems are able to go through large amounts of data very quickly, enabling the development of real-time facial recognition that can pick people out of a crowd. This technology can be used in positive or negative ways of course. Oppressive governments can use it to track people and determine where you are at any given time, but it can also be used to spot known terrorists in a crowd, and help law enforcement respond quickly to an event before it gets out of control. It is also being used for a government issued ID cards, so that people don't have to routinely get new drivers licenses or other documents. As we age, the visual appearance of our face changes, but certain key characteristics of the face are constant (in most circumstances) and can be quickly analyzed by technology to identify an individual. So you get one photograph on a license that is good for all time unless you have had a disfiguring accident.

Types of Data

In addition to learning the wide range of applications that are suitable for machine learning, if you are going to be involved in this field you need to have a solid grasp on the types of data that are used.

Structured Data

Many businesses and large organizations collect large amounts of structured data, and they have been doing so for many decades. Structured data is information that is organized into particular formats. The classic example of structured data is a relational database. It has various fields that characterize a record in the database, which can be indexed in different fields for the purposes of sorting, searching, and retrieving subsets of the data. Structured data can also take many other different forms, as long as it is collected and organized.

For example, a grocery store can collect point of sale data, when customers check out. This data can be arranged in a databased, identifying the customer through a so-called loyalty or discount card, and then combining that information with their purchasing habits in order to drive targeted marketing. Certain types of medical devices and other sensors can also be used to collect structured data. For example, you could collect the oxygen level of a patient in a hospital at different time intervals, and this information can be recorded permanently in a computer system with identifying information of the patient.

Another type of structured data that most people are familiar with is a spreadsheet. Structured data plays an important role in business intelligence, and it can often be extracted and presented visually in the form of charts and graphs, to help management make important data driven decisions.

Unstructured Data

The fact is that most data is actually unstructured data. When we have unstructured data, there is not a specific format and it may not be amenable to organizational structures like spreadsheets or relational databases. It might also have many mixed media types. For example, the Facebook postings of a given user can serve as a representation of unstructured data. Although a posting can be classified as to the user, date, and time of the posting, there are many different types of information in the posting such as images, video, text, and hyperlinks. The data in an image or video is something that is not suitable for a relational database, and hence it is unstructured.

Another type of unstructured data that large organizations collect is data related to internal operations. This includes recorded phone calls, memos, emails, and images among other things. Companies often collect reams of this data but have no idea how to use it, organize it, or access it. Unstructured data is definitely amenable to use with machine learning. There are many ways that the internal data of a company can be used, for example the company could determine which employees are spending a lot of time in the office idle (that is, not engaged in work related activities). The unstructured data that a company collects could also be used to reorganize teams or move people from one department to another.

The company can find out who is collaborating with whom, and then use that information to move employees around to better facilitate those communications, or make changes if the management feels that they are not communicating with team members they should be communicating with. Text documents can be analyzed by machine learning programs to detect patterns that management is not even aware of, and then this information could be used to reorganize company operations to increase efficiency and productivity. There are many types of unstructured data, but to give you an idea of what might constitute unstructured data, let's quickly give an overview:

- *Photo and video*: Images and videos of all types can constitute unstructured data. Consider the video surveillance footage collected by many businesses. That is unstructured data.

- *Traffic data:* One area that is now routinely tackled by machine learning is traffic patterns. Machine learning systems can help people by analyzing the unstructured data that is gathered on traffic patterns in busy locations, and this can then be used to suggest alternative routes.

- *Mobile data:* Unfortunately, depending on your point of view, the more dependent we become on our smart phones, the more large companies (and government agencies in some situations) are able to monitor our behavior. Your location data, usage data of apps and text messages, all constitute unstructured data that can be analyzed by machine learning systems to find hidden patterns that can be used for predictive purposes or classification.

- *Social media data:* Any data from your usage of Facebook, Twitter, Instagram, LinkedIn or other social media sites are a treasure trove of unstructured data that can be used to predict what products you are interested in or your future behaviors.

- *Satellite information:* Satellite imaging is a good example of unstructured data.

- *Transcripts of phone calls:* Whether it's an internal phone call between members of your sales staff or a transcript of a technical support call, the unstructured data in that transcript can contain a great deal of information that could be useful to the organization.

It is estimated that at least 80% of recorded information is unstructured data that is not contained in relational databases or other formats. Unstructured data is being generated constantly, every second of every day. By analyzing and utilizing unstructured data, companies can significantly improve competitiveness, efficiency, and productivity.

If you aren't using unstructured data, that means that you are leaving a lot of important information on the table.

Unstructured data can reveal trends before people even realize they are happening. For example, a company could discover that a trend is building in people abandoning a specific product, or the seemingly random posts on Twitter and Facebook might reveal a trend that was happening at large in society that is under the radar of most people.

Summary

The examples discussed in this chapter serve to illustrate the wide range of problems that can be tackled using machine learning. As you can see from these examples, the applications are quite diverse. This diversity is possible because of the general nature of machine intelligence. A human being can learn to become a doctor, or a financial analyst. They can learn how to ride a motorcycle or how to play chess. This type of general intelligence that human beings possess has been the inspiration for the development of artificial intelligence. Any given machine learning system will be quite specific as to what it learns and does, and once it's trained on something, that is what it's going to do. But by combining several machine learning systems together, we can create an integrated system like a robot that can be used to perform multiple tasks.

Chapter 3: Supervised Learning

A machine learning system must be trained. This is done by presenting it with data.

There are three ways that machine learning systems undergo training, or a learning phase. The two main methods that are used are known as supervised and unsupervised learning. A third method is available, which is called semi-supervised learning. In this chapter, we are going to learn the ways that these methods are used, the purpose of using them, and how they differ from one another. We will begin by considering supervised learning, since this is considered a bit more basic. However, the application, rather than any thoughts about complexity, is going to be what determines the types of learning that are used.

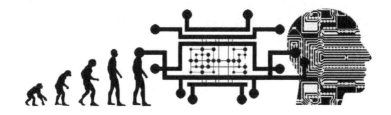

413

Supervised Machine Learning

The term supervised or unsupervised refers to the training portion in the life of the machine learning system. The first main technique that is used is called supervised machine learning. This is most appropriate when you have a large data set that has clearly defined inputs and outputs. Another way to put this is that given a certain input set of data, we know what the output, or correct answer is. We say that the data in this case is labeled. This simply means that the various fields in the data are labeled as an input or an output. Mathematically, we are considering a basic functional form in this case:

Y = f(X)

Here X is the input, and Y is the output, and f is an unknown functional relationship between the two. The point here is not to be thinking in terms of specific mathematical relations, but rather in terms of an abstract relationship that exists between the inputs and outputs. In some cases, there will be a precise functional relationship, but in many cases, we are not going to know what the relationship is, even though the computer system will "know" how the inputs and outputs are related. It will discover this relationship by detecting the hidden patterns that exist in the data that can be used to related inputs and outputs (and are probably unknown to the human observers).

As a simple example, suppose that we were selling our own smart phone, and we wanted to find out who the ideal customer was.

For the sake of simplicity, suppose that our data only records the gender, age, and zip code of each customer of our phone service. We can then simply label each customer as a yes or a no as to whether or not they purchased the smart phone. Our input vector is going to be gender, age, and zip code, while the labeled output—which is given to the system as a part of supervised learning—is a marker as to whether or not the given customer purchased the phone.

Prior to doing the exercise, we may not have any idea about what characteristics are most important in determining whether or not a given customer is likely to purchase the phone or not, but the system might determine that females aged 30-45 are most likely to purchase the phone.

With this information in hand, we can then target a larger share of our advertising budget to this group. The real world is complicated, and there are not going to be simple scalar relationships between the inputs and outputs, and they are not going to be simple scalar variables. Instead, the inputs and outputs are going to be in the form of vectors. A vector is a mathematical quantity that contains multiple elements. In the case of data that is used in machine learning, the vector will contain multiple fields of data. It is important to think in general terms, and so the data is not necessarily numerical in nature, although it could be.

The supervised learning process is often likened to an elementary school class that is guided by a teacher. For example, think about teaching children how to multiply two numbers together. This can be setup by thinking in terms of giving input vectors such as (2,2), (4,3) and (7,5), together with the known outputs (4), (12), and (35). This is an example of labeled data, where we have inputs, e.g. (4,3) and labeled outputs, e.g. (12).

In the same way, inputs and outputs are labeled for the computer system by the data scientist. Then the computer system goes through large amounts of data, in order to learn the patterns underlying the data and develop a relationship that can be used to predict outputs from future inputs. This is one of the core reasons that you would want to use supervised learning to train the system, in that you are hoping it will be able to predict future outputs. The output value during training is sometimes called the supervisory signal. A real-world example might be a data set of customers that got loans at a bank. Some of the customers will pay off the loan early. Others may default on the loan; some may keep making payments but be consistently late. The goal in this case would be to look at the input data on each of these customers, and then try to determine the relationships that exist between the inputs and the outputs.

In a complex real-world problem like this one, there are going to be many unexpected and hidden patterns in the underlying data that human observers could miss.

Some of the relationships that exist between the inputs and the outputs will help the system make predictions of how a loan made to a new client will turn out based on the inputs that are provided. Supervised learning can be thought of as a mapping process between input and output pairs. The purpose of training is to guide the system so that it can infer a relationship between the input and output vectors, and then that relationship can be used with any new data to predict the output. Of course, the training data is going to be limited in scope by necessity, and as a result the system is going to have to generalize to a certain degree in order to arrive at a relationship that can be applied to new data. This process can result in problems, and there is an issue faced by all supervised learning systems that are called the bias-variance tradeoff. We will talk more about that later.

General Types of Supervised Machine Learning

Machine learning can be generally classified as either regression type learning, or classification. Generally speaking, in regression, the output variable may have continuous mathematical values. In a classification problem, the labels are discrete and you can think of the input as being classified to belong to one group or another. Binary classification will assign a member to a group based on a 0 or a 1. In the earlier example where we considered whether a member of our phone service bought a phone or not, we could use binary classification, with buying the phone is a 1, and not buying the phone being a 0. However, classification problems can have more than two possible results.

The Process of Supervised Learning

The process of machine learning is going to be directed by a specialist on staff that is known as a data scientist. A data scientist is a professional that has training in multiple disciplines. At the very least, the data scientist should have training in computer science, especially in the fields of artificial intelligence and machine learning.

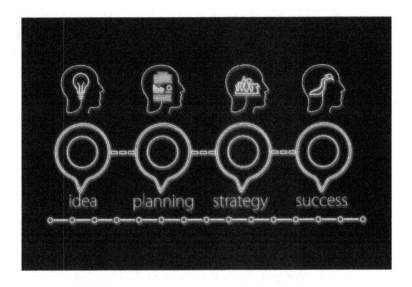

They should also have advanced training in statistics and probability, because these branches of mathematics have a large role to play whenever there are large data sets to be analyzed. Third, it is often desired that the data scientist has some business acumen, which will help them understand how the results of their work are going to be used by the organization and what the impact is going to be. There isn't really a formal definition of "data scientist" and until recently, there wasn't really any formal training or schooling for it. This is a multidimensional field of expertise that has arisen in the real world do the coming together of several forces in the business and technological worlds. The first skill that the data scientist must have is in the ability to select the best data sets available to use for learning, when faced with a specific problem.

Selecting the data can also mean refining the data, the data scientist may look at the fields of data and pare them down to a smaller number, that in the judgment of the human observer, seem more relevant to the problem at hand. As we will see, it is important to cut the number of fields down if there are a large number of them. Too many inputs for a system are going to make it harder for it to learn. When we discuss artificial intelligence and machine learning, people often have a mystical view of it and might have the impression that the computer has an infinite capacity to examine data and learn. In fact, computer systems do not have an infinite capacity, even though they can examine and analyze much larger data sets than humans can. There may even be theoretical limits to the capacity of any intelligent system to do analysis and arrive at the correct result when there are too many inputs. The problem of too many inputs causes issues because it becomes harder to determine the relationships between inputs and outputs. This is called the dimensionality problem. If there are too few dimensions, or fields representing an input to a problem, then there is not going to be enough information for the system to figure out the relationship between the inputs and the outputs. On the other hand, if there are too many inputs or dimensions, then the system is going to be confused, and unable to find out what the true relationship between inputs and outputs are. Again, you shouldn't be thinking of inputs and outputs as being strictly numerical in nature. For example, the problem at hand may be training a system in handwriting analysis. So, the input data might actually be images of handwriting. Human experts working on the problem are going to choose data sets to use in training that they believe is representative of the real-world situation. Again, this is another aspect of the problem that is going to depend on the judgment of the data scientists that are setting up the training. It is another illustration of the fact that even though a machine learning system is not programmed, in the sense of having human operators write line by line instructions for the computer, it is nonetheless still heavily influenced by human decision making and judgment.

Feature Vectors

A feature is what it means in plain English. That is a feature is some measurable characteristic of a given input to a system. If the input is an image, some of the features that describe it could include the color, tint, brightness, and so forth of each pixel. If we are talking about a loan application, the features in question would be of a completely different nature. They could include credit score, bankruptcy (y/n), zip code, years of education, monthly income, and so forth.

Inputs are called feature vectors, because a feature vector is a representation of some object in the real world, that contains a set of features for that object. For example, if we wanted to teach a system to recognize a truck or a car in a photograph, and determine the difference between the two, many aspects of the vehicle could be represented in the feature vector. It would be up to the data scientist to choose the features that they believe best represents the object of study. Since some of the computer algorithms that are used in machine learning are numerical in nature, such as linear regression, a problem often has to be boiled down to numerical data. It is up to the data scientists to get the right representation in order to use the right algorithm, and they also have to be able to select the best features to represent a given object that is being studied. Obviously, this process is never going to be perfect, and at times there are going to be mistakes made.

Picking the Learning Algorithm

Once the problem has been broken down into input and output vectors, and the proper set of features has been selected, the data scientists must choose the best algorithm that can be used in order to represent the problem accurately. There are many different functions that are used. There are several different learning algorithms that are used. Choosing the algorithm that is used is another step in the process that is directed by a human being, and so this is another way that human observers and trainers are involved in influencing the final machine learning product. Let's review the type of algorithms that are used.

Linear Regression

Linear regression is one of the most popular algorithms that is used in machine learning. The purpose of using linear regression is to model a relationship between inputs and outputs that can then be used to predict future outputs. We will discuss linear regression in more detail in a future chapter.

Logistic Regression

Logistic regression, like linear regression, is a type of statistical modeling of some phenomenon. In this case, the output assumes a binary form. Therefore, we expect the output to be a type of yes/no, pass/fail, or alive/dead type of output.

Decision Trees

A decision tree is an algorithm that asks a series of questions at nodes about the characteristics of an item. This then follows along, leading to a path through different branches of a "tree" that will allow the system to arrive at a resulting answer or classification of a question being asked. For a real-world example where this could be used, think in terms of a diagnosis program. A patient will present with a set of symptoms, and yes/no questions can then be posed about the symptoms and other characteristics to determine whether or not the patient has an illness and if so what kind of illness the patient is suffering from.

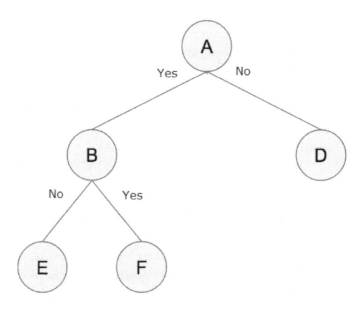

For example, you could use a decision tree in order to distinguish between allergies and a cold or flu. Does the patient have a fever? Is the patient experiencing body aches? And so on…the answer to one question will direct the system along a branchlike path in a tree to more questions. After several questions have been answered, eventually the conclusion is reached, in this case it would be a yes, the patient has allergies or yes, the patient has a cold/flu.

Naïve Bayes Classifier

In many cases, the purpose of machine learning will be to classify something. One common example of this that is used is spam email messaging, something we have touched on before. The point is that an email is classified as spam, or not spam. In recent years, email systems have become more sophisticated and they might classify email in more detail. So, we start with is the email spam or not spam, and if not spam, is it a personal email, a social email, or a promotion?

Of course, determining the difference between a promotion and spam is a more difficult problem, than determining whether an email is sent by a friend or whether it's a spam email. Nonetheless, systems like Gmail process such high volumes of email, and they have been doing it for large numbers of people over many years, that they are pretty good at sorting emails in this way (but of course, they still make many mistakes). Bayesian classifiers use probability in order to classify inputs. Naïve Bayes means that naïve independence assumptions are made with regard to the input features in the problem.

As the spam example illustrates, this type of algorithm can be used to label inputs. Supervised learning is suitable for this algorithm because the correct label would be the output of the system. So, the inputs to a system that was learning email via supervised learning would be the sending email address, the subject line used, the text of the email, and so forth. The possible outputs are the classifications of the email–is it from social media, is it spam, is it a personal email etc. These types of models use conditional probabilities, but the details are beyond the scope of this book.

Support Vector Machines

The next type of algorithm that is frequently used in supervised learning is called a support vector machine. Generally speaking, this type of algorithm is used when data can be classified as belonging to one data set or another. During training, the data inputs are provided, along with their classifications. This allows the system to build a model that represents the relationship between the input vectors and the classification. The beauty of this type of training is that although the human observer is somewhat involved, for example in selecting the inputs and outputs to present to the system, the human observer doesn't have to be involved in any way when it comes to determining the type of relationship that exists between the input and output data. Once the system has been trained, when it is presented with a new data point, it should be able to accurately classify the data as belonging to one classification or another.

K-Nearest Neighbor Algorithm

This type of algorithm can be used for classification or regression. In the case of supervised learning, regression is more likely to be important. The output in this case is some property of the object that is under study. The system will arrive at predicted outputs by observing the k-nearest neighbors, and then averaging the values of their outputs.

Some mathematical function is used in order to precisely determine the "distance" between two different data points in a data set. Conceptually, this is like a distance function between two points in space. The underlying assumption here is that when two data points in a set are close together, using the definition given in the distance function, they are going to have similar outputs. The neighbors can be weighted or unweighted. If they are unweighted, all neighbors that are used in the calculation are treated in the same manner, and so the predicted output is calculated using simple averaging techniques. If a weighted algorithm is used, then neighbors that are closer to the data point in question are given more weight than the neighbors that are more distant. It is believed that generally speaking, the latter method is going to provide more accurate answers. However, which method you use in a given situation is going to be a matter of judgment. So once again, we have another point at which human judgment is involved in the process.

Neural Networks

A neural network is a model that is based on the way a brain functions. Hopefully, it is able to model a human brain, but as far as we know all brains work in basically the same manner. In an actual physical brain, there are neurons or nerve cells, that are able to hook up with or connect to other neurons. There is a cell body near the top of the cell, and several branches or dendrites extend out of the top of the cell body in a tree like formation. These each includes individual nodes that can connect to many other cells.

At the other end of the cell body, there is a long extension that resembles (at least conceptually) an electrical cable. This is called the axon. At the other end is more tree like dendrites, which are connected to other neurons. The sum total of inputs from the neurons connected to the front of the cell body will determine whether or not the neuron 'fires', which simply means that an electrical current will travel down the axon, leading to the release of chemicals out the other ends, that will help determine whether or not succeeding neurons fire or not. Somehow, this process represents information processing, learning, and consciousness. While consciousness is not very well understood, the process of learning basically takes place as neurons form new networks among themselves, in order to represent information. Connections between neurons are strengthened or weakened, depending on experience and learning.

The goal of neural networks is to have a representation of this setup and the processes inside a computer. Compared to a real brain, neural networks are quite primitive, nonetheless the general features of the process are there.

A nerve cell is represented by a "node", which is a computer function that might do some simple task. Actually, it is going to output a nonlinear function of some type of the inputs provided to the node, if communication has taken place. Inputs to a given node, from other nodes that are in the system, will be weighted. The weights will change as the system is exposed to new data. This is analogous to a physical neuron forming stronger or weaker connections to other neurons that are sending it input.

The weights will either be larger, strengthening the signal input from another node that is in another layer, or it will be smaller, weakening the signal.

An input layer of nodes will accept or take in information from the external world. There can be one or more hidden or intermediate layers. The first hidden layer is behind the input layer, and it will take inputs from the input layer. The outputs will serve as inputs for the next layer. If that is the last layer in a simple system, that layer will produce outputs for the external world. Alternatively, you can have multiple hidden layers.

As a neural network is exposed to data, the weights will adjust, changing the interconnections between the nodes or "neurons" in the system.

A physical neuron will not fire unless a threshold is crossed with respect to electrostatic potential. In the same way, a node may have a threshold that must be reached before it will send an output signal to the neurons in the next layer.

Finishing the Process

We will talk about some of the more important learning algorithms in more detail in future chapters. It is important to recognize that you can't say one algorithm is better than any other algorithm. The judgment and experience of the data scientist must be used in order to determine the best algorithm to use in a given situation. Once the algorithm has been selected, the data scientist will expose the system to the data.

In some cases, the function used may be tuned by selecting the values of certain parameters that are used. These are called control parameters. The human observers will then evaluate the performance of the system, determining how well it performed. If it has not performed up to an acceptable level, then more training may be used, and there may be adjustments to control parameters to see if this will improve performance.

The Bias-Variance Tradeoff

One of the most important issues facing a data scientist and the use of supervised learning is the bias-variance tradeoff. These are errors in a prediction that result when a model is built. The goal when developing any computer model is to minimize errors. In the case of supervised learning, when you try to minimize variance errors, you will end up increasing bias errors. In turn, if you try to minimize bias error, you will increase error due to variance.

The key to success with supervised learning is simultaneously minimizing bias and variance. Of course, that means that we don't minimize either as much as we could minimize each in isolation. Therefore, a trade-off is made, in order to reduce the overall total error. In other words, you will have to accept that there is going to be some level of error in both cases.

When we are doing supervised learning, it is important to know what bias and variance refer to. Let's consider bias first. Simply put, bias is the difference between the prediction of the model, and the correct answer, on average. If the model is very accurate with the training data, this means that the error between the prediction and the correct answer is going to be very small, but at the same time that also means that the model is going to be very biased toward the training data. That could lead to errors in the real world, since the training data– to some extent–is not going to be representative of all the data that exists out there in the real world. This illustrates the importance of choosing representative training data. If the data scientist is able to choose training data that is highly representative of the data that the system is going to encounter in the real world when it is deployed, then there will not be as much bias.

Variance is the amount of spread, or variation in the data. Models with high variance will do very well on training data, but they will have problems with other data. The researchers developing the system will first present the system with training data, and then they will present it with test data. When the system has a high bias, it will produce large errors with both the training and test data, and presumably also with any real-world data that it would encounter when deployed, if no modifications are made.

If the system instead has high variance, it will have small errors with the training data, but will demonstrate high levels of error with the test data, and therefore with any real-world data that it encounters. There are four situations that we can encounter, when considering bias and variance together:

- *Low Bias and Low Variance*: In this case, the model will be very accurate. It will give accurate results with training, test, and real-world data.
- *Low Bias, High Variance*: In this case, the data will overfit the training data. So, in training it will give very accurate results. But in testing or real-world situations, it will have high rates of error. It has overfitted the data used to train it.
- *High Bias, Low Variance*: In this case, the system is underfitting. Therefore, it is not going to be accurate, even with the training data.
- *High Bias, High Variance*: Here, we will be all over the map. The predictions of the model will not be accurate.

426

Underfitting and overfitting during training are things to look for when using supervised learning. Again, the data sets that are selected by the human observer are going to be important here. If the data set provided to train the system does not have enough data in it to accurately draw conclusions, underfitting can result. That means there will be high bias, but low variance. The model might be too simple to recognize the patterns in the data. Models that are particularly prone to underfitting include linear and logistic regression. Another way to look at it is that if the model is too simple, it can be prone to high bias and low variance. Remember that earlier, we mentioned the problem of dimensionality. In this case, that means we don't have enough parameters to correctly describe the problem. Overfitting basically means that the system has fit the training data too closely. Any data set is going to have noise, or data that is intrinsically meaningless for the problem that is being studied. When the model overfits the data, it will fit the noise as well. So, it will perfectly fit (or nearly so) the training data set. But since it is being misled by the noise in the training data set, that means that in further testing on new data or in the real world, the model is going to be inaccurate. Decision trees are particularly prone to overfit the data. In this case, dimensionality may be a problem again. This time, we might have too many parameters. Ideally, you want to minimize both bias and variance as much as possible at the same time. This is done by minimizing the total error in the problem.

Matching Complexity to Bias and Variance

Any relationship between inputs and outputs is going to have its own level of complexity. If a problem is simple, that is the relationships between the features of the input vector and the output is simple, then a simple algorithm that has high bias and low variance might be able to learn the true relationship between inputs and outputs. Alternatively, the relationships between inputs and outputs may be highly complex. In that case, the algorithm needs to be flexible, and it will need a larger data set in order to learn the relationships between the inputs and the outputs. In that case, low bias and high variance algorithm will be better. These examples illustrate the problems that can arise and the amount of judgment that may be required in order to arrive at the best possible solution.

Dimensionality

The more features an input vector has, the more difficult the problem is to solve. Even if only a few features of the input vector are important to the output, if we don't know ahead of time which ones they are, this can create difficulties for the learning algorithm. The extra dimensions may serve to confuse the algorithm, by leading down the wrong direction. It may "detect" false relationships that don't actually exist. Mathematical procedures called dimensionality reduction may be used in order to try and eliminate features that are not important for determining the relationship between the input and output vectors in the problem. Alternatively, if not enough dimensions are provided as input, then the system may not be able to accurately predict future results, because not enough input features have been provided to the system.

Output Noise in Supervised Learning

Noise in the input data is one thing to worry about, and there is also a noise present in the output data that is used in supervised learning. There are many reasons that input data will have errors.

In the course of real life, errors are going to be a natural occurrence. If human operators are recording or collecting data, they may make mistakes while recording results. In the normal course of operation, electronic devices may report erroneous results as well, for one reason or another.

As discussed earlier, this is why you want to avoid overfitting the training data, because you become attuned to the errors that are present in the training data set, that is not going to be characteristic of the data generally. One way to avoid this problem is to do some preprocessing of the data. In this instance, an effort can be made to reduce the noise in the data that is used for training before it is presented to the system.

Chapter 4: Unsupervised and Semi-Supervised Learning

In the last chapter, we introduced the first way that machine learning systems are trained. This was called supervised learning, and the training process in that case involves presenting the system with a set of data where the outputs are known and labeled ahead of time. Presenting the known outputs to the system in order to help it learn is how supervised learning works. However, one of the main benefits of machine learning is that these types of systems are able to find hidden patterns in large data sets. This fact brings us to the next way that machine learning systems can be trained, and this procedure is known as unsupervised learning. In the process of unsupervised learning, the system is allowed to examine data and spot patterns within the data, drawing inferences about the data on its own.

This is done without human direction and without any labeling of outputs. Since the outputs are not labeled (indeed, they may not be, and usually are not, even known), we can say that they are unlabeled. Often, the choice of using supervised or unsupervised learning will depend on the framing of the problem at hand, and the question as to whether you know what the outputs are. If the outputs are known then it makes sense to use supervised learning. But they may not be known, in which case unsupervised learning may be more appropriate. Another type of learning attempts to mix the two. This will involve training on data sets using both supervised and unsupervised learning. In this case, we say that we are using semi-supervised learning.

In this chapter, we will learn about unsupervised learning, and then wrap up the discussion by considering semi-supervised learning.

What is Unsupervised Learning?

In order to use regression, you need to be able to know what the output values are for the purposes of training, so that the data can be fit to some type of functional relationship. But with some data sets, we may not know what the outputs are, or we may be interested in using a large data set in order to determine if there are any hidden patterns or relationships in the data that we didn't even know existed. Clustering is one of the main methods used in unsupervised learning, so that the system can determine relationships between different members in the data set.

Clustering

In a large data set, you are going to find that the member objects can be grouped together in one or more ways. Consider an image. The pixels that make up the image can be classified by color. Then you could group together all yellow pixels, all orange pixels, all green pixels, all red pixels, all blue pixels, and all violet pixels in the image. The key to clustering is grouping together data points that are more similar to each other than they are to other members in the data set. Algorithms are applied in order to do cluster analysis, clustering is the task that is to be completed, and not a specific way of doing the task.

When used with unsupervised machine learning, the machine is going to find the clusters on its own without human input. The human observers may not even know what clusters are present in the data, or they may only have a vague idea. A cluster is not even something that we can say what it is with any certainty. That will depend on the specific application, and in some cases, clusters may be defined with more or less rigor.

K-Means

K-means clustering gathers the data into k different clusters, determining which cluster a data point belongs to by how close it is to the mean of a given cluster. Often a human observer will look at the data to make an estimate of the number of clusters that should be used. The center or mean of each cluster is then calculated, and then as you sweep through the data, a distance function is used in order to find out which cluster the data point belongs to. This process is repeated in an iterative fashion, recomputing the mean values at each step.

Mean Shift Clustering

Mean shift clustering uses a window to sweep through the data. In this case, it begins by searching for areas with a high density of data points. The data is divided into different classes. As it sweeps through the data it attempts to find the center of each class. The center points are the mean of any data points that are inside the window. This algorithm will then sort the data into appropriate clusters. While k-means clustering involves determining the number of clusters, in this case, the algorithm determines the number of clusters for you.

DBScan

This means Density Based Spatial Clustering of Applications with Noise. This is another density-based clustering algorithm. The algorithm picks an arbitrary starting point in a set of data. A distance function is used to determine a neighborhood about the point. The first step is to determine whether or not there are enough points in the neighborhood for analysis. If there are, then a cluster is formed. If there are not enough points in the neighborhood to form a cluster, then the point is determined to be noise. Any data points that are within the distance that defines the neighborhood are determined to be members of the cluster. The algorithm will visit each of the points within the given neighborhood.

Next, the algorithm will search outside the neighborhood to find an unvisited data point. It then repeats the process, determining if there are enough points in the neighborhood of the new data point to consider it valid and defining a new cluster, or if not, the point is labeled as noise and ignored. There is no pre-set number of clusters, this is discovered by the algorithm. It is also able to determine if a data point is noise or not. Other clustering methods may not be able to do this. If the data has a high variance in the density of data points, the method may not be effective. The OPTICS method is an algorithm that was devised in order to address the density weakness problem of DBSCAN.

Hierarchical Clustering

This type of clustering can be either bottom-up or top-down. A bottom-up algorithm starts by considering every single data point to be a cluster. It then sweeps through the data, and then merges similar data points together to form new clusters. A distance function is used in order to determine whether or not two data points should be joined together to form a cluster. The sweeps through the system will continue, growing the number of points in each cluster. This type of clustering can be used to build a tree like structure. The leaves of the tree are the individual data points, and then going up each branch, you have each combination that was used to define a new cluster.

Anomaly Detection

One of the most useful ways that unsupervised learning can be used is with anomaly detection. Anomaly detection can be important in a wide variety of real-world circumstances. One of the most common ways that it is used is with the maintenance of security for computer networks. A machine learning system can examine past data that consists of attempts to access the network, and it can search for anomalies that are outside the statistically expected behavior of attempts at network access. When this occurs, then there is a certain degree of confidence that the access attempt is fraudulent.

When using unsupervised learning for anomaly detection, the central assumption that is made is that the majority of the collected data is completely normal. Therefore, the system will simply learn by searching for data that does not fit together with the rest of the data set. In other words, the system will search for outliers. It is then assumed that the outliers represent fraudulent activity.

Visualization

Systems trained with unsupervised learning can be used to determine hidden patterns in data, and then present the data in human readable form using visualization. In other words, the system will generate graphs and charts which will illustrate the relationships between features in the data.

Dimensionality Reduction

In the last chapter, the curse of dimensionality was mentioned several times. In some cases, the number of dimensions is excessive and having too many dimensions can make it difficult to determine the relationship between input and output variables difficult. Techniques of dimensionality reduction will attempt to cut down the number of features in the data set without losing important information. In the process of feature extraction, the system will merge together correlated features into one single feature. By cutting down on the number of features, the time required to determine relationships between the data can be reduced, and it will make it more likely that a problem can be solved accurately. Principle component analysis and singular value decomposition are two techniques that can be used for dimensionality reduction.

Semi-Supervised Learning

In some situations, semi-supervised learning may be appropriate. This type of learning is a hybrid training strategy. Simply put, both supervised and unsupervised learning is used in this case. It has been shown that at least in some circumstances, the accuracy achieved with semi-supervised learning is superior to that seen with unsupervised learning alone. The key is to enhance unsupervised learning by training the system on a small dataset using supervised learning first. This can be thought of as a way to "prime" the system. Then the system can continue learning, but in the second phase of training, a larger data set is used for unsupervised learning.

Reinforcement Based Learning

Reinforcement learning is another strategy that can be used in machine learning. In this case, the system will have software agents that act within some kind of environment. A video game is an example of where this can be used. Like unsupervised learning, this is another method that does not rely on using labeled input and output data pairs.

In machine learning, reinforcement learning is centered on getting the machine to follow the best possible path in specific situations. The training is done by providing rewards. There will be a reinforcement agent that has to decide on its own how to perform various tasks. There are not any training datasets or labels used when building a system that is based on reinforcement learning. A good way to understand reinforcement learning is to think in terms of a path through a maze. You can have a maze with obstacles that the agent must navigate around, and a reward somewhere in the maze that it must find. The agent will learn in the same way that a human being might learn, so you might imagine yourself in a corn maze trying to find a pot of gold. The agent will learn by trying different paths, and it learns solely through experience. When it tries a path and runs into an obstacle, then it will learn not to use that path again, and it will explore a different path instead.

434

By trying out all possible paths and learning where the obstacles are, the agent will find its way to the reward. The agent can be encouraged to find the correct path by giving it rewards at various steps along the way. Reinforcement learning is useful when there are multiple ways to solve a problem. A very simple problem like 2+2 has only one way to solve it, but in the real world, complex problems can often be solved in many different ways. In reinforcement learning, the agent will learn all the possible ways to solve the problem. When the agent is not performing in the right way, it can be punished and forced to start over. Every time that the agent is punished or rewarded, it will learn, and the next time it is sent back to the starting position, it will perform better so that it will be easier to reach its goal.

How Reinforcement Learning Compares to Supervised Learning

In supervised learning, we provide a set of data points and labeled answers to the system so that it can deduce the relationship there is between inputs and outputs. This is not done with reinforcement learning. Instead, the agent in reinforcement learning involves the agent making its own decisions, and then suffering the consequences of its own actions. This is how life is in reality, so it is a kind of model of real experience. You can think of supervised learning as the kind of training that you would get in elementary school, while reinforcement training is the kind of learning that you experience in day to day life.

When you start out now knowing very much, you are probably going to make many mistakes. But each time that you make a mistake, you learn not to pursue the actions that you took that led to the bad result. In the same way, the agent in reinforcement learning finds out which paths lead to punishment and which paths lead to rewarding. After it learns this, then it no longer takes the bad paths, and it gets better at solving the task that it needs to solve. Just like with real life, the behavior of the agent can be shaped using positive or negative enforcement, or some combination thereof.

Positive reinforcement involves giving the agent a reward for making the right decision, while negative reinforcement involves giving the agent a punishment for making the wrong decision. If too much positive reinforcement is used, it can lead to diminishing returns over time. Maximal performance, however, is achieved by using positive reinforcement. A minimal level of performance is achieved by training with negative reinforcement. A combination of the two can help the system learn without overwhelming it and leading to diminishing returns.

What Types of Systems Use Reinforcement Learning?

Reinforcement learning can be applied in many different circumstances. One of the main areas where it is used is with robotics. Machine learning systems can also be trained using reinforcement learning, and one of the main areas where it's used is in training machine learning systems to play games.

Is Reinforcement Learning Unsupervised Learning?

The answer is that reinforcement learning is not unsupervised learning. In unsupervised learning, the system is trying to find hidden patterns in a data set. In contrast, with reinforcement learning, there is a software agent, and we are trying to shape the software agent by rewarding it or punishing it when it exhibits certain behaviors while learning a skill. So, this is actually a completely different learning method as compared to unsupervised learning. The agent will use exploration strategies in order to learn and master a given skill.

Chapter 5: Regression Methods

Regression is a method that is used to predict the output value when it is numerical and continuous. As such, regression methods are particularly useful when it comes to a supervised learning problem. For example, given a set of characteristics of a patient, we might use a regression algorithm to predict their fasting blood sugar level. The inputs might include their age, race, height, weight, blood pressure, or any other measured value that might characterize the overall health of the patient and general tendencies. Another example that might be amenable to a regression type algorithm could be using age, occupation, level of education attained, zip code of home residence, city, and other data to make an estimate of their annual household income.

Regression is a basic mathematical problem. It is used to fit data to a curve, so it is attempting to derive a relationship of the form y = f(x) that is unknown prior to analysis. A regression problem may have multiple variables that can be fit to a curve, as the examples above illustrate. Care must be used with regression modeling because they are particularly susceptible to overfitting and underfitting. Remember that if you overcomplicate a problem, this can lead to overfitting. There might be a lot of collected data that is not related to the problem at hand, but if you include it, the computer system will attempt to find a relationship between the irrelevant data and the output. When real world data is then presented to the system, it will make erroneous predictions because the relationships it builds from the irrelevant data fields don't always hold.

And let's also remind ourselves that if the model is too simple, it will probably miss the actual relationships that are present in the data. In this case, it is going to underfit the data, and it will probably have a large error even with the training data set.

Types of Regression

The most common type of regression that is used in machine learning is linear regression. Specifically, simple linear regression is used. This is a simple mathematical relationship between inputs and outputs. It could take a form like this:

Y = a + bX

Here, X is an input vector that consists of one or more fields or vector elements, and Y is the corresponding output vector. Y may be a single parameter. The point of this model is to use the input vector to predict the value of Y. The training process is used to determine the values of the parameters a and b. In short, you are trying to fit a straight line to a cluster of data.

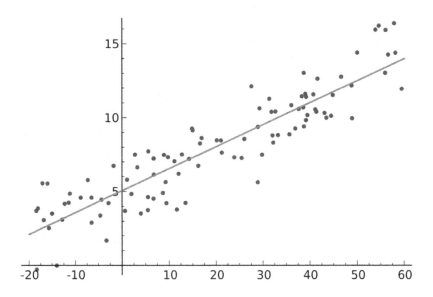

The goal of training is to determine the coefficients used to fit the training data as accurately as possible. There is always going to be some degree of error no matter how good your model is. Error can be calculated by simply taking the average squared distance between the predicted values and the measured values. Using a technique called gradient descent, the process begins by using randomly chosen parameters, and then as the data is analyzed the model updates the values of the parameters in order to minimize the error.

The size of the data set is going to be related to the level of accuracy that is achieved. Here, we are not talking about the number of fields used, which is what the dimensionality problem is about. Rather, we are simply noting that collecting more data is going to help us build a more accurate model, as long as the data is good data.

For example, if you were attempting to build a model that was predicting household income based on a given set of data fields, as you can imagine, the computer system would get more accurate if we had 1,000 data points rather than 100 data points, or if we had 10,000 data points versus 1,000 data points. Also, the more data you have the more specific you can get in our analysis. When you only have 100 data points, the error margin is going to be so large that you really can't say anything with much confidence. But if you have thousands of data points, each data point being a person with information that may be related to the salary they make, then you can glean a large amount of relevant statistical information while also possibly drilling down more deeply. Rather than just asking how household income is related to a number of years in school, you might also be able to ask if dog owners have a higher median income than non-dog owners.

When there are multiple input features, a more complicated relationship must be used. In this case, there are going to be multiple parameters used to fit the line. The general form is still going to be:

$$Y = a + bX$$

But this time, b is going to be an array of values, with one parameter for each feature in the input vector. If we have 6 features in the input vector, then it would be of the form:

$$Y = a + b[1]*x[1] + b[2]*x[2] ++ b[3]*x[3] + b[4]*x[4] + b[5]*x[5] + b[6]*x[6]$$

Mglearn

Mglearn is a set of helper functions that can be used in python to practice machine learning. It can be downloaded at this link:

https://github.com/amueller/introduction_to_ml_with_python

Installation instructions can be found here:

https://github.com/amueller/mglearn/blob/master/Readme.md

When using mglearn in python, you will need the following import statement:

import mglearn

You will also want to use basic plotting tools. You can include the following to generate the scatter plots that can represent test data sets:

import matplotlib.pylot as plt

import matplotlib

440

Since this is a tool that is designed to learn how to do machine learning, you can use it to generate datasets. To generate a dataset for the purpose of testing and learning, we can write:

X,y = mglearn.datasets.make_forge()

This will create a testing dataset that has an input vector X that can have multiple features together with labeled outputs y.

A good way to simulate the kind of data that you would encounter when faced with a linear regression problem is to make a wave of discrete points. This can be done using the make_wave command. We can label the input vector as the feature, and the output as the response. Then, you can setup an example with the number of samples that you want using the following code. Suppose that we wanted 50 samples:

X,y = prctlearn.datasets.make_wave(n_samples = 50)

plt.plot(X,y,'o')

plt.ylim (-4,4),

plt.xlabel("Feature")

plt.ylabel("Response")

This will give us something like this:

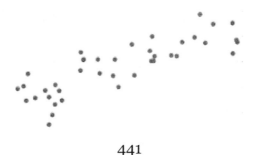

Another way to make a plot is to use linear_regression_wave. Sticking to one feature for simplicity. For example:

mglearn.plots.plot_linear_regression_wave()

The system will learn the values of the fitting parameters from the training data. This gives us:

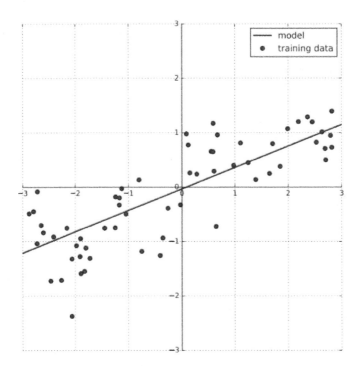

Ordinary Least Squares

Earlier we mentioned that one of the goals of our analysis is to minimize the error between the predicted values and the actual, measured values. One way that this can be done is by using what is known as the least squares method. This is what was described earlier. That is, we want to minimize the sum of the squares of the errors at each point—the error being the difference between the measured data and the value predicted by the model. Typically, least squares is a technique that is used when a system is "overdetermined". This means that there are more equations in the system than there are unknown variables.

It is useful for linear regression because the least squares will minimize the sum of the squares of the residuals. In the case of machine learning, this means that we are going to be able to build a model of the system that is able to minimize the errors.

Logistic Regression

In many problems, the result that we want to predict is not a continuous variable, but rather a yes or no answer. For example, we might have a set of medical patients with a large amount of data collected on every patient. We might know their age, their weight, their body mass index, fasting blood sugar, systolic and diastolic blood pressure, total cholesterol, and so on. We might want to use the data collected on a patient to predict whether or not they are going to be diabetic within five years.

This would enable the patient's doctor to help the patient take steps now in order to avoid becoming diabetic at some point in the future. In order to have the system learn how to make this prediction, we would have to feed it a large training data set on past patients. This data would be labeled data, but the answer would be binary. So, we would have a large number of features on the input vector, which would be the types of medical data that we just described.

The answer would be represented in binary form, with $1 =$ yes, the patient became diabetic within five years, or $0 =$ no, the patient did not become diabetic.

So, although we have a yes or no answer to the problem, this is still a regression problem. When the answer is a binary value, we call this logistic regression. Like linear regression, the goal is to fit the data using a set of parameters from the features of the input vectors. This type of model can be built around a threshold value. In fact, a system to detect spam email can be constructed using logistic regression. So, although the end result is the email is spam (1) or it is not spam (0), in reality there is a threshold of characteristics that will determine the end result. So, you might say that it is showing 51% of the characteristics of spam, and so then it is labeled spam. The same thing would happen in our model of diabetic patients, each patient could be assigned a score, with a certain cutoff point that would reasonably predict that the patient was going to develop diabetes. And of course, we recognize that this is a reasonable approach to use because in the real world there is never going to be any certainty that a given patient can be predicted to become diabetic, although in some cases the probability might be very high. So logistic regression can also be understood as being a kind of classification problem. Linear regression cannot be used for classification, but we can use logistic regression.

Once again, this is going to be a simple linear mapping function, and so it will have the form as a linear equation:

$Y = WX + B$

Threshold Functions

In order to arrive at a binary result, we need to use a threshold function. There are several choices that could be used, but the most common function that is used is called the sigmoid function. Basically, the sigmoid function is 1 if x is greater than 0, and it is 0 otherwise. The graph of a sigmoid function is shown below:

444

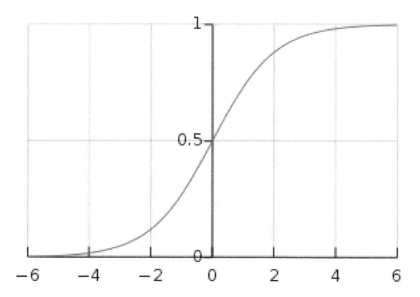

The sigmoid function can be shifted along the x axis, and so if we are calculating a probability that someone is going to be diabetic, we can set a threshold and then output a yes or no answer depending on whether or not the threshold is reached, by multiplying any result by the shifted sigmoid function. So, we could shift the origin of the sigmoid function to say 0.7, if we felt that we would want a 70% probability that a patient is going to become diabetic within five years to determine a yes answer.

The details of this don't concern us here, you can simply follow the instructions of whatever tools that you are using to implement the shifted sigmoid function that you need for your purposes. As you can see from the graph, the sigmoid function also gradually slopes down to zero. By making further adjustments, you can construct threshold functions that have a sharper boundary.

Binary and Multinomial Logistic Regression

We have already discussed the basic point of binary logistic regression. In that case there are only two possible outcomes. Of course, not every situation is that simple. If there are three or more possible ways that we can classify something, then you can use multinomial logistic regression. Suppose that we developed a machine learning system that could examine a photograph of a skin tumor and determine the type. There would actually be four different possibilities in this case.

First of all, the lesion in the photograph might be benign. It could be a plain mole that is not cancerous. Alternatively, it might be a basal cell carcinoma. It could also be a squamous cell carcinoma, and finally it might be a melanoma. Based on different values that could be calculated by the model, it would place each image that it evaluated in one of the four bins. We say that there is no order here. Of course, the doctor and patient would have their preferences, but mathematically speaking there is not any order.

If there is a problem with ordering, then we use what is known as ordinal logistic regression. In this case, the ordering of the outcomes matter, but we are still going to be sorting the data into different bins, based on the cutoff points that are assigned and the result of the regression analysis.

Chapter 6: Classification Methods

In this chapter we are going to examine some of the classification methods that are used with unsupervised learning. These are going to include things like clustering and anomaly detection. There is a little bit of overlap, in that neural networks can be used for supervised or unsupervised learning. If you are wondering why that would be–think to yourself about what a neural network is. In short, a neural network is just a brain. It is a generalized intelligent entity that can learn anything. So that should tell you that it is not a surprise that a neural network could be used to solve a problem where different types of learning are involved.

Data Transformation

Data transformation is a process of using unsupervised learning to simplify a data set. One of the most common examples of data transformation is dimensionality reduction. When data is gathered for a given problem, it may be the case that the data contains frivolous or duplicate features. Of course, if a human being is looking at the data, then it becomes a judgment call and that is something that could turn out to be wrong. However, you could take an approach of letting the machine find all the patterns in a data set, and have it throw out the features that are not predictive. Data can also be consolidated together. Sometimes multiple features of an object can be combined together in order to arrive at a simpler representation of the data.

Clustering

Data in most situations can be clustered. If you go to a restaurant that is busy and filled with a couple of hundred people, there are many different ways that they could be sorted out. For example, you would sort everyone by age, in five year intervals, creating many clusters.

Or you could divide people by gender. Or you could ask everyone their salary and then divide up people by their income. That is all clustering involves, it takes a data set and then divides up the members of the data set into different groups. When using clustering, a distance function is used to determine who is similar to whom. The idea of a distance function is based on the calculation of actual physical distance in mathematics. That is, it will have the same mathematical form, but it will use some measure of distance that is related to the problem at hand. For example, in a given color image, each pixel is going to have a specific color value. We could start examining the data by picking out a pixel, and then building a cluster by defining a level of distance that we want to use as a threshold to say another pixel is the same color as the first one, and then group all of them together. After we have passed through all the data and pulled out all the pixels that are the first color, we do another pass and build the next cluster based on the color of the next pixel that we find. As you can see in clustering, there is no labeling involved. The system goes through the data itself and arranges the data points into the groups that it finds, but nothing has been labeled. It is important to recognize that there are not any hard rules when it comes to clustering. In other words, the application and those involved will determine what to use to cluster the data and what the distance criteria are going to be.

Partitioning

Partitioning is a way to do clustering in machine learning. In this case, the data points are partitioned into k clusters. A distance function is used for partitioning. An example of this is k-means clustering.

Grid Methods

When using a grid method, the data space is divided up into grids. The grid like structure will consist of a large number of cells. Then clustering operations are done on the individual cells in the grid.

DBSCAN

This is a density-based clustering method. In this case, the space that the data is in is checked for density, and high-density regions are taken to have similarity as opposed to low density regions. For example, if we had a database of people from a city, we might form clusters based on age. Those with a similar age would be assumed to be similar in other ways.

Applications

Clustering methods can be used to classify data and divide it up in many applications. One of the most popular ways that this is used in the business world is to create market segments. These are clusters of people that are assumed to have similar tastes and so forth that would be related to marketing. For example, you could form a cluster of Hispanic women aged 18-25 living in the southeast United States. Clustering is used in many scientific applications of machine learning. For example, biologists often use clustering techniques for the classification of living organisms. Earthquake zones are determined by using clustering methods. Areas that are ripe for oil and natural gas exploration can also be determined using clustering methods. In fields like insurance, clustering can be used to spot anomalous behavior, which can indicate identity theft or the filing of fraudulent claims.

K-Nearest Neighbor

The k-nearest neighbor algorithm is one that is often used for classification purposes. This process uses a "voting" method by looking at the k-nearest neighbors to a given data point. The basic idea of this algorithm is that similar objects are going to exist in proximity to one another. Like clustering, it will use a distance function in order to determine whether or not a given data point is close enough to another object in order for us to say that they can be classified as being the same. Simple Euclidean distance is used with the k-nearest neighbor algorithm most of the time.

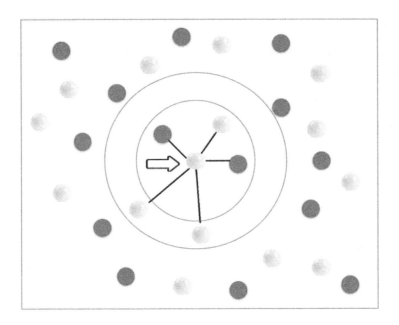

K is a value that tells the system how many neighbors to examine as a part of the algorithm. You pick an object in the data set, and then calculate the distances of the other objects from it. Then you sort the objects based on distance from smallest to largest, and then take the top K of them. The objects in the data set used here will have some labels. So, for the K elements that have been selected you gather the labels. In a classification problem, you get the mode of the labels. For those who don't remember, a mode is the most frequently occurring data value. So if we were doing classification by color, and our k nearest neighbors were (orange, yellow, green, orange, orange, blue, orange, green, orange), the mode would be orange. Since the nearest neighbors are orange, we choose this as our classification. The k-nearest neighbor algorithm can also be used on a regression problem. In that case, to find the value, you compute the average of the k labels.

Random Forest

A random forest is related to decision trees. In the case of a random forest, multiple decision trees are constructed during the training process. Then classification is used by having the decision trees output values, and the mode of the values returned by the decision trees is used.

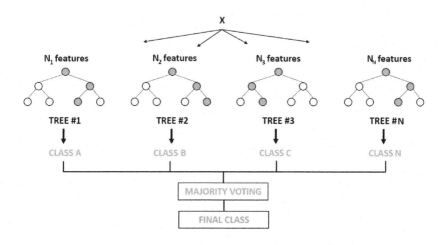

Chapter 7: TensorFlow

Tensor flow is a library built for machine learning that can be used in python. It also serves as a backend for Keras, a deep learning neural network library that we will discuss in the next chapter. The goal of TensorFlow is to make the implementation of machine learning easier. It was created by Google, and it is free to use as it is an open source library. The front-end API for TensorFlow is written in python, so you can easily use TensorFlow with programs coded using python.

Neural Networks and TensorFlow

TensorFlow is designed to work with a special type of machine learning, that is implemented using neural networks. In TensorFlow, you create graphs and data flows through the graphs. This is not anything new, the graphs that are described in TensorFlow are nodes, the same kind of nodes that are used in neural network models. In TensorFlow, a node that is in the model is going to be a snippet of code that will implement a mathematical operation on the inputs. Then it will produce an output, that is then multiplied by a threshold function (see the following chapter) that will either let the output pass to the next layer in the network, or it will stop it from continuing forward. Connections in TensorFlow are represented by multidimensional arrays. In mathematics, these multidimensional data arrays are called tensors.

The API is a Front End

TensorFlow helps you build fast neural network models because the interface to python is nothing more than a front end that makes using the library easy and user friendly.

Rather than being interpreted like python, the TensorFlow library is compiled C++ code, and so you are actually utilizing a compiled binary file when you use TensorFlow in your models. Python is merely used as an interface to transfer data back and forth and tell the TensorFlow library to execute various operations.

Multiple Ways to Access Computing Power

One of the most powerful features of TensorFlow is that you can use different computing targets to actually perform the calculations. It is possible to use your local machine, but you can also use a cluster of computers in the cloud, and you can even utilize mobile devices to run your codes. Once you create a full working model using tensor flow, it can be deployed to any computational device. This can include a desktop computer, the cloud, or mobile devices.

TensorFlow Puts You a Step Away

The main benefit of using TensorFlow is that it does all the dirty work for you. So you don't have to sit down and actually code the tools that are used to build neural networks and do computations. Instead, these tools have already been built for you and therefore all you have to do is access them. For readers that have used tools like Mathematica or Matlab, think of it like that. You could sit down and write your own python program to compute triple integrals, or you could just set one up in Mathematica and let it calculate it for you. The same principle is at work here. TensorFlow is created so that you don't have to reinvent the wheel, and instead you can just use the tools that are used over and over again in the construction of neural networks. Then, when the technology changes behind the scenes, suppose that some brilliant computer scientist comes up with a better way to make neural networks, you don't have to worry about that. The people that run TensorFlow will fix things up for you behind the scenes, and you can just focus on using the library.

This is a standard "black box" model of computing. You are using the black box, passing data back and forth to it, and you don't have to worry about what is inside the black box.

TensorFlow and Keras

Since TensorFlow is used in conjunction with a library called Keras, we are not going to go into the details of TensorFlow. It provides the raw power behind Keras, which is a tool that makes working with neural networks super easy. In the next chapter, we will show how to use Keras and setup tensor flow as the backend.

In fact, if you look at the examples on the TensorFlow website, they are using Keras to do many of the tasks.

Chapter 8: The Keras Library

The Keras library is a python library that can be used for deep learning. Remember that deep learning is based on neural networks, which are designed to simulate the workings of the human brain in order to build systems that are capable of learning how to solve various problems and that operate autonomously. The Keras library allows you to build stand-alone models, that can be used in a "plug and play" fashion. So, you can design a model and then use it within some other context as a node that you plug in. Keras can run on top of TensorFlow.

Types of Neural Networks Used with Keras

Keras is used to create neural network building blocks. It uses standard neural networks, but Keras can also use convolutional neural networks and recurrent neural networks. The main purpose of Keras is to use python to do deep learning.

Installing Keras

In order to install Keras you must have python and the SciPy library. Keras also requires either TensorFlow or Theano.

It is not necessary to install both, but at least one must be installed. Keras can run on top of either TensorFlow or Theano but can't run by itself. You can install Keras at the command line using the following command:

sudo pip install Keras

457

If you have installed Keras and need to upgrade it, this can be done using the following command:

sudo pip install–upgrade Keras

This will create a configuration file for Keras in addition to installing it. The configuration file will be found in your home directory. If you open the file, you will find an entry called backend that can be used to specify whether or not it runs on TensorFlow or Theano. Alternatively, you can run this command at the command line and it will tell you to want the setting is. You can change it if needed:

python -c "from Keras import backend; print(backend.backend())"

If you want to force it to use a different backend, then you can specify it at the command line. This example shows how to tell it to use TensorFlow and then print to confirm:

KERAS_BACKEND=TensorFlow python -c "from Keras import backend; print(backend.backend())

Creating a Deep Learning Model

A model in Keras is called a sequence. In short, this will be a stack of layers used to build a deep learning neural network. You start by creating a sequence and then adding the layers you want to add to the sequence. Next, you will specify loss functions and optimizers. Once the setup is completed, you can train your model. Using data that you have selected as training data, you can then execute the model. The model can then be tested after training is completed. This will be done using a test data set where you know the answers.

You can run the Keras model on the test data set and then compare the predictions it makes to the actual correct answers.

In order to use Keras, you will need to use numpy (see the last chapter). The backend used by Keras does not need to be specified in your python programs. So you will set up some import statements to use the library:

```
from numpy import loadtxt

from Keras.models import Sequential

from Keras.layers import Dense
```

The first step when creating a model using Keras is to load a dataset. You can use comma separated value files to import your data. Let's suppose that we are doing a classification problem, and we have a set of data in a file called testdata.csv. Assume that the data is divided into a feature vector X that has 10 features, and an output y.

The steps to load the data are:

```
# we have a comma delimited file

Mytestdata = loadtxt('testdata.csv',delimiter=',')


#extract the input features X and the output variables y

X = Mytestdata[:,0:10]

y = Mytestdata[:,10]
```

Sequential Models in Keras

Keras uses sequential models, which are deep learning models with a sequence of layers. We will create an input layer that is going to have the correct number of inputs. For each layer, we will specify the number of neurons in the layer. Some people refer to the "neurons" in a neural network as nodes. We need to determine the number of nodes in each layer. The output layer is going to have a single note, and we need to determine an activation function to use with the node. If you recall from our discussion on neurons in a real human brain, they have a threshold that determines whether or not the neuron is going to fire and produce an output. The threshold in a human neuron is going to be determined by the electrostatic voltage. To mimic this in a neural network, we need some kind of threshold function, that will either allow information to pass or not pass. A sigmoid function is typically used.

This is a function that looks like this:

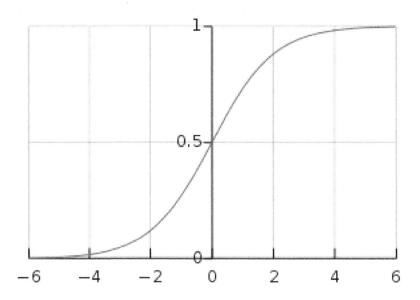

You can multiply the output by the sigmoid function, and you can see if it has not passed the threshold value (the origin in this case) the output is not passed on. We can also use a rectified linear activation function or "relu". This is sometimes called a ramp function.

The details of how it's constructed are not important for our purposes, but you should have an idea of what it looks like to get some understanding of how things are working behind the scenes:

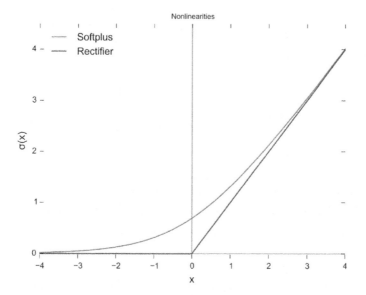

Now let's define our Keras model. At each layer, we are going to define the number of neurons to add. In the first layer the dimensions of the input are specified, and then you need to have one output layer with a single code at the end. We will have two layers in the middle. These are called hidden layers. Remember that we have 10 inputs.

```python
Neural_model = Sequential() # initialize the model
```

Now add the first layer, specifying the number of nodes, the number of inputs, and the activation function

```python
Neural_model.add(Dense(16, input_dim=10, activation = 'relu')
```

```python
#Add two hidden layers
Neural_model.add( Dense(8,activation = 'relu'))
Neural_model.add( Dense(8,activation = 'relu'))
```

```python
#Finally, add the output node
Neural_model.add( Dense(1,activation = 'sigmoid'))
```

Once you have specified the construction of the model, you can compile it, using the compile command. When you compile your model, you will have to specify a few parameters. These are the loss function, the optimizing function, and metrics. A neural network needs to use weights to determine the strength of connections between different nodes, so the optimizer that is specified tells it how to determine the weights. Suppose that for our example we have a binary classification problem, which is actually quite common for neural networks. The loss function in that case that you want to pass to Keras is binary_crossentropy. Adam is an optimizer for weights that uses gradient descent. Finally, we use accuracy for the metric when doing binary classification. The full setup, specified when executing the compile command in your python program, is as follows:

```python
Neural_model.compile( loss = 'binary_crossentropy', optimizer = 'adam', metrics = ['accuracy')
```

Training the Model

After the model has been defined and compiled, then you will train it on some data. This is done using the 'fit' command, which will attempt to fit the training data that you expose to the model. In Keras, training is done using epochs. An epoch is a single pass through all the rows in the training data set. You are going to specify multiple epochs, which simply means that it will pass through the data multiple times. As the model passes through the data, at some point as it's being exposed to the data it may want to update the weights inside the model. You use a batch size to tell it how many data samples to pass through before it updates the weights. This is done by setting the batch size. So, an epoch is really nothing more than an iteration where the model revisits the data with multiple passes. By exposing it to the data many times, you can make the model better. Think of it as studying, if you read a chapter you are going to be tested on once, you might not do so well. If you read chapter 3 times and study it, then you are likely to pass the exam. The same principle sort of applies here, each time that the model goes through the data, the weights will be adjusted, making the model better.

Of course, at some point we are going to get into a situation of diminishing returns, in other words continuing to pass over the data no longer causes significant updates to the weights. You have to use judgment, based on experience, to know what works. If you expose the model to testing data after this process and it is not very accurate, then you might conclude that you didn't use enough epochs to train the data, or your batch size was not appropriately chosen.

In any case, you can train the model with a single line in your python program:

Neural_model.fit(X, y, epochs = 200, batch_size = 10)

When you are working with deep learning neural networks, the error is going to settle down to some value. There is always going to be a degree of error, it is not possible to create an error free system. However, when it settles down to the minimal error that is possible given the data and the setup that you have created, this is known as convergence.

Testing a Keras Model

The next step after training is to test the model. This is done using the evaluate command, and you can get an estimate of the accuracy of the model at this point to determine if the model is where you want it to be. In order to evaluate a Keras model, you can use a new testing data set in the same way that you would with any other machine learning program. Again, this is going to be a one-step command, but first we have to load our test data.

When you evaluate a model, it will return a single float value, the accuracy.

#Load Test Data

Test_data = loadtxt('test_data.csv', delimiter = ',')

X_t = Test_data[:,0:10]

y_t = Test_data[:,10]

result = Neural_model.evaluate(X_t,y_t)

print('Accuracy is : %.2f' %(accuracy * 100))

Making Predictions with a Keras Model

Finally, you can use a Keras model that has been trained to make predictions. You will do this assuming that the model has attained an acceptable level of accuracy. This is done by passing it an input data set, but no output values (after all, it is a prediction and you don't know what the output values are). Predictions can be returned in pairs so that you can see the prediction y for every input X.

464

Assume that X_i is some new input data that we have loaded into the system from a csv file of input data. Assume also that we have 100 elements.

```
Predictions = Neural_model.predict(X_i)

For i in range(100):

    Print(predictions[i],y[i])
```

Summary

As you can see, if you want to build deep learning neural networks, Keras makes it pretty simple. Of course, doing it the right way is something that you are going to have to work towards by gaining more experience as time goes on. The nice thing about Keras is that it makes it very easy to build, train, and test neural networks and then get the information that you need out of them. And even better it's free to use.

Chapter 9: The Scikit-Learn Library

In this chapter we are going to introduce the Scikit-learn library. This is a set of tools for python that are used for the purposes of data mining and data analysis. These tools are reusable and the library is able to perform many of the common tasks used in machine learning. For example, it can do regression, classification, dimensionality reduction, clustering, and preprocessing.

Background: What is Data Mining?

In short, data mining is examining large data sets in order to extract the patterns, anomalies, and correlations that are hidden in the data. Data mining has been used in the business world for a long period of time, and although it is a task that is well suited for machine learning, it's not specifically associated with machine learning. That said, for our purposes we will want to look at it from a machine learning perspective. There are several ways that data mining is used in business. For example, an analysis of large data sets can help a company cut its costs, or it can be used to help provide better customer service. The range of applications for data mining is large, any task that you can think of for a business that is important is something that can be solved with data mining provided that the large data sets that are required exist and are accessible.

Data mining simply refers to going through large data sets in order to find the patterns in the data that can describe useful relationships or make predictions. In short, this is nothing new. Different types of modeling are used in data mining. These include descriptive modeling, predictive modeling, and prescriptive modeling. Descriptive modeling involves discovering shared similarities or clustering in historical data. Clustering is used to group similar data points or records together. Descriptive modeling can also be used to identify anomalies, by finding outliers that don't fit into any of the clusters that can be built in a large data set. Descriptive modeling is also used to find previously hidden relationships that might exist between members of a data set. In predictive modeling, we move from an analysis of historical data to use past data in order to predict future results.

When we move into predictive modeling, we are encountering many of the familiar methods that are used in machine learning. Tools used in predictive modeling include neural networks, regression models, decision trees, and support vector machines. Finally, prescriptive modeling seeks to utilize unstructured data in predictive models.

The Data Mining Process

Data mining goes through a series of steps designed to select, modify, and gather the information that may be contained in large data sets. The first step is selection of the data to be used. Then it will go through a process of preprocessing in order to prepare it for the data mining process. This may include assembling data from many different sources or data warehouses, and assembling it into a new and unified form that is suitable for the analysis. Dimensionality reduction and other techniques may also be used in order to make the data more suitable for machine learning methods. Then, the various methods used for data mining are applied to the data set.

Datasets in Scikit-Learn

Scikit learn has several data sets that can be used for the purposes of practice. These are available in the dataset loading utilities. They are referred to as toy datasets. The data sets that are currently available include:

- *Boston:* This includes a dataset of Boston house prices that is suitable for regression problems. It includes a large number of fields that may or may not be relevant for something you are analyzing. For example, it includes the per capita crime rate and a median value of homes in the area, but also includes the concentration of nitrous oxides in the neighborhood.
- *Iris:* The iris data set contains information about iris flowers. The purpose of this dataset is to learn about using classification methods.
- *Diabetes:* The diabetes dataset includes ten features that may be relevant to diabetes, including age, sex, body mass index and other parameters. The dataset includes data on 442 patients. This is another regression dataset.
- *Digits:* the purpose of this dataset is to study optical recognition using handwritten digits. It has 64 features and 5620 elements. This is to study classification.

469

- *Linnerrud*: this is a dataset that can be used to study multivariate regression. It is a small dataset with only 20 instances, with 3 features, but there are two sets, physiological features that measure weight, waist circumference, and pulse, with the other set containing exercise performance results.
- *Breast Cancer*: this is another classification data set. It includes 569 members, each with 30 features that describe a breast cancer tumor.

Several real-world datasets are also available on the site. To load a data set, you first need to import sklearn and the appropriate libraries into your python code. It is also necessary to import numpy. For this example, consider using the diabetes dataset.

The necessary import statements are:

import matplotlib.pyplot as plt

import numpy as np

from sklearn import datasets, linear_model

from sklearn.metrics import mean_squared_error, r2_score

Next, we need to load the data set:

diabetes = datasets.load_diabetes()

Splitting Data into Training and Testing

The next step is to select data that will be used for training the machine learning system, and then for testing it. The first step in scikit is to specify what features are used. In this example, we can pick a feature to use:

diabetes_X = diabetes.data[:, np.newaxis, 2]

Now you can split the data into subsets, one for training and one for testing. This needs to be done for inputs X and outputs y.

diabetes_X_train = diabetes_X[:-20]

diabetes_X_test = diabetes_X[-20:]

diabetes_y_train = diabetes.target[:-20]

diabetes_y_test = diabetes.target[-20:]

Doing Linear Regression and Training

Using scikit, doing linear regression and testing is extremely simple. Everything that you need for doing our analysis is already built for you, you simply need the data to run it on. For the example given here, we use a linear regression model in order to build a predictive model based on the features used in the analysis. Training the model is done with one line of code.

regr = linear_model.LinearRegression()

regr.fit(diabetes_X_train, diabetes_y_train)

Now that the model has been trained, we can test the model by having it make predictions, and then comparing that to the known results. A variance of 1 would be a perfect prediction, so the distance between the reported result and unity will tell us how good the model is.

```
diabetes_y_pred = regr.predict(diabetes_X_test)

print('Coefficients: \n', regr.coef_)

print("Mean squared error: %.2f"

    % mean_squared_error(diabetes_y_test, diabetes_y_pred))

print('Variance score: %.2f' % r2_score(diabetes_y_test, diabetes_y_pred))
```

Here we plot the output:

```
plt.scatter(diabetes_X_test, diabetes_y_test, color='black')
plt.plot(diabetes_X_test, diabetes_y_pred, color='blue', linewidth=3)
plt.xticks(())
plt.yticks(())
plt.show()
```

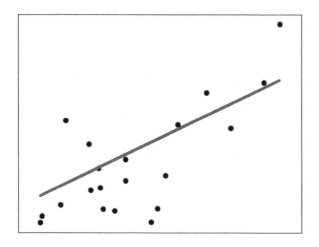

Using SciKit for Solving Other Types of Problems

Many of the toy and real-world datasets provided with Scikit can be used to do classification problems, clustering analysis, anomaly detection, and more. In this example found on the scikit-learn.org website, we see how to use outlier detection. The data used for this example is the Boston dataset with housing data. Covariance methods are considering two different relationships. In the first case, an anomaly is found considering the pupil-teacher relationship versus the accessibility to highways. In the second example, we look for anomalies in a dataset that is distributed quite differently, considering the average number of rooms per household against the % lower status of the population. This will show you how to use classifiers in order to detect outlying or anomalous data. We begin by importing the needed libraries. As always you will need to import numpy, and the plotting and dataset libraries. You will also need to import the covariance library. The example code here was created by Virgile Fritsch.

import numpy as np

from sklearn.covariance import EllipticEnvelope

from sklearn.svm import OneClassSVM

import matplotlib.pyplot as plt

import matplotlib.font_manager

from sklearn.datasets import load_boston

We begin by loading the data. It is helpful to look at plots of the data now, so that we can understand what the programmer is referring to. First, you see the two-cluster data, with a significant outlier. Below, we see the banana shaped data

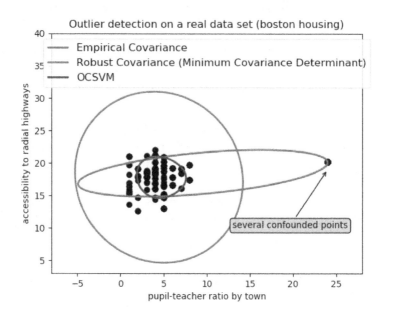

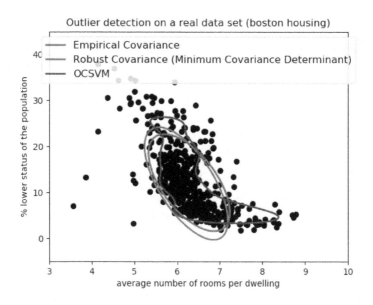

Here is the code that is used to load the data. The values used indicate the particular features and outputs that we want to use in each data set.

X1 = load_boston()['data'][:, [8, 10]]   # *two clusters*

X2 = load_boston()['data'][:, [5, 12]]   # *"banana"-shaped*

Next, the classifiers are defined.


```
classifiers = {

    "Empirical Covariance": EllipticEnvelope(support_fraction=1.,

                            contamination=0.261),

    "Robust Covariance (Minimum Covariance Determinant)":

    EllipticEnvelope(contamination=0.261),

    "OCSVM": OneClassSVM(nu=0.261, gamma=0.05)}
colors = ['m', 'g', 'b']
legend1 = {}
legend2 = {}
```


In order to detect outliers, you need to have the computer learn where the 'frontier' is so that it can then detect outliers. This is accomplished with the following statements:


```
xx1, yy1 = np.meshgrid(np.linspace(-8, 28, 500), np.linspace(3, 40, 500))

xx2, yy2 = np.meshgrid(np.linspace(3, 10, 500), np.linspace(-5, 45, 500))

for i, (clf_name, clf) in enumerate(classifiers.items()):
```

```
plt.figure(1)

clf.fit(X1)

Z1 = clf.decision_function(np.c_[xx1.ravel(), yy1.ravel()])

Z1 = Z1.reshape(xx1.shape)

legend1[clf_name] = plt.contour(
    xx1, yy1, Z1, levels=[0], linewidths=2, colors=colors[i])

plt.figure(2)

clf.fit(X2)

Z2 = clf.decision_function(np.c_[xx2.ravel(), yy2.ravel()])

Z2 = Z2.reshape(xx2.shape)

legend2[clf_name] = plt.contour(
    xx2, yy2, Z2, levels=[0], linewidths=2, colors=colors[i])


legend1_values_list = list(legend1.values())
legend1_keys_list = list(legend1.keys())
```

Now we can plot the data. First, we plot the two-cluster data:

```
plt.figure(1)  # two clusters
plt.title("Outlier detection on a real data set (boston housing)")
plt.scatter(X1[:, 0], X1[:, 1], color='black')
bbox_args = dict(boxstyle="round", fc="0.8")
```

```python
arrow_args = dict(arrowstyle="->")
plt.annotate("several confounded points", xy=(24, 19),
        xycoords="data", textcoords="data",
        xytext=(13, 10), bbox=bbox_args, arrowprops=arrow_args)
plt.xlim((xx1.min(), xx1.max()))
plt.ylim((yy1.min(), yy1.max()))
plt.legend((legend1_values_list[0].collections[0],
        legend1_values_list[1].collections[0],
        legend1_values_list[2].collections[0]),
        (legend1_keys_list[0], legend1_keys_list[1], legend1_keys_list[2]),
        loc="upper center",
        prop=matplotlib.font_manager.FontProperties(size=12))
plt.ylabel("accessibility to radial highways")
plt.xlabel("pupil-teacher ratio by town")


legend2_values_list = list(legend2.values())
legend2_keys_list = list(legend2.keys())
```

Then plot the banana shaped data:

```python
plt.figure(2)  # "banana" shape
plt.title("Outlier detection on a real data set (boston housing)")
```

```
plt.scatter(X2[:, 0], X2[:, 1], color='black')
plt.xlim((xx2.min(), xx2.max()))
plt.ylim((yy2.min(), yy2.max()))
plt.legend((legend2_values_list[0].collections[0],
        legend2_values_list[1].collections[0],
        legend2_values_list[2].collections[0]),
        (legend2_keys_list[0], legend2_keys_list[1], legend2_keys_list[2]),
        loc="upper center",
        prop=matplotlib.font_manager.FontProperties(size=12))
plt.ylabel("% lower status of the population")
plt.xlabel("average number of rooms per dwelling")
plt.show()
```

The plots show that the outliers have been detected.

Summary

Scikit is a very comprehensive but easy to use tool that can be used with python for machine learning and data mining. The tool is free to use and there are many coding samples that can be downloaded to help you learn how to use this tool to do many of the common tasks that are done in machine learning. Rather than having to write many lines of code in order to implement testing and other tasks, Scikit-learn enables you to use its built-in functionality in order to write clean and short code snippets that can do some pretty sophisticated analysis.

Chapter 10: NumPy

Numpy is a library of scientific computing routines that are used in Python. The main purpose of NumPy is to allow you to perform many operations that are used on matrices. It will enable you to do faster calculations and build more sophisticated models, because the arrays used in NumPy go beyond what is available with standard lists in Python. NumPy is a library that you are going to need to use with many of the tools that have been described in this book. NumPy can actually be thought of as a wrapper. There is pre-compiled C code that works underneath the NumPy interface that you see as a Python programmer. The pre-compiled code enables NumPy to perform calculations with large matrices and vectors very quickly.

Ndarray

Ndarray is the most fundamental object in the NumPy library. The label simply means an N-dimensional array. Every element in a ndarray is the same data type. So, while you may be used to mixing up data types in lists with Python, you can't do that with an ndarray. An ndarray can be initialized in code using the array method and specifying the data elements that are in the array. First, you have to import the NumPy library into your python code.

This is done like this:

import numpy as mynumpy

Now, mynumpy is an object that we can refer to and use throughout our code. For example, we can create a simple vector with three elements like this:

my_vector = mynumpy.array([1.3, 4.1, 10.8])

Notice that all three elements in the array are the same data type. So, we could not type:

my_vector = mynumby.array([1.3, 'sam',10.8])

We could also create a matrix, by specifying the two rows in the matrix. This is an example of a 2x2 matrix:

```
import numpy as mynumpy
2d_matrix = mynumpy.array([[1,2],[3,4]])
```

Now let's create a 2 x 3 matrix:

```
2by3 = mynumpy.array([[3,8,2],[5,2,7]])
```

The shape command will give the number of rows and columns in the matrix. You can also extract the number of dimensions, and the shape and size of the array, along with the data type of the elements. These examples are illustrated with this code:

```
print("Shape of 2d: ", 2d_matrix.shape)
print("Shape of 2 by 3: ", 2by3.shape)
print("Size of the 2 by 3 ", 2by3.size)
print("Dimensions of first array: ", 2d_matrix.ndim)
```

The results are:

Shape of 2d: (2,2)

Shape of 2 by 3: (2,3)

Size of the 2 by 3: 6

Dimensions of first array: 2

To get the data type, use the dtype command:

print(2by3.dtype)

This will print int64. Arrays can be created for any numerical data type in python, such as float or complex. You can also use the zeros command to create an array (or technically a matrix) that has a specified number of rows and columns that are all initialized to zero. For example:

voltages = mynumpy.zeros((5,7))

That has created a 5 x 7 matrix filled with zeros called voltages. There is one exception to the rule that the elements of an array have to be the same data type, you can create an array of python objects using NumPy, and each object can contain data of different types. In the context of machine learning, you are going to be using arrays that contain the same type of data.

Creating a Column Vector

Creating column vectors is something that is routinely done in the context of linear algebra. To create a column vector using numpy, simply follow the syntax shown here. In the first example we create a column vector with two elements, and in the second example we create a column vector with three elements, and then we create a row vector with three elements:

import numpy as my_numpy

vector_2 = my_numpy.array([[3],[6]])

vector_3 = my_numpy.array([2],[7],[9])

row_vector = my_numpy.array([1,6,9])

Size of NumPy Arrays

It is important to note that the size of a NumPy array is fixed when you first declare it. The reason that we need to mention this is that python lists can grow dynamically when the program is running, and so those who have experience with python will find that this is not the kind of behavior that they are used to.

High Level Operations on Arrays

NumPy is also used to perform high level operations on arrays, which facilitates the use of NumPy arrays in the context of advanced and complex mathematical operations.

Dot Product

In many contexts, calculating the dot product between two vectors is a common calculation that must be carried out. First let's set up two vectors and then use the dot command to print out the result. Remember that the dot product produces a scalar result.

```
import numpy as my_numpy

vector_A = my_numpy.array ( [1,4,5] )

vector_B = my_numby.array ( [2,3,5] )

print(my_numpy.dot(vector_A,vector_B)
```

Get the Eigenvalues and Eigenvectors of a Matrix

NumPy can use the linear algebra library *eig* function to return the eigenvalues and eigenvectors of a matrix simultaneously.

```
import numpy as my_numpy

#Create a Matrix
matrix = my_numpy.array([[2,2,3],[1,5,9],[11,8,8]])
print(matrix)

# Calculate the Eigenvalues and Eigenvectors of the Matrix
eigenvalues ,eigenvectors = my_numpy.linalg.eig(matrix)
print(eigenvalues)
print(eigenvectors)
```

Matrix Inversion

Another common task that is used with square matrices is to invert a matrix. Again, you will use linalg, and this illustrates how NumPy wraps complicated mathematical operations into simple one-line statements.

```
import numpy as my_numpy

Matrix = my_numpy.array ( [1,2,3], [4,5,6], [7,8,9] )

Print(Matrix)
#invert the matrix

Inverted_Matrix = my_numpy.linalg.inv(Matrix)

Print(Inverted_Matrix)
```

Trace of a Matrix

In many scientific contexts. The trace of a matrix is an important piece of data. This can be found by using the trace command.

```
import numpy as my_numpy

#Create a Matrix
matrix = my_numpy.array([[1,2,3],[4,5,6],[7,8,9]])

print(matrix)

print(matrix.trace())
```

Random Number Generation

Finally, it can be useful to generate random numbers. In this case we generate four random numbers ranging over 1 and 20, and then we generate five numbers from a normal distribution with a mean of 5.2 and standard deviation of 1.3:

```
import numpy as my_numpy

my_numpy.random.seed(1)

print(my_numpy.randint(0,21,4))

print(my_numpy.random.normal(5.2,1.3,5))
```

Creating a Neural Network Using Numpy

One of the powerful features of numpy is that you can use the matrices and mathematical operations that are built into the library to create neural networks. In the following example, which is borrowed from python-course.eu, a simple network with one hidden layer is developing using numpy and python alone. Of course, doing this without using one of the libraries that have been described in the book means that you are going to be doing a lot of coding yourself that isn't really necessary. In my view you may as well use a library that is already fully developed for this purpose. However, we will include their example here so that you can see that it is possible to build up a neural network using python alone, and you can do other tasks like linear regression.

In the example used, a neural network class is defined. Weight matrices are created to calculate the weights between the nodes that are in the neural network. The threshold used is the sigmoid function.

The entire code is here:

```
import numpy as np

@np.vectorize

def sigmoid(x):

    return 1 / (1 + np.e ** -x)
```

```python
activation_function = sigmoid

from scipy.stats import truncnorm

def truncated_normal(mean=0, sd=1, low=0, upp=10):
    return truncnorm(
        (low - mean) / sd, (upp - mean) / sd, loc=mean, scale=sd)

class NeuralNetwork:

    def __init__(self,
                 no_of_in_nodes,
                 no_of_out_nodes,
                 no_of_hidden_nodes,
                 learning_rate,
                 bias=None
                 ):
        self.no_of_in_nodes = no_of_in_nodes
        self.no_of_out_nodes = no_of_out_nodes
        self.no_of_hidden_nodes = no_of_hidden_nodes
        self.learning_rate = learning_rate
        self.bias = bias
        self.create_weight_matrices()

    def create_weight_matrices(self):
        """ A method to initialize the weight matrices of the neural
        network with optional bias nodes"""
```

```python
        bias_node = 1 if self.bias else 0
        rad = 1 / np.sqrt(self.no_of_in_nodes + bias_node)
        X = truncated_normal(mean=0, sd=1, low=-rad, upp=rad)
        self.weights_in_hidden = X.rvs((self.no_of_hidden_nodes,
                            self.no_of_in_nodes + bias_node))
        rad = 1 / np.sqrt(self.no_of_hidden_nodes + bias_node)
        X = truncated_normal(mean=0, sd=1, low=-rad, upp=rad)
        self.weights_hidden_out = X.rvs((self.no_of_out_nodes,
                            self.no_of_hidden_nodes + bias_node))

    def train(self, input_vector, target_vector):
        # input_vector and target_vector can be tuple, list or ndarray
        bias_node = 1 if self.bias else 0
        if self.bias:
            # adding bias node to the end of the inpuy_vector
            input_vector = np.concatenate( (input_vector, [self.bias]) )
        input_vector = np.array(input_vector, ndmin=2).T
        target_vector = np.array(target_vector, ndmin=2).T
        output_vector1 = np.dot(self.weights_in_hidden, input_vector)
        output_vector_hidden = activation_function(output_vector1)
        if self.bias:
            output_vector_hidden = np.concatenate( (output_vector_hidden,
[[self.bias]]) )
```

```python
        output_vector2 = np.dot(self.weights_hidden_out,
output_vector_hidden)

        output_vector_network = activation_function(output_vector2)

        output_errors = target_vector - output_vector_network

        # update the weights:

        tmp = output_errors * output_vector_network * (1.0 -
output_vector_network)

        tmp = self.learning_rate * np.dot(tmp, output_vector_hidden.T)

        self.weights_hidden_out += tmp

        # calculate hidden errors:

        hidden_errors = np.dot(self.weights_hidden_out.T, output_errors)

        # update the weights:

        tmp = hidden_errors * output_vector_hidden * (1.0 -
output_vector_hidden)

        if self.bias:

            x = np.dot(tmp, input_vector.T)[:-1,:]    # ???? last element cut off,
???

        else:

            x = np.dot(tmp, input_vector.T)

        self.weights_in_hidden += self.learning_rate * x

    def run(self, input_vector):

        # input_vector can be tuple, list or ndarray

        if self.bias:

            # adding bias node to the end of the inpuy_vector
```
488

```python
    input_vector = np.concatenate( (input_vector, [1]) )
input_vector = np.array(input_vector, ndmin=2).T
output_vector = np.dot(self.weights_in_hidden, input_vector)
output_vector = activation_function(output_vector)
if self.bias:
    output_vector = np.concatenate( (output_vector, [[1]]) )
output_vector = np.dot(self.weights_hidden_out, output_vector)
output_vector = activation_function(output_vector)
return output_vector
```

Conclusion

Thank you for making it through to the end of *Python Machine Learning*, let's hope it was informative and able to provide you with all of the tools you need to achieve your goals whatever they may be. Machine learning is an exciting and rapidly evolving field. While mastery of the subject can involve many years of study, it is possible to get started quickly by gaining some basic familiarity with the methods and goals of machine learning. Many of the machine learning methods, despite the mysterious aura that surrounds the field, are actually relatively simple mathematical tools that have literally been around for centuries. It is just now that they are being applied to the massive amounts of data, the so-called big data, that is being collected by companies and other large organizations.

Python is an excellent tool to use for learning about–machine learning. Python is a very simple programming language that most people are able to pick up rather quickly. Libraries have been developed for python that is specifically designed for machine learning, and so it is easy for a developer to play around with the tools and actually solve simple machine learning problems. The way to go forward is to actually practice and study more. Begin by going through any exercises that you can find that entail covering all of the major algorithms that are used in machine learning.

Using both supervised and unsupervised learning is important, as anyone who wants to understand machine learning needs to become intimately familiar with both. You should also practice by using many of the standard algorithms like linear regression and k-nearest neighbors.

Something that I would suggest is to avoid getting trapped into only using generated test data. To enhance your learning and development, get a hold of real-world data sets that you can run your algorithms on so that you can gain an even greater familiarity with the practice of data science. Many people who are new to the concept of machine learning ask what specific educational credentials they need in order to get into the field. While there are some general guidelines, the truth is there are no specific rules.

We can begin by saying that in all likelihood, anyone who is involved in a scientific or technical field of study would be in a position to get involved in machine learning. That certainly applies to electrical or computer engineers. However, some people that might be better placed to get into machine learning are mathematicians that are experts in statistics and probability. Some crossover knowledge can be helpful, but in some ways, when it comes down to the day-to-day practice of a data scientist, the field of machine learning is really a statistical field. Certainly, a high level of knowledge of statistics and probability is helpful.

Since it is considered a crossover discipline background in computer science can be helpful. The ideal candidate would be someone who has a substantial background in computer science that has also demonstrated a high-level education in statistics. The more advanced your education, the more deeply you can go into the field, including doing AI research and designing more advanced systems. If you are just playing around with some models, you are not going to be designing machine learning systems for use in some new robotic systems. That will require advanced education in computer science.

However, there are varying roles and levels of machine learning. Those who study computer systems in business school, provided that they have a good understanding of statistics, are going to be well-suited for doing machine learning tasks as a data scientist at many companies. Simply analyzing customer data or internal company data for trends and patterns is not something that requires a deep understanding of artificial intelligence, and your role is to use the tools of machine learning that are available in order to extract the kind of information that is useful for the enterprise. So, machine learning and data science are fields that have a wide range of complexity and application. There is virtually some level of expertise that is going to be suitable for many different levels and types of education, background, and taste. It is definitely a growing field for the future. In this book we have learned what machine learning is, and how it is applied today by businesses to many different tasks.

We learned that there is supervised and unsupervised learning, and how they are different. We also learned the issues that might crop up with various tradeoffs in machine learning. We also learned many of the major algorithms that are used in machine learning, including regression methods, k-nearest neighbor methods, and decision trees.

A large part of building a solid and reliable machine learning system is selecting the most appropriate training data sets and the best algorithm for a given situation. This in part is going to be determined by your experience, and the more experience that you get practicing machine learning, the better you are going to be when it comes to selecting the right algorithms for a given problem. We also saw how python could be used to implement some of the most common machine learning tasks. We used python for regressing, k-nearest neighbors, and other classification methods.

We looked at the TensorFlow library, the Sciikit learn library, and the Numpy library.

We also learned about Keras, and saw how to build a neural network. The power of Numpy lies behind many of the tools used to build machine learning models with python.

So where to go from here? The first step is to keep learning. You should keep practicing by building more models, and using different tools to build your models. However, there is more to machine learning than simply playing around with tools. You should read as many books as you can and watch videos from reputable sources, so that you can learn the theory and fundamentals that lie behind the concept of machine learning. If you go further than this, it will in large part depend on your current situation and your goals for the future. If you are already a working professional, you might not need to go to school and get a degree in computer science. You might be learning the tools described in this book for the sake of practical application at your current job. If that is the case, then practice along with self-study is the best path forward for you, although of course if you are willing and able to return to school to get an in-depth education on the subject, that is always an option.

For those that are just getting exposed to the field and looking to it in order to pick a career path, getting a college degree in computer science or a related subject is probably the best way forward for you, especially if you are hoping to attain employment. The fields of data science and machine learning are not likely to be fields where too many people are able to get employment without some kind of college degree in a related field. If possible, find a school that will let you get a concentration in artificial intelligence and machine learning.

I would also advise taking many math classes that are focused on statistics and probability. Some "business acumen" is often advised, so it can't hurt to take some management classes as well. This is recommended even though many technical types are not that enthusiastic about business school. You are not going there to become an MBA, but you should get some idea of business operations at a large corporation and learn about many business concepts like business intelligence, predictive analytics, and data mining, since these are useful concepts for corporations and they prefer people that have some understanding of this to join their team, ready to hit the ground running.

Computer engineering is a related field that can also be pursued, and you can even consider mechanical engineering. That might not come to mind right away, but remember that in mechanical engineering there is a lot of research in the area of robotics. But remember that college is nothing more than an entry ticket. Machine learning is a very practical field, and many of the tools described in this book are what is going to be used in the real world. I hope that this book has stimulated your interest in machine learning, and that it will help propel you to continue your education and development in this exciting area.

Finally, if you found this book useful in any way, a review on Amazon is always appreciated!